THE GOD MAKERS II

ED DECKER & CARYL MATRISCIANA

HARVEST HOUSE PUBLISHERS
Eugene, Oregon 97402

128718

All Scripture quotations in this book are taken from the King James Version of the Bible.

THE GOD MAKERS II

Copyright © 1993 by Harvest House Publishers
Eugene, Oregon 97402

Library of Congress Cataloging-in-Publication Data

Decker, Ed.
    God makers II / Ed Decker, Caryl Matrisciana.
        p.   cm.
    ISBN 1-56507-137-9
    1. Mormon Church—Controversial literature.   2. Church of Jesus
Christ of Latter-Day Saints—Controversial literature.
I. Matrisciana, Caryl, 1947–   .   II. Decker, Ed. God makers.
III. Title.   IV. Title: God makers two.
BX8645.D382   1993
289.3—dc20   93-18872
                                                                        CIP

Printed in the United States of America.

We dedicate this book to the memory of two special people...

... our very dear friend Dolly Sackett, whose courage and determination motivated her to engage in "the good fight" and spread the gospel's truth to potentially millions of people. She valiantly spoke out against the deception of Mormonism and lovingly presented the alternative—a message of grace and freedom in Jesus Christ. Today she lives with Him in heaven.

... and we fondly remember Lillian Chynoweth. We thank her for her encouraging inspiration and testimony. Even while she is with the Lord, her voice and face are a reminder to us of the grace of God. She continues to reach the hearts of hundreds of thousands, just as she hoped, with her heartrending message in the film The God Makers II.

CONTENTS

A Truly Modern Religion 7

1. Mass-Marketing Mormonism 13

2. The Other Side of Family
   Home Evening 33

3. The Changing Face of Mormonism 45

4. Reach Out and Touch Someone 61

5. Astonishing Changes in the
   Unchangeable Temple 75

6. Purging the Radicals 87

7. The Birth of Heresy 99

8. False Prophecies of Joseph Smith 109

9. A Tangled Tale of Scripture 127

10. Present-Day Polygamy and
    Blood Atonement 141

11. The Satanic Connection 161

12. Secrets of a Wealthy Kingdom 175

13. The Hinckley Affair 187

14. Back to Basics 203

    Appendix—Testing the Book of Mormon 217

    Notes 231

A Truly Modern Religion

As THE BILLY GRAHAM CRUSADE CAME TO A CLOSE, the camera panned back from the pulpit area to show the vast arena. The altar area in front of the speaking platform was filled with people surrendering their lives to the love and grace of the Lord Jesus. We sat there quietly watching it on television, each of us lost in our private thoughts, contemplating those many lives changed by biblical truths, families renewed by biblical principles, marriages restored by biblical concepts. Suddenly our thoughts were pulled back to reality as the scene switched from the crusade to a TV spot encouraging us to remain in our seats and watch the special program to follow.

What came next was a half-hour presentation created by the Church of Jesus Christ of Latter-day Saints (LDS) and timed to capture the Billy Graham audience when so many viewers were spiritually vulnerable. The pitch drew them into dialing an 800 number for one of several free videos. The catch was that any offered video would be delivered by two young LDS (Mormon) missionaries.

The broadcast, "What Is Real?" asserted that the Latter-day Saints are a Bible-believing church centered in Jesus, and was aired in 77 cities. As the Mormon 800 number scrolled along the bottom of the screen,[1] we couldn't help but wonder how many hurting people, hearts breaking for a relationship with the Creator God after the crusade, watched that program, called the number, and were snatched away from the arms of the waiting Christ, drawn away into spiritual deception.

These impeccably produced LDS specials and the follow-up videos are designed to reach people with words and pictures that seduce troubled hearts into believing the Mormon deception. They are filled with phrases such as "we wanted more of something...we didn't know what it was...we were empty...I

7

wanted to feel alive . . . I didn't get married to get divorced . . . God had a plan for people like us, forever . . . if the Lord could only help us . . . listen to your heart." No wonder so many people fell prey to that sweet imitation of truth. Even the soothing music promised peace.

Nothing in the program so much as hinted that the message being proclaimed was anything other than a compassionate evangelical plea to begin a relationship with God. And what could be wrong with that? Nothing, unless there's more to the story than is being told, unless the words being spoken have double meanings. It's not what LDS programs *say* but what they *don't say*. Mormonism stands in direct opposition to evangelical Christianity, yet it deliberately uses Christian terminology to mislead people. Why is it that not one of the Mormon Church's special programs, paid advertisements, or public service campaigns ever tells people what separates Mormonism from orthodox Christianity so viewers can decide for themselves?

Why doesn't the LDS Church ever run a TV spot that says, "We believe that Jesus Christ was the brother of Lucifer." Or a warm family show that says, "Someday soon you could be a god, on the same level as the God of the Bible." Or advertise that if you are a woman, you could become one of many wives to a god and spend eternity bearing his children? Why don't they tell people that the death of the LDS Jesus on the cross wasn't sufficient to pay for every sin, or that they believe that the words that their own prophets speak today supersede the Holy Bible?

Why don't they show these contradictory things? Because using well-accepted Christian words and images *works*!

In this modern world of state-of-the-art television communications, it is the rare American who has not seen at least a dozen moving TV spots promoted by "Your Friends/the Church of Jesus Christ of Latter-day Saints." For those few who have missed out, the same spot advertisements are showing up all over the country on radio, in newspapers, and in magazines.

The people who manage the public relations outreach for the Mormon Church have become masters of their trade. Their material is on a par with the Pepsi Cola Super Bowl commercials. The ads they have produced are working, and they are giving an ever-growing army of Mormon missionaries a ready list of anxious buyers.

These Mormon advertising strategies look so professional that no one would even think that he or she had been deceived. Mormon missionaries are still pedaling down the streets of America on bicycles, but today's Mormon missionaries are no longer casual visitors to your neighborhood. They are working from computer printouts generated by these high-tech media campaigns.

The professional eye of a savvy hunter was never more apparent than in the tendersweet pitch we viewed just after the Billy Graham Crusade ended. It was like watching destructive wolves silently slip in among the flock.

These LDS recruitment methods are successfully reaching into the very sanctuaries of Christianity. Even when forewarned, the unsuspecting church seems unable to cope with the new sophistication of the Mormon proselytizing techniques.

A Case of Mistaken Identity

For most of its history Mormons have struggled to be separate and distinct from the "apostate" Christian church. "Come out from among them!" was their early battle cry. They were a strange, easy-to-identify group, set apart from the real world by their peculiar habits and doctrines.

No longer!

Today's Mormons are now declaring that they are part of the Christian brotherhood. They are serious about joining pastors' groups and showing up for community prayer meetings and Bible studies.

Mormons have made inroads into secular venues as well. We heard recently that Mormon missionaries showed up at one Florida middle school in response to a public plea for volunteer help. They claimed that they needed a certain amount of public service to fulfill the service requirements of their mission. There was little that could be done legally to prohibit these young Mormons from doing their volunteer work, and today they spend several hours three mornings a week working among the youngsters. At the school, they are not going by their usual rigid titles of Elder Smith and Elder Jones. The kids know them as Tom and Mike. A special relationship is being created in that town between the Mormon missionaries and a school full of impressionable kids who live in the houses Tom and Mike will be visiting with the Mormon gospel. Successful? You bet it is!

What is alarming is that the Mormons are starting to look almost more like Christians than the Christians themselves. The Mormon Church has a new emphasis in its approach. Its leaders have corporately decided that the old days of separation from orthodox Christians is just not going to work over the long haul. They see that they must bring Mormonism into the new age and be all things to all people. Above all else, they must appear to be the epitome of Christianity to that segment of the population that generally considers itself Christian. *Christians are the Mormon target population of the nineties in America.*

Christians must realize that the Mormon hope of appearing Christian is not reflected in their historic or current teachings. As we will show, the numerous recent changes are only cosmetic.

Don't be deceived by the pretty new face.

New Strategies

To make its plan for assimilation into the Christian mainstream work, the LDS Church must stop people who educate and warn the public through movies and books such as *The God Makers* and *The God Makers II*. The new approach to dealing with those who expose and oppose the false doctrines of Mormonism is to aggressively work to close the doors of *Christian* churches to them.

This massive effort of the Mormon Church in developing warm interfaith friendships is starting to pay off. Ministries that expose the dark side of Mormonism are now often told by these neutralized Christians that real Christians don't attack other faiths. They say that Mormons can be won to Christ *only* by quiet, nonconfrontive, lifestyle evangelism. They say that Mormons will see the life of Christ in us and eventually be converted.

It's a nice theory, but it just isn't effective, and it just isn't true.

Even some groups that minister to the Mormons have begun to believe that it is wrong to expose the false doctrines of Mormonism (leaders who are unfamiliar with Mormon teachings may want to browse through Chapter 14, "Back to Basics," for a brief overview). They say it is all right to discuss our differences and demonstrate the problems we see with the LDS teachings, but looking a Mormon in the eye and calling him or her to repentance is too aggressive, too confrontational. Mormons smile and nod their heads in agreement, giving credibility to an ineffective approach that they can live with.

While the general Christian body sits quietly by, happily greeting the Mormons now showing up among them, the highly energized, heavily supported LDS missionary effort is stealing sheep from the same Christian flock by the hundreds of thousands. As we will see, the false doctrines of Mormonism are leading millions of precious people into a Christless eternity.

1

Mass-Marketing Mormonism

CONTRARY TO THE IMAGE IT PRESENTS TODAY, the Church of Jesus Christ of Latter-day Saints, which was founded in 1830, spent its first hundred years or so shaking its corporate fist at the Christian world and condemning it in strong rhetoric. The LDS prophets, Temple rituals, and scriptures denigrated orthodox Christianity. The true believer was required to separate himself from corrupted Christianity and step under the mantle of the only true prophet, Joseph Smith, and the only true authority of his "restored" Church. According to the Book of Mormon:

> There are save two churches only; the one is the church of the Lamb of God, and the other is the church of the devil; wherefore, whoso belongeth not to the church of the Lamb of God belongeth to that great church, which is the mother of abominations; and she is the whore of all the earth.[1]

One of the bedrock doctrines of Mormonism is that there is no salvation outside the Mormon Church. In his definitive encyclopedic work on LDS doctrine, the late Mormon apostle Bruce R. McConkie declared, "If it had not been for Joseph Smith and the restoration [of the true Church], there would be no salvation. There is no salvation outside The Church of Jesus Christ of Latter-day Saints."[2]

It is not an oversimplification to say that this position has created a double frustration in the minds and actions of the

Mormon leaders. On the one hand, they must zealously seek converts out of that "whore of all the earth," apostate Christendom. On the other hand, they must be able to survive and flourish in a world very different from the one in which Joseph Smith first lured his converts. Today's Mormon Church must quietly melt into what it has long considered to be that same church of the devil.

Concerning this difficult metamorphosis, an article in a recent *U.S. News & World Report* noted:

> Until a few decades ago, it [Mormonism] was a small and obscure sect, a religious oddity ensconced in the inter-mountain West and isolated from the rest of Christendom by its heterodox beliefs and a history tinged by violence, persecution and polygamy. Today, The Church of Jesus Christ of Latter-day Saints, better known as the Mormon Church, is one of the world's richest and fastest growing religious movements. Since World War II, its ranks have quadrupled to more than 8.3 million members worldwide. With 4.5 million U.S. members, Mormons already outnumber Presbyterians and Episcopalians combined. If current trends hold, by some estimates they will number 250 million worldwide by 2080 and surpass all but the Roman Catholic church among Christian bodies.[3]

According to Rodney Stark, professor of sociology and religion at the University of Washington, as a result of such continued growth:

> Mormonism stands on the threshold of becoming the first major faith to appear on earth since the prophet Mohammed rode out of the desert. . . . Yet along with its growth from a regional sect to a worldwide church come both political and doctrinal conflicts.[4]

There's an old saying, "You can take the boy out of the country, but you can't take the country out of the boy." That's the position the Mormon Church finds itself in today. The Church's internal mindset is cemented to its original doctrines, which clearly and completely separate it from orthodox Christianity.

Latter-day Saints can't let go of their esoteric doctrines without forfeiting their unique identity. Yet Mormonism can't take its place within the standard bounds of orthodoxy without dropping those same doctrines. The result is a hodgepodge of affirmations and denials, and a corporate decision to hide the complete theology and agenda of Mormonism from the public.

The purpose of this book is to expose this great paradox of Mormonism. We are going to look under the polished surface of their public image and bring to light the many things Mormon Church leaders wish to hide from the public.

The Saints Want *You*

No organization can successfully and continually swell its ranks without a highly effective recruitment program in operation. The LDS Church has become the acknowledged master of the proselytizing game, bringing it almost to an art form. From the outside looking in, recruitment clearly seems to be the highest priority item in the corporate budget.

The Church spends enormous amounts of money pursuing its converts with both overt and subtle recruiting tactics. Its missionary program alone costs an estimated $550 million per year![5] In addition to its successful paid media campaigns, the Church has been quietly but actively planning and pursuing numerous other image-enhancing programs. These range from many Church-operated Cultural Centers to the highly visible Tabernacle Choir tours. While their corporate focus is generally on promoting the missionary programs, these newer strategies are steadily changing the world's perception of the LDS Church.

In order to further the pristine image it has so carefully cultivated, the Mormon Church maintains its own very active Public Communications Department headquartered in Salt Lake City. Its full-time staff is dedicated to telling the world about the joys of

Mormonism on one hand and minimizing bad press on the other. To ensure proper dissemination of what Mormons believe is the correct perception of the gospel, the Church has called together a virtual army of workers in the field. As one Mormon source, the LDS-oriented *This People* magazine, notes, a corps of 1400 men and women throughout the world have accepted calls to be Public Communication Directors. These people are assigned to work at every level with the local LDS church system. These functions are spiritual *callings* in the Church, requiring a formal *laying on of hands and a setting apart.*

On the Air

One of the responsibilities of the Church communications department is to keep radio stations supplied with free, high-quality information:

> To further support the local effort, the Church supplies nearly 250 stations with a 15 minute weekly news service, guests and topics for radio talk shows, and a program called Times and Seasons, an award winning thirteen-part series of public affairs programs on topics ranging from pornography to fasting.[6]

Any radio station needing professional, broadcast-quality programming need only call an 800 number in Salt Lake City, punch in an extension number, and have the data sent to them exactly as their system requires.[7]

Most of the spot announcements that television and radio audiences immediately recognize as Mormon are part of the Mormon Church's Home Front Public Service Announcement (PSA) campaign. The Home Front PSA's, which depict ways families can work and grow together, are among the most successful in the history of religious media campaigning. As *This People* magazine reported:

Perhaps the Church's most effective media programs over the years have been the Home Front campaigns. These are highly produced radio and television spots celebrating family in the most vibrant and lovable images. . . . These public service spots, which are run at the pleasure of the radio and television stations that use them, have walked off with every major advertising and film award available to them in the past few years. According to several surveys, their soft, sometimes humorous approach has firmly identified the Church with the family in the minds of the public.[8]

In virtually every bit of LDS advertising and programming, the viewer, listener, or reader can call an 800 number to request a free book, audiotape, or videotape relating to the piece. Unless the caller is adamant about being left alone, his name will soon appear on a computer list sent to the LDS Missions office nearest the caller's home.

By using PSA's, the Church saves literally tens of millions of advertising dollars. John Heinerman, an active Mormon and the author of *The Mormon Corporate Empire*, says:

When the Church wants to get airtime in Brazil, or somewhere else . . . all they need to do is to go and [say to] the government people, "We would like to present a half-hour program on the family, and on increasing patriotism," and right away they'll get airtime. Two years ago, Hungarian television came over and did a nice story on the Mormons, and over 400 million people learned about the Mormons. The Church didn't have to pay for it, and the ironic thing is that these big television evangelistic ministries have to pay out millions of dollars. The Mormon Church has it down to a science, and they are probably the best PR people of any religion that I know.[9]

In the News

Another facet in the marketing of Mormonism is the written word. Few regional newspapers have been spared the opportunity to publish an expensive four-color insert on the many benefits of Mormonism. These are always sent out with the weekend or Sunday deliveries to assure maximum home distribution. In addition, paid Mormon advertising saturates the pages of many best-selling publications, including *TV Guide* and *Readers' Digest*. While the word *saturate* may seem a bit provocative, in media terms it describes the intense penetration being achieved by these LDS campaigns.

In response to this media blitz, hundreds of thousands of free Mormon videos and their holy scripture, the Book of Mormon, are requested annually. In 1989, for example, the number of Books of Mormon requested totaled 259,943. In addition, 86,000 of those people requesting the book asked for follow-up by Mormon missionaries.[10]

Along with their regular promotions, Church public relations people have tied major advertising in *TV Guide* to the showing of the television movie "Going Toward the Light," which depicted a Mormon family with a child who died of AIDS. As with the Billy Graham special, the timing was meticulous.

All of the expensive and strategically placed advertising is professionally designed with deliberate intent on reaching certain viewer segments. It has successfully marketed Mormonism as a bastion of domestic strength and middle-class respectability. The sought-after image Mormons want to be associated with is the epitome of all that is family-centered, wholesome, and *Christian*.

The idea of Mormonism being portrayed as the perfect answer to happy family unity is the obvious goal of Mormon media penetration. However, a six-year study by Brigham Young University's Family and Demographic Research Institute, which the *Salt Lake Tribune* reported as "one of the most extensive efforts ever to collect international information about LDS membership," showed that only about 20 percent of all Mormons fit the ideal picture of the family with a husband and wife married in the LDS Temple and children at home.[11]

Brigham Young University (BYU) sociologist Tim B. Heaton notes with reference to the findings of the study: "Some [couples] have no children; some are married outside the temple, about a fifth are married to non-members. And, of course, there are many single-adult households, some with children." Heaton also noted that "Mormons are not immune from divorce" and estimated that over one-third of U.S. Mormons will be divorced before age 60. He added that divorce is currently less common among U.S. Mormons while just the opposite is true in other countries.[12]

Tracing the Family Tree

The Mormon Church isn't leaving it to just the public relations people to get their message out. The Church's famous genealogical library in Salt Lake City is the world's largest repository of genealogical information. It houses *hundreds of millions* of microfilmed records that help Church members to identify their non-Mormon ancestors in a bizarre Mormon belief that they must posthumously baptize their dead into Mormonism. It is for this reason that Mormons so energetically trace their ancestral lineage as far back as possible.[13]

Mormons believe that spirits of dead people should have the opportunity to accept Mormonism in the afterlife. Therefore Mormons practice LDS Temple rituals, such as proxy baptism, for their dead. Members are encouraged to have the faith's ordinances performed for all their ancestors in the hope that they will embrace the faith:[14]

> For nearly 100 years, the international Mormon church has been compiling a vast library of personal-status records from more than 200 countries: birth records, death records, marriage licenses , immigration and emigration rolls, church membership, government censuses, Social Security cards. The Salt

Lake City Mormon library has some record of more than 2 billion individuals, held in millions of microfilm reels and more than 5 million books. Two years ago the Vatican gave the Mormons permission to put all Catholic church membership records on microfilm.[15]

But the genealogical library serves another purpose. It also lures other genealogists to Mormonism who, while searching for their family roots, are proselytized right there in the Mormon archives. According to the *Philadelphia Inquirer*:

Some non-Mormon users (out of the of the 3,000 people who use the library each day, about 40 percent are non-Mormons) complained that after visiting the center, they were put on the church's mailing list and received a small flood of Mormon literature.[16]

In another bit of free advertising, in early 1989 the United States Post Office published a Family Tree Chart as part of one of their postal service campaigns. On it they listed the Mormon Church as "a source for genealogical information" and referred Post Office patrons to the Mormon Family History Library in Salt Lake for further information.

At regional and local levels, Mormons regularly sponsor genealogy classes and workshops through the local libraries and city recreational departments, often using Mormon church computers, libraries, and genealogy worksheets to assist the non-Mormons.

Top Draw—Mormon Cultural Centers and Visitor Centers

Tourists are a recruiting gold mine for Mormonism, and the art of enlisting them has been mastered at major Mormon tourist attractions and cultural events, where visitors receive a slick barrage of Mormon information, films, tours, and literature, plus a follow-up call from Mormon missionaries when they return home.

The Polynesian Cultural Center, Hawaii's top paid-admission attraction, hosts more than 1 million people each year. Since the Cultural Center opened in October 1963, about 18 million people "have experienced its living museum format of meeting Pacific islanders in recreated South Pacific villages and enjoying authentic pan-Polynesian performances."[17]

Many of the actual Polynesian performers working at the center, as well as most of the service personnel, are LDS students who have been recruited from the nearby Hawaii campus of BYU.

The Polynesian Cultural Center is located at the LDS Hawaiian Temple site, and an easily accessible shuttle tram transports visitors the short distance to visit the Temple Visitor Center. While there, pleasant hosts and hostesses make it convenient for guests to sign the visitors' book and leave a comment or thought behind. Those people who do sign their names in the book can reasonably expect Mormon missionaries at their doors not long after they return home, asking them how they enjoyed the Polynesian Center and Temple tour.

The LDS Temple Hill in Los Angeles, east of the San Diego Freeway and just north of the Santa Monica Freeway, is one of the most effective missionary tools in Southern California, especially at Christmastime, when its 40,000 lights twinkle on the trees and shrubs while carolers perform on the grounds. Sixty thousand people pass by the Temple every day, making it a showplace for the Church. It is a city landmark and appears on air and sea navigational charts. Nearly 9000 people tour the Temple Visitor Center each month, learning that Latter-day Saints are Christians. It is probable that about a tenth of those leave their names and are followed up as missionary referrals.

These are but two examples of the drawing power of Mormon tourist attractions. Without a doubt, the crowning jewel of Mormonism is Temple Square in Salt Lake City, Utah. Visitors can't help but be impressed by the two Visitor Centers, the flower-filled walkways and gardens, the Tabernacle, the Assembly Hall, and the actual Salt Lake Temple itself. More than 1.8 million visitors each year are caught up in a whirl of programmed "good-ness" and an image of purity of heart and soul that flows from the smiles and comments of the ever-present tour guides. Guides fluent in the native languages of a major portion of the world's people groups are available. Again, guest books are prominently displayed and tourists are encouraged to sign them and leave a comment about their visit.

The Case of the Missing Statue

Not all comments are appreciated, however, especially when they are vocalized rather than written quietly in a guest book. A few years ago, after we had released the film *The Temple of the God Makers*, I (Ed) was in Utah filming material for the follow-up film, *The Mormon Dilemma*, when a telling incident occurred.

For *The Temple of the God Makers* the film crew had shot a scene in the Visitor Center that featured a statue of Adam and Eve kneeling at an altar. On the altar was an offering of fruits and vegetables, and a little lamb sat happily untethered at its base. In the film, we pointed out that the offering of the fruits and vege-tables displayed there was an integral part of the actual LDS Temple ceremony. We explained that these offerings of Cain were rejected by the God of the Bible as unworthy and unaccept-able sacrifices (see Genesis 4) because they were the handiwork of man. It was a shock to the system for many Mormon viewers to see this major theological flaw in their Temple ritual.

When I walked by the statue in the Visitor Center, I stepped into a group of tourists there. A tour hostess stood in front of the statue, describing the way in which Adam and Eve had come to be at that altar and how important the offerings were to the Lord. About two seconds after she had finished her memorized speech, and as she waited in silence for the group to be duly impressed, I gasped loudly and began pointing at the statue, crying, *"Look! Look!"* Sheer terror sprang into the eyes of the guide, and every eye became riveted to the statue. *"Look! Fruits and vegetables! The offering of Cain!"* The place turned to bedlam.

A few weeks later, I and others had the opportunity to revisit the statue and stood amazed. All that remained was a dent in the plush carpet outlining where Adam and Eve once knelt. We asked the man greeting visitors at the entry what had happened to that statue. His response was that there had *never* been a statue there! By the following summer a new and more biblically correct first couple were back on the site, without their altar and offering.

Home Improvements

On Sunday morning, July 29, 1990, the final morning of the Capstone Conference (the annual Saints Alive conference for ministries to the Mormons), several of us walked through Temple Square during a break in the nearby meetings. As we walked through the North Visitor Center, we were amazed. That building once housed the many displays dealing with the restoration of the LDS gospel. Mormons believe that there was an apostasy or falling away at the time the last apostles died. The legal authority of the Church was lost, and God had to restore it. So the true gospel of Jesus Christ was lost until God "restored" it through Joseph Smith. Although the restoration is the foundation of the Mormon faith, every single thing that dealt with Joseph Smith and the restoration had been removed from public view.

Now the main floor displays centered on the prophets of the Old Testament. The second floor, with its gigantic statue of Christ, focused on Jesus, and the lower floor was converted to theaters showing films about Christ, families, and our relationship with God. One must suppose that there must be *some* restoration material stored in plain wrappers somewhere under a counter that could be had if you flashed a Temple recommend (a pass that certifies that a Mormon has been found "worthy" to participate in Temple rituals), but who knows?

The South Visitor Center displayed some historical information on the construction of the LDS Temple and Solomon's Temple, and downstairs you could hear about the Book of Mormon, but we found only one mention of Joseph Smith on the main floor: Under a picture of Jesus was a written statement from LDS scripture with a heading that said something to the effect of "Jesus Testifies of Joseph Smith."

Conrad Sundholm, from Truth in Love Ministries in Oregon, asked an older man who looked like a supervisor what had happened to all the original displays. The man, perhaps thinking that he was talking to an upset Church member, confided that when they had all the restoration of the gospel displays, they averaged about 5000 missionary referrals each year. Now with this "Jesus only" approach, *they had surpassed that number each month!*

One other thing shocked us. Almost all the usual older men and women guides had been replaced by very pretty young women who were not dressed according to the usual code.

Mormon Tabernacle Choir

Perhaps the best-known ambassador of goodwill for the Mormon Church is the Mormon Tabernacle Choir. Listening to the choir is an overwhelming sight and sound experience, with over 300 voices selected from the very best talent within the Church. The choir's weekly broadcasts from Temple Square, "Music and the Spoken Word," backed by the mighty Tabernacle organ, have been a familiar sound and sight to several generations of Americans.

The choir has toured in 16 foreign countries, sung at numerous worldwide broadcast and special events, and performed at the inauguration of four U.S. presidents. During a celebration of the choir's 60 years of continuous broadcasting, former President George Bush called the choir "one of America's greatest treasures."[18]

It would be impossible to calculate the positive public relations impact the choir has had on the recruitment efforts of the Church. Just their name alone brings immediate positive recognition when mentioned in a proselytizing encounter.

Many of the albums of the great hymns of the Christian church are produced by the choir. These albums are scattered throughout the Christian world. Notably absent in these recordings for the general public are hymns that are pointedly LDS in nature, such as "We Thank Thee, O God, for a Prophet."

When Ed walked into a church one Sunday a few years ago to

do a three-day seminar on the cults, the prelude music being piped through the church's sound system was classic Mormon Tabernacle Choir, an outreach of the very cult the people had come to study!

Everyone Loves a Parade

From the holiday pageantry at the Mesa Temple in Arizona to the annual Hill Cumorah Pageant in Palmyra, New York, tens of thousands of visitors gather in streets across the nation to see outdoor dramas and famous Mormon pageants play out broad themes relating to Mormon history. These visitors are exposed to Mormonism in a light and festive atmosphere.

In Utah, the Pioneer Day Parade has largely taken over the usual Fourth of July pageantry. Every July 24, the anniversary of the Mormons' arrival in the Salt Lake Valley, the streets of downtown Salt Lake are lined with the faithful. Many of them have camped out since the afternoon before, holding down a favorite family curbside viewing spot. There is a tremendous Mardi Gras spirit as the city prepares for the parade, a spectacular procession of floats extolling the pioneer birthright of Utah. Most floats have an obvious LDS theme, and the Prophet and President of the Mormon Church is driven down the parade route as one of the featured celebrities.

Although these pageants draw many visitors into the Mormon net, ministries to the Mormons have learned to use the parade and the gathering masses as a time to move along the streets and witness to the crowds. It has been a fruitful ministry. One year, a Saints Alive (Ed Decker's ministry to Mormons) team projected the movie *Temple of the God Makers* onto the upper portion of a two-story building they were renting on South Main, just two blocks from the Temple. The people who were anchored to spots they were saving became a captive audience, and the film drew people from up and down the parade route. After a few too many showings, the Salt Lake police politely asked the Saints Alive team to turn off the projector or they would do it for them.

The New Gideons

The Church's missionary zeal has led members to place the Book of Mormon (recently subtitled *Another Testament of Jesus Christ*) in more than 10 percent of the homes of the Washington D.C. South Mission area. The effort was so successful that seven Church stakes (regional divisions) have each committed to donating 10,000 more copies each year to expand the effect of the project.[19]

Scouting Young Recruits

Some of the most profitable *local* missionary outreaches are through the LDS troops in the Boy Scouts of America.The Boy Scout program of the Mormon Church is an integral part of their young men's program. Every LDS boy is automatically involved. A boy's first Aaronic priesthood duties are often tied to his work in the scouting program. (Each young LDS boy steps into the Aaronic or lower priesthood at age 11.) Many non-LDS school and neighborhood friends come into the Scout troops, where their parents naturally become involved with LDS parents and the influence of the Mormon Church.

The LDS Church is very open about its control of a major segment of the Boy Scouts of America:

> The LDS presidency, speaking with the *Church News* in connection with the 78th anniversary of the partnership between the Church and Boy Scouts of America, emphasized that scouting continues to play a strong role in fulfilling Aaronic Priesthood objectives of preparing young men for full time missions, temple blessings and righteous manhood. . . . All members of the Young Men general presidency, along with President Monson of the First Presidency and other Church leaders on the general and local levels, serve on national BSA committees. The Church does have a voice in decisions made by Boy Scouts of America. . . . It's not running us: we're working together as a companionship.[20]

Olympic Helpfuls

Athletic programs and sponsorship of athletes are other avenues through which the Mormon outreach thrives. In one unique, regional approach in 1988, 500 members of the LDS Church in Alberta, Canada, volunteered to help behind the scenes at the Winter Olympics with "transportation, helping with security, hosting athletic delegations, working in food services and other areas, and singing and dancing in the opening and closing ceremonies. . . . The city's 12,000 Church members constantly are looking for ways to participate in community projects."[21]

The program was considered a great success by both the Olympic organizers and the Mormons. The LDS *Church News* now regularly runs articles about other high-profile LDS good-will programs, including soup kitchens and aid to the homeless, flood victims, and earthquake and hurricane survivors.[22] We know that help is vital to those who need it, but we feel that the LDS Church orchestrates much of this highly publicized action in order to achieve public approval as never before.

"Hello, We're from the Church of Jesus Christ of Latter-day Saints"

No foray into the recruiting tactics of the Mormon Church would be complete without taking a look at those front-line soldiers of the faith, the Mormon missionaries. You would have to be living on another planet not to have experienced meeting a pair or two of these missionaries. They always travel in twos, the clean-cut young men dressed in dress slacks or suits, white shirts, and conservative ties, standing out like beacons of light. Some of the missionaries are paying their dues to God and family, knowing that failure to put in their time serving on a mission would bring the tinge of spiritual deficiency and disgrace into their parents' home. For the greatest part, however, these young men (and increasingly women) serve their missions with vigor and honor and minimal public complaint.

In the decade of the nineties, the LDS missionary force numbers over 40,000 active participants at any given time. Most of them are between 18 and 22 years of age and have delayed college and career plans to go wherever they are sent to spend two grueling years spreading the Mormon gospel. As *U.S. & World Report* states:

> No group works harder at proselytizing than the Mormons; last year some 33,000 young men and 8,000 young women served as volunteer missionaries in the US and 94 other countries and 26 territories. Each spent from three to eight weeks at LDS Church's Missionary Training Center in Provo, or at one of 14 satellite centers in other countries. Last year Mormon missionaries won nearly 315,000 new converts.[23]

Once in the field, missionaries live rigidly controlled lives. A recent article in a California newspaper shared the story of several Mormon missionaries in the Los Angeles area. It talked about the deep commitment required to submit to the 12-hour days, the six-day weeks, and the missionaries' struggle to avoid the distractions of normal life.[24]

The article noted that Church rules of conduct for missionaries forbid watching TV, calling home (it isn't all bad news: they can call home twice a year—on Christmas and Mother's Day), and reading newspapers or listening to music (other than Church-approved tapes). Dating or even standing within arm's length of the opposite sex is banned. Moderate exercise and some sports are permitted on a very small scale, but things like full-court basketball are unacceptable. Usually, missionaries are assigned to new partners and cities every several months.

According to the article, virtually every moment of missionary life is carefully plotted by Church officials. Rising at 6:30 A.M. and going to bed by 10:30 P.M., the missionaries follow an intense program of praying, studying, teaching, and door knocking. They are supposed to meet weekly quotas for Books of Mormon distributed and potential converts or inactive Church members counseled.[25]

I Remember...

In an incident that occurred a few years back, I (Ed) was on a ministry trip in the South Pacific island nation of Tonga. My companion on the trip was Tom Bauer, the head of the Youth with a Mission (YWAM) base in Maui, Hawaii. On this particular day, we were off in a very remote area of Tonga. I am sure that only our guide knew for sure where we were, and maybe Tom had some suspicion. I didn't have a clue! I recall that we were at a spot that overlooked a little bay where boats came in and out, some connecting with an island that was just a tiny speck on the horizon—an unnamed place where a few hundred Tongans lived without electricity or anything else remotely related to what an American would consider the comforts of life.

A few hundred yards out from shore was a tiny native boat with an ancient putt-putt gas outboard motor slowly pushing through the swells in the direction of the remote island. They were in for a long day, I thought. It held three passengers. The Tongan at the helm, one Mormon missionary who was seated in the center, holding onto the sides of the boat, looking back toward shore, and another Mormon missionary standing in the bow, eyes riveted ahead to the work that lay before them. In spite of my adversarial position with the LDS Church, I was deeply touched. I wished I had a camera at that moment and the addresses of the families of those two young American Mormons.

Tom and I watched as they grew smaller and smaller in the distance. Tom was close to tears when he finally spoke. "Ed, if only we could see Christians going forward like that, with a zeal for the real gospel as earnest as the zeal of those two."

Hank Hanegraaff, president of the Christian Research Institute (CRI) in Irvine, California, is a man with that same kind of zeal. He put out a ministry brochure a few years ago that nailed it on the head. In part, it said, "Will you do for the Lord what others will do for a cult?" He understood the problem exactly. While the cults grow in size and power, the Christian church is afraid of offending people by talking about the Jesus of the Bible!

These Mormon missionaries are the classic example of misplaced zealousness for the doctrines of man. The apostle Paul cried out:

> Brethren, my heart's desire and prayer to God for Israel is that they might be saved. For I bear them record that they have a zeal of God, but not according to knowledge. For they being ignorant of God's righteousness, and going about to establish their own righteousness, have not submitted themselves unto the righteousness of God (Romans 10:1-3).

Missionary Burnout...the Pit

We were interested to see that the missionaries in the *Contra Costa Times* article were open with the reporter, Roy Rivenburg, about an area of their lives they almost never mention to an outsider, a period of depression known as "the Pit":

> That [the Pit] is shorthand for the depression and burnout that can strike from encountering repeated hostility and rejection. The latter doesn't just come from non-believers. Dear John letters are a major bane of missionary life. Brigham Young University's mission center [located adjacent to BYU] devotes an entire wall to I've-met-someone-else missives from home. To escape the Pit, most missionaries redouble their efforts.[26]

In our own experience and by gleaning from statements made by Mormon leaders, we estimate that 25 percent of the missionaries called each year leave the mission field before their scheduled time. This is *not* good news at home, where the family has already had the parental joy and spiritual blessing of hearing their son or daughter speak at church during a sacrament meeting, saying goodbye to the local congregation before leaving home to do the Lord's work. Nor will the folks at home have the usual homecoming party to match the joyous missionary farewell that everyone in the ward (the local church assembly) attended. To put this dropout rule in perspective, the LDS missionary program ejects over 5000 failures per year—and that's a lot of saying you're sorry.

Further, Church leaders say that 50 percent of those who fill a full-time mission for the Church are still active (pay their tithes, attend meetings, hold Church office) two years after returning home. That may sound good on the surface, but it also means that of every 20,000 missionaries who come home from a successful mission each year, 10,000 fall by the wayside into inactivity soon after they return home. If one were to carry out those figures over a decade, it would represent a tremendous number of failures sitting at the edge of Mormonism, and how many families in disarray?

Why would the Church let such a festering hole eat away at its underbelly? It is simply a matter of numbers. Each successful full-time missionary replaces himself several times over each year. The generally accepted average convert rate is seven converts per missionary per year. Even in the worst scenario, the Mormon Church is seeing a *net gain* of approximately 300,000 persons per year. Tough on the few, but for the corporate body, the missionary program is a great success.

From the biblical perspective, however, it is all wrong. Remember what Jesus had to say in this matter:

> He spake this parable unto them, saying, What man of you, having an hundred sheep, if he lose one of them, doth not leave the ninety and nine in the wilderness and go after that which is lost until he find it? And when he hath found it, he layeth it on his shoulders, rejoicing. And when he cometh home, he calleth together his friends and neighbors, saying unto them, Rejoice with me, for I have found my sheep which was lost. I say unto you that likewise joy shall be in heaven over one sinner that repenteth more than over ninety and nine just persons which need no repentance (Luke 15:3-7).

Special-Interest Groups

Proselytizing minority ethnic groups seems to be a growing trend in the Mormon missionary program. American Indians, because they are said to be descendants of the Book of Mormon civilizations, have always been a prime target, but increased conversions with other minority groups attest to Mormon success elsewhere. For example, Latinos are a targeted group in the Los Angeles, California, area. In 1991, 1337 Latinos were converted, bringing the total number of Latinos in the Los Angeles area to 24,000. (By comparison, Los Angeles has a total of 350,000 Mormons to 650,000 in Salt lake City.)[27]

Today the Book of Mormon can be read in 80 languages, and by 85 to 90 percent of the world's population. Well over half, 46, of these translations of the Book of Mormon appeared for the first time in the 1980's in regions such as Greece, Ghana, Islands of the Lesser Antilles, the Philippines, and south-eastern South Africa where Zulu is spoken.[28]

It would appear that where little is known of the LDS Church, it grows fast. And where the Church is better known, it grows more slowly. The *Encyclopedia of Mormonism* shows that the annual rate per 100 baptized members is much higher in the less developed countries of Africa and Asia than it is in European or North America. In Africa, for instance, the convert rate is approximately 13 people per hundred Church members. By comparison, in the western United States, the convert rate is just over one per 100 baptized members.[29]

To increase these numbers, the Mormon Church has entered the marketing game with gusto. What Mormons are selling so successfully is an *image*, an image of goodness and well-being that now permeates the American subconscious. Before buying stock in the company, however, let's compare the image with reality.

2

The Other Side of Family Home Evening

Although Mormonism is highly regarded for its involvement in social concerns, statistics from the State of Utah, where the population is overwhelmingly Mormon, indicate that Mormonism cannot produce a lifestyle that is any freer from societal ills than the rest of the country. That "Happiness Is Family Home Evening" image of Mormonism doesn't go over so well at home in Utah!

Their high-profile goodwill programs may include soup kitchens and aid to flood victims, yet their own members often suffer neglect due to poor management practices of the LDS welfare program. Even secular welfare systems in Utah have the same problems: Some disabled people in Utah have had to sell everything just to survive, while others have waited up to five years for payments of benefits. Early in 1992, disabled Utahns claimed that the terrible management of the Utah Division of Determination Services caused delayed benefits to over 4000 people.[1]

Bill Schnoebelen, author of *Wicca, Satan's Little White Lie*, and coauthor of *Mormonism's Temple of Doom*, is a former Mormon and former Satanist. When interviewed for *The God Makers II* film, Bill commented:

> We are seeing in Utah the fruits of the teachings of Mormonism reflected in social statistics. We are seeing homosexuality running rampant among people in Utah; we are seeing child abuse and teenage suicide.[2]

John Heinerman, an active Mormon, is the coauthor with Anson Shupe of *The Mormon Corporate Empire* and director of the Anthropological Research Center in Salt Lake City, Utah. John fully affirmed Bill Schnoebelen's fears about the social problems faced by the Church in his own interview for *The God Makers II*:

> The Mormon Church is caught up in the dilemma of having to, for the first time, face the reality that there are major problems within its organization, with its membership, that are just not going to go away. One of these [problems] is homosexuality. In 1981, homosexuality was in another category called "other moral offenses." In '82 it was taken out and put into a category by itself. . . . Homosexuality has increased by 50 percent, 100 percent, 200 percent, and it has just gone upward.
>
> Also adultery. The number one reason that the Church excommunicates is for adultery, and its numbers are staggering and increasing every year. Another area of concern is the rising amount of child abuse within the LDS Church. . . . It is a growing problem.[3]

Among Heinerman's other concerns are the growing amounts of prescription drug abuse and other crimes at Brigham Young University (BYU), in Provo, Utah, which is the showcase of Mormonism:

> Here [at BYU] you have runaway abuse of prescription drugs. I quoted (in a talk I gave last night in La Mirada, California) from an FBI report that now Brigham Young University is not as safe as the University of Utah in Salt Lake City. Brigham Young University has more aggravated crimes and assaults . . . they smoke, and drink, and have gay clubs and lesbian clubs.

Heinerman concludes: "So what it shows is that all is not well in Zion, and that there are major problems confronting our religion."[4]

Homosexuality at BYU

Heinerman's comments about homosexuality at BYU were not surprising. As early as 1982, students at BYU published a two-part series on LDS homosexuality and the gay lifestyle and the ways BYU and the LDS Church have chosen to deal with the phenomenon.

The report was published in an off-campus student paper called the *Seventh East Press.* Staff writer Dean Huffaker presented an extremely balanced look at the collision course between homosexuality and Mormonism. Centering on the problems gays have at BYU, he interviewed "gays and homosexuals on and near campus—including a former BYU instructor, a former BYU professor, and former and current BYU students." He reported on the weekend exodus of gay BYU students to one of the most popular gay bars in Salt Lake City and their regular visits to a gay bath there. For the students, the danger was always that BYU Security, with its undercover agents, was always trying to ferret out gays who would then be targeted for immediate disciplinary action.[5]

Huffaker reported that one homosexual, a former BYU professor named Steve, said that he struggled with the obvious inner turmoil for ten years while teaching at BYU. According to Huffaker, "While Steve was teaching at BYU, he was receiving help from the counseling center. His therapist told him that he was seeing three hundred students with the same problem."[6]

Readers of the articles were left with no doubt that the LDS missionary program was a cradle of homosexuality. The *Seventh East Press* reported that in one group of 15 homosexuals alone, 13 were returned missionaries.

The Church was taken back by the *Seventh East Press'* blatant disregard for the unwritten but well-known rules for propriety or protocol in dealing with Church "problems." Those responsible for the indiscretion were called in and warned. In a follow-up issue, an article dealing with Book of Mormon discrepancies pushed Church leaders past their level of tolerance. Key people on the *Seventh East Press* staff were transferred out of BYU, and the *Press* died a quick and ignominious death. But the secret was out: Mormonism was a hotbed of homosexuality. Unless the problem was dealt with directly, it was going to come back and haunt Church officials. Little did they realize that it would come back anyway. Less than a decade later a man named Charles Van Damm would refire the boiling caldron by throwing the acting president of the Mormon Church into the pot. We will deal with the Hinckley affair in a later chapter.

In the spring of 1990, Evergreen, an organization of Mormons, ex-gays, and friends, held a private, by-invitation-only meeting in Salt Lake City touting cures for homosexuality. The conference, "LDS Men Overcoming Homosexuality," attracted about 150 participants,[7] including Mormon bishops and gay men. Obviously, there is more than just a small problem in Utah when gays, ex-gays, and LDS Church leaders are meeting to come up with answers to the homosexual dilemma in which they now find themselves.

Alarming Statistics

In a state monopolized by a religious group that advertises marital harmony, recent marriage and family statistics are staggering. Utah's divorce rate is higher than the national average.[8] Fifty-five thousand women are abused annually by their partners.[9] Child abuse and neglect has increased 212 percent in the last decade, with more than 10,000 new cases in 1991.[10] Rape and sexual assault for adults has increased 93 percent during the same period.[11]

In child labor law violations, Utah ranks number one in a six-state region.[12] The Utah Department of Health admits pregnancies of unwed teenagers are a growing problem. In 1988, 48 percent of all births to teens were out of wedlock.[13] In addition, Utah's prison system was ranked fourth for rate of inmate population growth in 1989, with a 21 percent increase.[14]

There has also been a staggering 379 percent increase in child sexual abuse to children under 14. Much of the abuse is incestuous, and sadly the perpetrators are given lenient sentences because of an oddity in Utah law which accommodates sexual abuse by a *Mormon* relative.[15] While state law provides stiff penalties for people who abuse children to whom they are not related, if a father sexually abuses his *own* children, the judge has the option of waiving any sentence and letting the Church step in and deal with him through their ecclesiastical system.[16]

God in the Courtroom

A case in point was the appeal of Allen Hadfield in 1989. Hadfield had been convicted of sexual abuse of his 12-year-old son and 10-year-old daughter and was appealing to the State Supreme Court. The *Salt Lake Tribune* reported that Hadfield's attorney claimed that his client's children were influenced to lie about him by a therapist. Hadfield, who is LDS, had been convicted on four counts of sodomy and three counts of child abuse in a ritual satanic form.

In spite of the heinous nature of the crimes, Hadfield served only six months on a work-release program. Usual mandatory sentencing for such crimes is ten years. But Hadfield was under *Church* counseling. As we noted, Utah law allows judges like staunch Mormon Cullen Y. Christensen of Provo's Fourth District Court to invoke an incest exception. Christensen found Hadfield qualified for probation under this exception, since he was being counseled for his deviant behavior by the Mormon Church.[17]

In looking at the particular section of the referenced Utah Code, it is obvious that the Mormons manipulate even the *intent* of the exception. The actual wording states:

> The defendant has been accepted for mental health treatment in a recognized family sexual abuse treatment center which specializes in dealing with the kind of child sexual abuse occurring in this case.[18]

Nevertheless, when a defendant walks into court with his bishop and letters of affirmation by other leaders in the Mormon hierarchy, and the bishop advises the Mormon judge that the Church will handle the counseling, the deal is as good as done. The Mormon god and his priesthood have entered a plea on behalf of the defendant. What LDS judge would dare risk his own exaltation to godhood or his reelection to the court by disagreeing?

Another example of the power of the Mormon religion to control decisions in Utah courtrooms was reported in an article "Did God Influence Jury? Court Asked to Decide":

> The Utah Court of Appeals has been asked to determine if God's influence in a jury room is an improper interference of jury deliberations during a criminal trial. Two people charged with conspiracy to hide evidence of an office-building burning were found guilty after a male in the jury "asserted his spiritual authority in the said religion" [Mormonism] and thereby "influenced his fellow adherents to submit the question of guilt to *the will of God* by joining him in group prayer," claimed the defense attorney, Loni Deland. "Immediately following the prayer, the said juror expressed the 'answer' to the prayer—that [the defendants] were guilty." After that, Mr. Deland said, all prayer participants changed their opinions to adhere to the will of God, and a 6—2 vote in favor of acquittal became a 6—2 vote in favor of conviction without further evidentiary considerations (emphasis added).
>
> In his brief he said, "It is an undeniable fact of life in the state of Utah that one religion dominates virtually all aspects of life. The State Legislature openly acknowledges that the approval of the Mormon Church's hierarchy is a prerequisite to successful passages of proposed laws touching on that religion's tenets. It is also common knowledge that the church adheres to a

male-only priesthood which governs on the premise that the church president is a prophet and rules with divine inspiration and authority which flows from him to the faithful via the priesthood." ... De Land said, "The juror who asserted his spiritual authority" manipulated his client's verdict.[19]

We have just taken you through a minefield of social problems that are out of control in Utah, problems that the LDS Church pretends do not exist. *The fruit doesn't fall far from the tree.* If the Mormon Church were really the only true church, operating with divine, holy revelation on a daily basis, then the LDS Church, its prophet of God and its social, welfare, and religious systems would have turned Utah into a virtual Garden of Eden. But it hasn't.

Worse, because the LDS Church would rather that the sins of its common people not be there, *they aren't.* The good LDS people live in a perpetual state of denial, and when sin does push its ugly head through the roof of the house so all can see, then it is blamed on the failure of the individual to live up to the standards of the Church. The Church is *always* right, *always* pure, *always* without spot or wrinkle. LDS people end up either as robots or broken people unable to see a way out of this paradox.

Years ago, in the early days of the Saints Alive ministry, Ed was doing a daily radio program that was broadcast into most of Utah. While the program generated a lot of correspondence in most areas, there were certain rural pockets from which not a single letter came. Saints Alive had no idea if anyone even listened to the show in those areas. When time and scheduling problems made it impossible to maintain the daily program, it was eventually closed down.

Not long after the program went off the air, Ed received an unsigned letter with no return address. The postmark on the envelope was from one of those "silent" towns. The writer told of how she was a physically abused Mormon wife and mother who was a virtual prisoner in her own house. She shared how she had tried to get help and counseling from the local bishop. He had told her husband that she was complaining about him, which only brought on more beatings. Her own parents told her she was not working hard enough at being a good Mormon wife. She thought about suicide often.

One day, alone at home, she turned on the radio and tuned into the Saints Alive program, "Dialogue." She listened as Ed and his cohost, Jim Witham, talked about the love and grace and joy of knowing Christ. She gave her life to Jesus a few days later while listening to them call the lost to Calvary. The program became her one hope, her only contact with reality. She organized her schedule around those 15 minutes each day, and her life became a new one, centered in Jesus, filled with peace. In spite of all the turmoil in her life, she had found joy and a solid anchor in a raging storm. She wanted Ed to know how much good that program had done for just one Mormon woman. She wanted him to know that he and Jim had been carrying the bulk of her heavy burden in the love and caring they had shown each day on the air.

That's the way we feel about our roles in creating *The God Makers* and *The God Makers II* films and books. Someone has to speak for these silent victims; someone must be their voice. Someone needs to stand up to this giant "Big Brother" masquerading as a benevolent family-centered church that preaches Christ.

On the Road with *The God Makers II*

The reader needs to understand that when we released the original *God Makers* movie a decade ago, relatively little was known about Mormonism in mainstream Christianity. The film hit like a bombshell and was being shown in as many as a thousand churches per month. Scores of ministries to the cults were showing the 16-mm version of the film almost nonstop throughout the country for several years. Even today, ten years later, the video version of the film is still one of Jeremiah Films' all-time bestsellers.

Today, Mormonism is no longer a quiet, quaint little Quaker-type sect tucked away in the mountains of Utah. It is a major business conglomerate/religion with tens of thousands of missionaries wielding the power of success around the globe.

Mormon leaders may have been asleep when the first *God Makers* film hit, but they were ready and waiting for the new one! The first copies of the *God Makers II* video went out of the mail rooms at Jeremiah Films and groups like Saints Alive without covers or jackets. Too many people were waiting to see this new look at the Mormonism of the nineties to wait. The initial response was tremendously positive. In early December 1992, Ed took the new video into Utah for three premier showings scheduled for Salt Lake City, Brigham City, and Ogden.

Even before Ed arrived in Utah to premier the film, all the stops were pulled out by its detractors. The day before Ed was to arrive, an organization called the National Conference of Christians and Jews (NCCJ) issued a widely distributed news release attacking the film that went out across the country over AP wires. It was as follows:

A STATEMENT FROM THE NATIONAL CONFERENCE AND THE UTAH CHAPTER: FOR RELEASE DECEMBER 10 AT 10:00 AM: A statement by Gillian Martin Sorensen, President of the National Conference, about God Makers II: [Contact Chris Bugbee (1-212-206-0006)]

"Like its predecessor, God Makers II presents an intemperate polemic against the Mormon faith disguised as an objective documentary. Using a carefully selected mix of sensational and unsubstantiated first-person accounts, lurid allegations, and a highly subjective interpretation of Mormon teachings, God Makers II draws upon the incendiary arsenal of religious bigotry."

"Frank discussion of the truth claims of different faiths is a legitimate avenue of inter-religious dialogue," Sorensen acknowledged. "But, base appeals to fear and hatred have no place in such efforts, and must be condemned wherever they are encountered."

"With its depiction of the Mormon Church as an evil empire founded upon sexual exploitation, predatory greed and Satanism," Sorensen said, "God

Makers II carries the odious scent of unreasoning prejudice. Let the public beware."

"President Sorensen's statement reflects the feelings and has the endorsement of the Utah Chapter of the National Conference of Christians and Jews," said presiding Co-Chair Ted Speros. "A statement of our mission is to promote understanding and respect among all races, religions and cultures through advocacy, conflict resolutions and education. God Makers II is an affront to religious understanding."[20]

What the AP report did not say was that the NCCJ was the same group that claimed the very same things about the first movie in 1984. At that time they claimed to have exerted a major effort in researching the movie before they concluded it was "religious pornography." Yet the NCCJ *failed then and failed now* to contact Jeremiah Films, Saints Alive, or any single participant for a single document to support a single statement. We would guess that their only input in a blatant attempt to discredit this film was the public relations office at the Mormon church.

The NCCJ failed to identify more than a dozen Mormons in the first study group and failed to mention that there wasn't a single Orthodox Jew or conservative Christian on the team, then or now. They also failed to state who the Mormon members of their board presently are or how they had managed to get this statement ready for release in Utah on December 10, the day before Ed was to arrive there. It had taken them nearly a year to release their report on the first *God Makers* film. This one was out within a month of the first videos being shipped out from Jeremiah Films. The Mormons can sit back and smile while this unorthodox group, led by Mormons within it, does their cleanup work. The NCCJ news release and its authors are without merit! Who gave them the authority to judge what specific lines of doctrine separate any group from Christian orthodoxy when they themselves aren't even part of it?

The one sad part of the matter is that several *ministries* to Mormons joined in with the NCCJ to take some shots at the film and at us. These groups feel we should be strictly intellectual in our statements. A lady from one such group in Utah was interviewed both in the press and on television and stated that "the things [they] object to [in Mormonism] can be laid out and documented. I can present logical reasons not to believe in Mormon claims. The Decker film appeals more to emotion in a supermarket tabloid style."[21]

The fact is, the movie clearly stands on its own merit and is more than well documented, as we will show.

Ed wanted to face these accusations in Utah. If something was out of order, it was far better to face it openly and honestly right at the start. He read the NCCJ report in full and the negative public statement by the fellow Christian ministry after each showing and took a vote on who was telling things straight. By show of hands the film easily won by a ratio of well over 50 to 1 over the accusations. *The people in Utah already know Christian fact from Mormon fiction.* They have to live with this dark side of Mormonism every day. The film was a welcome bit of reality.

We wish you could have been with Ed in Utah as the movie was shown. The audience participation times were alive and positive. He had great, enthusiastic response in the very place where the film would obviously meet its severest criticism, virtually at the front door of Mormonism.

In one of the meetings, a man in the audience stood and said he had a statement to make. He said that he had been a Mormon for many years and he had just one thing to say about the movie. Ed fully expected to be called to repentance by the man, but was in for a surprise. The man stated that he had watched the film with great intent and "every single thing in that film is . . . absolutely true!" He said that he had been gathering notes on the Church over the years and had more than 1200 pages of documentation that supported the exact things the film pointed out. He was amazed that we had not made the film from his own notes.

Someone in the audience asked him why he was still a Mormon if he believed the things the film revealed were true. He was silent for a moment and then responded. He said that his wife was bedridden, an invalid for whom he did everything from clothing and cleaning to feeding. But his wife was a Mormon and had told him that if he released his data, she would leave him even if she had to crawl out of the house. He told Ed later that he can never get anyone from the Mormon Church to come to help him, even for a few hours. Yet even though she relied on him for everything, the Church had a death grip on her that was stronger than anything he could offer her.

Yes, the film is hard-hitting and *yes*, the Mormons are less than thrilled. But this is not a witnessing tool for wooing Mormons. It is a film to warn the Christian church! To warn an apathetic church, a church that has gone back to sleep, a church that is ignoring the wolves ravaging its own flocks! It is time to wake up that slumbering church once more to the shouts of danger!

3

The Changing Face of Mormonism

A LOT CAN HAPPEN IN A HUNDRED YEARS. At the turn of the century, the possibility of having a Mormon senator from the recently and reluctantly admitted state of Utah was more than the country could handle. Sending Reed Smoot off to the United States Senate all but brought the Federal troops back into Utah. That's a bit of an exaggeration, but it may have appeared that way to the Mormons who had to live through what probably seemed to them like the Spanish Inquisition.

Reed Smoot's story is important to our understanding of the changing face of Mormonism because it was from that incident that the LDS Church caught a glimpse the future struggle it would face in changing its direction from one of isolationism toward a path that would link it with the rest of humanity. The highly publicized Smoot Hearings of 1903–1907 had an impact on the Church with repercussions continuing to the present time.

The new *Mormon Encyclopedia* gives us penetrating insight to the issues involved from the LDS perspective:

> The 1890's had seen the Church pass through some of its most challenging times, including the tumultuous political fight for Utah statehood following the Manifesto of 1890 (officially curtailing new plural marriages) [in the United States] and Presidential amnesty for Church Officers who had practiced polygamy,

initiating the process of accommodation and accultura-
tion to mainstream America [emphasis added]. Eu-
phoria, however, was short lived.

The election to the U.S. Senate of Reed Smoot, a
highly visible Church leader, unleashed intense anti-
Mormon sentiment, which had subsided after statehood ... creating a furor that forced the Senate to
examine the case. The prosecution focused on two
issues: Smoots' alleged Polygamy and his expected
allegiance to the Church and its ruling hierarchy, which
it was claimed would make it impossible for him to
execute his oath as a United States senator. ... It soon
became apparent that it was the Church that was on
trial.[1]

Church leaders were called and questioned about the power
the Church wielded over its members—especially over the General Authorities, of which Smoot was a member. Again from the
Mormon perspective:

Some of the testimony revealed situations and circumstances that put the Church in an unfavorable
light. President Joseph F. Smith received especially
harsh treatment in cross-examination. ...

The victory for Elder-Senator Smoot was a victory
for the Church, providing the legitimacy it had been
seeking since 1850. ... Perhaps more than any other
individual, Reed Smoot molded and shaped the positive national image the Church was to enjoy throughout the twentieth century.[2]

This victory held the answer to the deep dilemma in which
the Church was mired. A few years earlier, Mormons had come
out of their hiding place in the desert and asked the government to
grant them statehood, *just as they were*, polygamy and all. It
never happened. They had to first shake themselves loose from
the stigma of polygamy and their unique brand of "Kingdom of

God" theocracy. Only after the Manifesto of 1890, which was not a revelation from their living prophet but a politically expedient declaration, were they marginally accepted into the brotherhood of States.

Then came the massive, unexpected blowup over Reed Smoot. We can only imagine the first closed-door meeting with the Council of the Twelve Apostles on the return to Utah of Prophet Joseph F. Smith after he had been raked over the coals on the witness stand regarding the strange quirks of his faith. It is our personal opinion that a policy of some sort was made at that time to accede to public pressure from time to time on serious doctrinal issues, which, if greatly publicized, could affect the Church's assimilation into mainstream American society.

From that time until World War II, Utah and Mormonism quietly sat on the back burner, avoiding most controversy. Meanwhile, another major change was secretly taking place behind the closed doors of the LDS Temple.

An Oath of Vengeance

During the LDS Temple ritual, certain oaths and covenants are made before God that are said to be both solemn and eternal. All participants are required to verbally take every oath. One such oath, which was part of the ritual until it was removed in early 1927, was called the *Oath of Vengeance*.[3] It was actually sworn against the United States of America in retribution for the deaths of Joseph and Hyrum Smith:

> You and each of you do solemnly promise and vow that you will pray, and never cease to importune high heaven to *avenge the blood of the prophets on this nation*, and that you will teach this to your children and your children's children unto the third and fourth generation[4] [emphasis added].

You can imagine that following the humiliation of the Smoot Hearings, The Brethren could only shudder at the thought of what the public disclosure of this oath would bring. (The very highest officials of the LDS Church are referred to by the faithful as The Brethren. This includes the Prophet, the First Presidency, and the Council of the Twelve Apostles.) There had been some chewing around the edges of this issue since the time of the hearings and The Brethren wanted no more of it. The oath was quietly removed from the ritual without ceremony or announcement.

While this oath was removed and Mormonism moved further into general acceptance, the oath itself was an *eternally binding one*, given in the holiest of places, under the power of the Mormon Church's eternal Melchizedek priesthood. Under these *eternal* circumstances, the vow once taken could not be undone.

Every LDS president from Brigham Young to and including Ezra Taft Benson in 1993 have been of an age to have taken that oath when they "took out their own endowments" (that is, they had gone through the Temple for the first time, learning the secret oaths and words that will gain them admittance into "celestial glory") prior to 1927, and are therefore still bound under these oaths.

Have they officially renounced the oath? Or are they still under its power? If they have *not* renounced it, how can they presume to lead approximately 4½ million American citizens under Article 12 of the LDS Articles of Faith ("We believe in being subject to kings, presidents, rulers and magistrates, in obeying, honoring and sustaining the law") and still be bound to call heaven to curse our nation?

If they have renounced it, how do they justify having sworn such a bitter, eternal oath in their sacred Temple before their god and then reneged on it? This surely places all the LDS people who have gone through the Temple and sworn oaths of total obedience to these very same leaders in an untenable dilemma. What of the Mormons who hold office in our government or serve in the military? There is an obvious conflict of interest between their oaths of office and their higher loyalty to a group of men who are sworn to seek vengeance against this great nation.

Mormon apologist Bruce R. McConkie states that "while the oaths of the saints have furthered righteous purposes, similar swearing by the wicked has led to great evil."[5] What is this oath if it isn't evil? In the Bible, Jesus states:

> Again, ye have heard that it hath been said by them of old time, Thou shalt not forswear thyself, but shalt perform unto the Lord thine oaths. But I say unto you, swear not at all, neither by heaven, for it is God's throne, nor by the earth, for it is his footstool (Matthew 5:33-37).

That should be plain enough, yet in their oath-taking, these unrighteous Mormon leaders have denied the strong admonition of Jesus Christ and reverted to exactly what He has told us not to do!

The biblical gospel has a different way of dealing with enemies. Christ said:

> I say unto you which hear, Love your enemies, do good to them which hate you. Bless them that curse you and pray for them which despitefully use you (Luke 6:27,28).

Paul instructed the church to "bless them which persecute you: bless, and curse not" (Romans 12:14).

We have no personal vendetta against a group of elderly men who swore ungodly oaths in their youth, but it is important to point out that the Mormon Church has been in the cleanup business for more than 100 years. Having had their hands stung in the Reed Smoot fiasco, they spent the next 40 years in near isolation, until their service in World War II drew them back into the heart of American life.

Storm Clouds on the Horizon

When I (Ed) joined the Mormon Church in 1957, the Church was experiencing a time of peaceful growth and enjoying strong societal favor. In fact, I really couldn't recall a single time that the Mormons were the subject of *any* public debate. Privately, people may have thought some of their outward habits were odd, but what was said about the Mormons was generally positive, dealing with the wholesome attributes they tried to communicate. They were known as "the people who took care of their own." If there were any anti-Mormons out there, I never saw or heard of a single one. Only once did a Christian couple in my neighborhood attempt to sit down with me and try to discuss the Mormon faith from their viewpoint. They were horribly unequipped to do so.

Most of the Church's growth during that time came from white Anglo-Saxons. According to Mormon teachings, the blacks were still under the curse of Cain, and the gospel was not presented to them.

Once, in the mid-sixties, a group of blacks picketed the Mormon church building I attended. It was during the Sunday school hour. Several of the Mormons went out and invited the picketers in so that they could see what they were objecting to firsthand. The protesters left rather quickly, but even then we could see the gathering storm clouds on the horizon.

An Incredible Revelation

On June 9, 1978, Mormon President Spencer W. Kimball announced to the Saints that he had received a *revelation* ending the Church's ban on blacks in the priesthood. President Kimball said that he had received the revelation "after extended meditation and prayer in the Salt Lake Temple. That same revelation came to his counselors and to the Quorum of the Twelve Apostles in the Temple, and then it was presented to all of the other General Authorities who approved it unanimously." The revelation declared that the "long promised day has come when every faithful, worthy man in the Church may receive the holy priesthood."[6]

Shock waves reverberated through the Church membership. An eternal doctrine of the Church had been reversed. However, time and a good deal of public relations on the doctrine of progressive revelation (which says that new eternal revelations can supersede older eternal revelations) brought the clamoring to an end. Today, the revelation, actually now called a declaration, and apparently one step below an actual revelation, is Mormon scripture (*Doctrine and Covenants, Declaration 2*).

It had earlier been believed that blacks would never hold the priesthood in mortality because they bore the "mark of Cain" and had been born through his lineage as a punishment for their failures in the Pre-existence (the Pre-existence is covered more fully in a later chapter).

According to Mormon scripture, when Cain rebelled and rose to slay his brother, God cast him away from His face and cursed him to be a vagabond and a fugitive. A mark was placed upon him that would make him known to all who see it: "I the Lord set a mark upon Cain, lest any finding him should kill him" (*Pearl of Great Price*, Moses 6:40).

Early prophets of the Mormon Church taught that this mark of Cain was a black skin. They also taught that the real curse on all who bore the mark of Cain was that they would be forbidden to hold the Mormon priesthood. In the LDS scriptures attributed to father Abraham, we are told that this curse of black skin was carried across the flood through the black-skinned Egyptian wife of Ham, the son of Noah. The LDS scripture again confirms this when it states, "Now, Pharaoh, being of that lineage by which he could not have the right of Priesthood . . ." (*Pearl of Great Price*, Abraham 1:21-27).

Early Mormon Church leaders had many racist and bigoted things to say about the blacks under the guise of their special, revelatory spiritual knowledge. Joseph Smith especially felt that something needed to be done with the blacks.

> Had I anything to do with the Negro, I would confine them by strict law to their own species, and put them on a national equalization.[7]

Brigham Young, second prophet of the Church, was quite vocal in his opinion of the blacks:

> You see some classes of the human family that are black, uncouth, uncomely, disagreeable and low in

their habits, wild, and seemingly without the blessings of the intelligence that is generally bestowed
upon mankind. . . . Cain slew his brother. . . . and the
Lord put a mark on him, which is the flat nose and
black skin.[8]

Shall I tell you the law of God in regard to the
African race? If the white man who belongs to the
chosen seed mixes his blood with the seed of Cain, the
penalty, under the law of God, is death on the spot.
This will always be so.[9]

John Taylor, third prophet of the Mormon Church, explained
how and why the blacks survived the flood:

After the flood we are told that the curse that had
been pronounced upon Cain was continued through
Ham's wife, as he had married a wife of that seed.
And why did it pass through the flood? Because it was
necessary that the devil should have a representation
upon the earth as well as God.[10]

Joseph Fielding Smith, tenth prophet of the Mormon Church,
put it in full perspective when he wrote:

Not only was Cain called upon to suffer, but because of his wickedness, he became the father of an
inferior race. A curse was placed upon him and that
curse has been continued through his lineage and
must do so while time endures. Millions of souls have
come into this world cursed with a black skin and have
been denied the privilege of priesthood and the ful-
ness of the blessings of the gospel. These are the
descendants of Cain. Moreover, they have been made
to feel their inferiority and have been separated from
the rest of mankind from the beginning. . . . We will
also hope that blessings may eventually be given our
Negro Brethren, for they are our Brethren—children

of God—not withstanding their black covering emblematical of eternal darkness.[11]

President Joseph Fielding Smith was a little kinder when speaking about this doctrine publicly. He told one national magazine reporter:

> I would not want you to believe that we bear any animosity toward the Negro. Darkies are wonderful people and they have their place in our church.[12]

Revelation or Public Relations?

Mormons had been taught that Negroes were doomed to the curse until after the return of Christ for His millennial, thousand-year reign. Therefore, they could not enter the Mormon Temple or receive the priesthood. Eventually, civil rights legislation brought the Mormon Church once again into conflict with American standards. LDS leaders were forced to reconsider earlier racist pronouncements against the blacks. In the mid-seventies they hired one of America's largest general management and consulting firms, Cresup, McCormick and Paget (CMP) of New York, which subsequently recommended "a careful review" of certain potentially embarrassing doctrinal policies such as the Negro issue and "a serious reconsideration" of such policies in light of past public relations problems.

The report strongly urged that Mormon Church leaders reassess the race issue and its "relevancy" for the future. Following these suggestions Prophet Spencer W. Kimball conveniently received a "divine revelation" and once again a clumsy Mormon policy was rescinded.[13]

This change of heart over admitting blacks to the Mormon priesthood brought the desired response. *Time* and *Newsweek* magazines stopped their presses to include the "revelation," and the president of the United States, Jimmy Carter, commended Kimball for his "compassionate and courageous" decision.[14]

In reviewing these last few decades of turmoil, *U.S. News & World Report* stated:

The doctrines with the greatest potential for divisiveness concern Blacks and women. For most of its history, the Mormon Church relegated Blacks to a position of inferiority and divine disfavor. Only in 1978 when Spencer W. Kimball, then the church's president, received divine revelation did the church declare Blacks eligible for the priesthood—a title bestowed upon all faithful males.[15]

The High Road to Change

By the mid 1970s, a great many ex-Mormons who had become orthodox Christians began to surface and suddenly represented a very vocal threat to their former church. While the movement was dismissed as a ragtail army of rejects, it soon became apparent that it would not go away and it would not be quiet. For the most part, these former Mormons had a real zeal to bring the true gospel of grace to their former brethren. By the end of the seventies, the many single groups of former Mormons had loosely joined into a nationwide network that was gaining the ear of the general public. In 1979, several dozen leaders in this movement met to strategize a campaign of deliverance for those still lost in Mormonism. By the mid-eighties, the annual Capstone Conference, sponsored by Saints Alive, was drawing hundreds of group leaders from around the world.

It was the first time in the history of the Mormon faith that an organized movement of former Mormons, people who knew the innermost secrets of the Church, had begun to grow. These crusaders knew the Church's weaknesses and dared to challenge the LDS Church publicly on its many areas of unorthodox, anti-Christian doctrine. During the next decade the Mormon Church would make more changes of greater scope than in all its preceding 150 years. We are strongly convinced that because of the LDS Church's desire to slip quietly among mainline Christian groups, it cannot publicly defend itself against the severity of the ex-Mormon charges. It is easier to quietly change the aberrant doctrine and put their efforts into creating friendship ties with ecumenical organizations and churches.

Their plan is working. Many of these groups already consider the Mormons as Christian brethren and the bolder, more evangelistic ex-Mormons as a radical fringe group that should be shunned.

The changes in Mormonism are far from over. Quite probably one of the next "eternal" practices to go will be the daily wearing of the LDS Temple garment, a holdover from the days of long johns. We fully expect that while this book is still in active circulation, a new decree will be issued mandating that the garment be worn only during Temple rituals.

While we are on the subject of Mormon Temple underwear, it too has had a long history of surreptitious change. It started out as an ankle-to-wrist long-john-type garment, with string ties and secret markings on the breast, navel, and knee. It has worked its way down to a mid-calf, short-sleeve, buttoned outfit, available in several styles, including a modernized two-piece model. So much for another "God-given," unchangeable mandate about man's holiest piece of sacred clothing.

The Changing Role of Mormon Women

For women in the Mormon Church, changes have come more slowly. A small but growing feminist movement in the Church is making little headway against the patriarchal power structure. Feeling disenfranchised, some Mormon feminists made it known they were praying not to God the Father, as is tradition, but to God's wife, of whom Mormon scriptures say next to nothing. When officials denounced the practice, the women agreed to stop but said they would ask God to reveal more about His wife. [16]

In 1990 the Mormon Church revised its Temple marriage ritual, substituting a woman's pledge to obey her husband with a pledge to obey God. Many women have stayed away from the Temple because they felt "discomfort and alienation," says Lavina Fielding Anderson, editor-elect of the *Journal of Mormon History*. While women's rights advocates applaud the reforms, they say the Church has a long way to go. Women are still barred from the priesthood and from top leadership posts and are excluded from participating in child-christening ceremonies. [17]

Priesthood Power?

Mormon historian D. Michael Quinn has written some startling things in a 44-page essay in a new work called *Women and Authority: Re-emerging Mormon Feminism*. The volume, edited by Maxine Hanks and published by Signature Books, has 16 other contributors. However, none have stirred the corporate beehive like Quinn has. According to an article written for the Provo, Utah, *Daily Herald* by reporter Vern Anderson:

> There is compelling documentary evidence that Joseph Smith gave women priesthood power in the temple "endowment" ritual, in which women are anointed to become queens and priestesses. "It is an explosive issue," Quinn said ... particularly at a time when church leaders face growing pressure from Mormon feminists for a more active role in a faith dominated by its male priesthood. Mormons define priesthood as the literal power of God and as the authority to act in God's name. They believe the "keys" to the priesthood came to Smith through heavenly intermediaries from Jesus Christ and have been passed on to the church's 12 successive presidents. Quinn said there is no evidence a woman was ordained to specific priesthood offices such as elder, high priest, bishop, or apostle. But in the early church there was clear distinction between priesthood power—available to women in the temple endowment—and priesthood office. ... Still, for nearly 100 years after Smith's death in 1844, Mormon women were authorized to perform the priesthood function of healing other women by anointing and blessing. ...
>
> Two weeks before Smith organized the Female Relief Society of Nauvoo, Ill, in 1842, he told the women that "the Society should move according to the ancient Priesthood" and he was "going to make this society a kingdom of priests as in Enoch's day— as in Paul's day."

Much later in printing the official minutes of Smith's remarks, the official "History of the Church" omitted Smith's first use of the word "Society" and changed the second "Society" to "Church." "Those two alterations changed the entire meaning of his statement," said Quinn.[18]

Church officials are not happy about talk of women having more recognition in the early Church to be coming at a time when the problem with women in Mormonism is a tender subject. In one careful response to the above article, Elder Boyd K. Packer of the Council of the Twelve Apostles gave the following insight:

It should not disturb either men or women that some responsibilities are bestowed upon one and not the other, duties of the priesthood are delegated to men and are patriarchal which means "of the Father." From the very beginning this has been so. The scriptures plainly state that they were "confirmed to be handed down from father to son." . . . There are differences among men and women but there is no inequity. . . . Intelligence and talent favor both of them, but, in the woman's part, she is not just equal to man, she is superior. She can do that which he can never do, not in all eternity can he do it. There are complementing rewards which are hers and hers alone.[19]

A Woman's Place

In the old days, when the average family could get by with one paycheck and most men were secure in their workplace, Mormon women stayed at home and lived the life of the happy homemaker—baking, sewing, and waiting at the door with a warm welcome for their breadwinner.

The goal of every young Mormon girl was to be there waiting for her missionary to return home to his family and rush with her to the Temple to be married for "time and all eternity." Even if

the young woman went to college, it was to advance her perfor-
mance as a wife and mother. Careers for women were not greeted
with smiles by The Brethren.

However, in today's world, where two paychecks are barely
enough to keep food on the table and job security is a rarity, even
the most faithful Mormon women are being pulled into the work
force—and it is tearing apart a vital cord within the very structure of the faith.

LDS President Ezra Taft Benson spoke to this issue in a special
television address that was broadcast to more than 1000 Mormon
meetinghouses throughout the United States and Canada. President Benson urged young wives to stay in their homes and not
seek a job in the workplace. "There is no more noble work than
that of a good and God-fearing mother," he said. "The counsel of
the Church has always been for mothers to spend their full time
in the home in rearing and caring for their children." He said that
young Mormon wives should not delay in having their children
nor limit the size of their families to obtain household luxury
items.[20]

Unfortunately, most LDS mothers are working to help put
food on the table and to pay the LDS tithes and other offerings
that often add up to 20 percent or more of their gross income.
Most can't even think in terms of luxury items. A week later,
President Benson said that a mother's role (at home) is vital to her
exaltation and to the salvation and exaltation of her family.[21]

Splinter Group Ordains Women

While the Church of Jesus Christ of Latter-day Saints has drawn
a line with regard to giving Mormon women the priesthood, one
early Mormon splinter group, the Reorganized Church of Jesus
Christ of Latter-day Saints, threw in the towel on the matter:

> Emily Fern "Bunny" Spillman, in 1985 was ordained
> as one of the first female elders of the Reorganized
> Church of JCLDS, one of 85 women nationwide to be
> ordained in the RLDS . . . the culmination of a life-
> time of work in the church. "I just want to be a worthy

servant." The Missouri-based RLDS church split off
from the main Mormon Church in the 1840's over
who should lead the church, Brigham Young or the
descendants of Joseph Smith the founding prophet of
Mormonism. In 1984, church president Wallace B.
Smith, the great-grandson of Joseph Smith, decreed
that women should be ordained into leadership roles.[22]

Whether or not Mormon women should be ordained to the
priesthood is really only part of the larger and more important
question: Why does the Mormon Church continue to promote an
unbiblical priesthood in the first place? We will look at the
Mormon priesthood more closely shortly. For now it is important
to note only that the long history of change in the Mormon
Church is at its core a problem of faulty doctrine.

Whether it is polygamy or vengeful oaths, or as we will show,
"eternal" Temple ceremonies and doctrines of blood atonement,
the Church of Jesus Christ of Latter-day Saints finds itself in
the position of continually trying to fix or modify doctrines that
were wrong from the beginning. At the same time, the Church
must convince faithful Mormons that it is God, not false Mormon
prophets, who has changed His mind.

4

Reach Out and Touch Someone

ONE OF THE VOICES YOU HEAR as *The God Makers II* film opens is the frustrated voice of a young ex-Mormon named Lisa as she says, "The biggest danger was that they took me in, and I was thinking it was a Christian church, and it wasn't a Christian church; it was a cult." Lisa had bought the lie. She fell victim to the seductive spirit of Mormonism, and it wasn't until she had been in the system for some time that her strong Christian background sent out enough danger signals that Lisa paid attention and left the Mormon Church.

Lisa isn't alone. She is in a fellowship that spans the globe. The word "cult" conjures up images of Charlie Manson or saffron-robed Hare Krishnas with shaven heads bobbing up and down in mindless chantings. More recently, the whole world watched as federal agents waited outside a heavily armed compound near Waco, Texas, while polygamist cult leader David Koresh waited for a divine word from God. To many people, Mormonism seems mild in comparison. In light of such divergent cult forms, let's define what we mean by the word.

Defining a Cult

Billy Graham characterizes cults this way:

> In general, I would say a cult is a group which follows religious ideas (usually taught by a strong leader) which are not in accordance with the Bible.

Sometimes cults will have certain writings for which they claim supernatural authority in addition to the Bible. Often the leader of the cult will demand total, blind obedience to his word and may even separate children from parents.

While cults differ greatly with each other, they have in common one thing: they reject Jesus Christ and the Bible as their authorities and therefore reject faith in Jesus Christ as God's way of salvation. Often, they attempt to disguise this by talking a great deal about Jesus. But frequently, the test of a cult is found in their answer to this question: How can I be saved? If the answer is anything other than trusting Jesus Christ, then the group may be a cult. This is particularly true if they say they alone have the truth and salvation is found by joining their group.[1]

Mormonism surely fits that definition. Mormon Church leaders have added to the Word of God with the *Book of Mormon, Doctrine and Covenants,* and the *Pearl of Great Price.* They have detracted from the Bible's authority with their priesthood and the doctrine that God must have a prophet in place directing His Church on earth. Full salvation is found only in Mormonism. Surely one must beware of such wolves in sheep's clothing who come among the flock to steal and destroy!

While Mormons may wish to gloss over any objective criteria for distinguishing *religions* from *cults,* we use the term *cult* to designate "a religious group which claims authorization by Christ and the Bible but neglects or distorts the gospel, the central message of the Savior and the Scriptures."[2]

No matter how nice a group appears, *nice* isn't on the list of criteria for determining orthodoxy. That standard Mormon test for truth, the warm "burning in the bosom," isn't on the list either, but in spite of that, Latter-day Saints are trying to sell the burning-bosom softness of modern Mormonism to the world as evidence of orthodoxy. The frightening thing is that it appears to be working. It has been stated that 60 to 80 percent of all converts to Mormonism come from evangelical Christian backgrounds.[3]

It is certainly a lot easier for someone to move from one Christian church to another than it is to move from an orthodox Christian church to Mormonism. First, one doesn't have to renounce one's profession of faith to jump a denominational fence, but leaping over into Mormonism is a jump over a pretty high wall. The Mormon Church of today is putting all its efforts into motivating people to get over that wall. In fact, many shepherds—pastors who are supposed to be protecting their flocks—are inviting in the wolves to play with the sheep. *The Mormons are leaving with the sheep.*

In a sense you can't blame the cults any more than you can blame the wolves: They are both doing exactly what they are bred to do. With marauding wolves, the problem lies more with the shepherd and the flock. A shepherd who isn't keeping an alert, protective eye on the flock is going to lose sheep, and the sheep who do not keep an eye on the shepherd but instead wander near the edge of the flock are prime candidates for the wolf's supper.

Remember what the Lord said in this regard: "Verily, verily, I say unto you, He that entereth not by the door into the sheepfold, but climbeth up some other way, the same is a thief and a robber" (John 10:1).

In the *Latter-Day Sentinel*, a now-defunct "Mormon" newspaper, the Mormons boasted:

> A recent study by the Southern Baptists revealed that an average of 282 members of their church join the LDS church each week. Coincidentally, the average Southern Baptist congregation has 283 members. ... The Baptists lose 52 congregations each year to the Mormons.[4]

When we read this kind of report, it's hard to understand how any Christian minister can comfortably sit down for a casual interfaith lunch with the Mormon bishop down the street and not be a little nervous. Yet in the new ecumenicalism of the nineties, it would seem rude for him not to fellowship with the Mormon.

A Case in Point

In the mid-eighties Ed accepted an invitation to visit a local Baptist minister at his church office and answer his many questions regarding Mormonism. They had a long talk. His name was Walford Erickson, and he wrote a religion column every now and then for the *Journal American*, a local daily newspaper in Bellevue, Washington. Ed could say without fear of contradiction that those articles were ecumenical.

One day he wrote a column that gave Ed some insight to the losses that Erickson's denomination had been having to the Mormons. In an article entitled "Mormon Tries to Reach Out to Other Faiths," he reported about the Mormon missionary who had visited one of his minister friends. This Mormon, Darl Anderson, just wanted to make friends with the pastor. Erickson was smitten with the idea that this Mormon not only wanted to reach out and engage in friendly dialogue with non-Mormon clergy but had the backing of the LDS Church to encourage and train other Mormon bishops in the area to do the same.

Wally Erickson is a fine man, but it would seem he lacked discernment in this area, since he wrote that he and a few of his pastor friends around Bellevue took delight in drawing Darl into their inner circle.[5]

In a local letter to the editor, Ed responded that Darl Anderson's attention to Erickson and his friends was "no accidental experience, but part of an LDS program to neutralize ministers and civic leaders to the covert, predatory program of the Mormon Church. Darl and his missionary buddies steal sheep for their church! That's their job."[6]

Darl Anderson conducts an in-house Mormon lecture series he calls "Win a Minister and Influence a Thousand" and is the Mormon author of *Soft Answers to Hard Questions*, which illustrates the strategy LDS leadership has adopted to gain acceptance among the American Christian community. He says that the purpose of public communications is to "promote public goodwill and positive attitudes [toward Mormonism] so that people will be more receptive to the blessings of the glorious Restoration." In other words, he wants local Mormon leaders to conduct themselves among Christians in a way that will make it possible to proselytize people who already are members of Christian churches.

Anderson devotes the book to ways to dialogue with Christian ministers in an attempt to get them to perceive Mormons as something other than a threat. He relates that when he began to develop this approach, local ministers were openly hostile to him, but after a while they warmed to his gentle tactics. He tells how he eventually persuaded them to let him join the local ministerial association.[7]

The fact is, Darl Anderson had been "called and set apart," with the official backing of his Mormon Church to lower barriers between Mormons and people of other churches. The purpose of the discussions of "friendshipping" is to draw attention to points that pastors and Mormons can agree on.

The design of such strategy ultimately sways naive Christians into the path of the Mormon agenda. Darl Anderson has already brought disruption to the evangelical Christian community in Mesa, Arizona, where one pastor, Roger Keller, invited the Mormons to come in fellowship. He also spoke to LDS missionary groups about the things they held in common. He was the perfect example of what Anderson felt could be accomplished through his program. Keller ended up as a Mormon, and his Presbyterian church was shaken to the core.

Anderson was then sent to Palmyra, New York and was quoted in a Church-related article as saying:

> If you can change that minister's attitude, you can change the attitude of hundreds. . . . Now if the minister is saying unkind things, it's turning people against the (Mormon) church. I look to the day when whole congregations will come into the church through their own leadership. We see quite a few ministers come

into the church. There isn't any reason a minister couldn't lead them in the truths we teach.[8]

Christian ministers aren't always treated so kindly, especially if they take a stand against the LDS doctrines. Michael Warneke has pastored the Bible Baptist Church in Salt Lake City since 1979. In a letter to John L. Smith of Utah Ministries (a ministry to Mormons), he told of some of the frustration that came after a bit of a confrontation with the Mormons:

> The next Sunday, the LDS church sent many carloads of missionaries to our church. They went in and out of the services, to disturb us. Four or five would come in for five minutes and then get up and leave, slamming the doors as they went out. They kept this up through Sunday school and the morning worship service.

This was not unexpected, as the pastor explained:

> Upon moving to our neighborhood and buying our current home, upon finding out I was a Baptist teacher, the Mormons pulled out the trees in our yard and egged our house with rotten eggs. Since we have built our church we have been robbed eight times in eight years. The windows have been knocked out of our bus three times, and we've been vandalized many times. Our boys play baseball. . . . It is nothing to see a Mormon kid with a .200 batting average picked to play over a non-Mormon with a .600 batting average.[9]

Mormons Join VISN Interfaith Network

In 1988, the Mormon Church jumped at the opportunity to join the beginning of a new interfaith religious television network. Vision Interfaith Satellite Network (VISN), a cable network, agreed to carry some Mormon programming. This programming included times for direct Mormon gospel messages in addition to "Music and the Spoken Word," Mormon Tabernacle Choir specials, and reruns of some of the dramatic films and TV specials done in the past.[10]

LDS activity on VISN has not only opened up the living rooms of literally millions of cable viewers, but has produced strong gains in common ground with the 22 other religious groups with whom they share network time.

VISN makes no pretense of being a Christian network. While many old-line denominations of historic Christianity are involved, so are other religions, notably Judaism. Additionally, several cults are represented, including the Mormons, the Christian Scientists, and the Unitarians. VISN also has the blessing of the National Council of Churches. A Mormon, Ralph Hardy, sits on the board of trustees of VISN.

Recently a pastor in the Seattle area called Ed's office to say that he had received an invitation from a local LDS Director of Clergy Relations to attend a promotional dinner at a nearby Mormon church building being held to introduce local clergy to the work of VISN cable network.

Sent by form letter on LDS Church letterhead to "all the pastors between Renton and Bellevue, and from Mercer Island to Snoqualmie Pass," Richard A. Hamilton, Director of Clergy Relations for the Renton Washington North Stake, invited the pastors to a special orientation and teleconference at one of the larger LDS churches in the area. Mr. Hamilton also invited the pastors and their spouses to "be our guests for dinner following the teleconference."[11]

Dear Pastor

Where once the Mormon Church positioned itself as clearly outside the realm of mainstream Christianity, today it is making an effort to be conciliatory. Overtures like Richard Hamilton's contact with Seattle area pastors promote the position that Mormonism and other streams of Christianity have more in common than not. Throughout the country, Mormon leaders are soliciting the friendship of Christian clergy and in some cases even applying for membership in the local ministerial associations. Books such as *We Are Christians Too!* and *Are Mormons Christian?* are arguing that Mormons and Christians are brothers in the Christian faith.

And the Mormons aren't waiting for Christian pastors to walk into LDS bookstores to find such books. Not only are the many Directors of Clergy Relations dropping off gift copies, but the authors are also getting the books out in direct force. Don and Brennan Kingsland, authors of *Are Mormons Christian?* sent a direct-mail piece out to Christian pastors, telling them:

> The Christian community has enough problems today fighting Satan—without weakening itself by divisions within, from attacking each other. Unfortunately, many persons today are more interested in fighting over "who is right" and "who is wrong," than they are in promoting unity in the Body of Christ and spreading the Good News to those waiting to hear it. . . .
>
> Don't be misled by attackers of the Church of Jesus Christ of Latter-day Saints. These individuals, incidentally, have developed affluent ministries and made lucrative businesses out of creating divisions in the Body of Christ.
>
> We are firmly convinced that Satan is behind the "divide and conquer" strategy we see being used so effectively by anti-Mormon leaders. To enable you to ascertain the TRUTH about our church, we are offering "MORMONS ARE CHRISTIANS, TOO!" at a special price to pastors.[12]

Interfaith Inroads

In an Associated Press release which recently came out of Salt Lake City, the writer reported on how the Mormon Church was trying to smooth its relations with other denominations and enter into informal dialogue:

The issue of interfaith relations with the Mormon Church was brought to the forefront by the Presbyterian Church (USA), which held its General Assembly in early June in a land where Mormons outnumber Presbyterians more than 200-to-1. In response, Mormon leaders issued an appeal to set up informal meetings with Presbyterian officials, and the denomination's Theology and Worship Ministry Unit and Utah Presbytery both submitted reports on Mormon-Presbyterian relations. . . .

Signs of change exist: a recently revised ritual no longer portrays non-Mormon clergy as agents of Satan, for example. But some ecumenical officials and church observers say the Church of JCLDS has not entered the mainstream of American religious life.

"Mormons' exclusivist claim toward truth and being God's church is as strong as it's ever been," said the head of a liberal Mormon group who spoke on condition of anonymity. "That's probably the major stumbling block toward improving relations with other churches."

Jan Shipps, a professor of religious studies at Indiana University, said the recent elimination of the part of the church's endowment ceremony where Satan hired a non-Mormon preacher to spread false teachings "is a very important signifier the LDS church is moving away from its position that all other churches are false."

Shipps said though *no official policy* encourages ecumenical relations, there has been "a kind of relaxing" of rules allowing some local Mormon churches to get involved with councils of ministries.[13]

The pattern is there in every corner of the Christian community. LDS leadership has reversed its elitist nature in the past decade in areas that the Mormon faithful would have considered unbelievable 20 years ago. For example, in early 1989 a mailer went out from the pastor of one of the downtown churches in Bellevue, Washington, inviting local pastors and their congregations and choirs to participate in an interdenominational Easter morning procession of walking the Stations of the Cross, which would take place in various downtown locations. Ed's home church sits on the edge of that area, and its members were therefore invited to participate. Ed was shocked to see the Mormon Church listed as having already been assigned one Station where *they* would have the responsibility of leading the prayers and singing. He knew that they would have full freedom to lead the participants in Mormon prayer and singing.

Ed was provoked by such antibiblical compromise to directly challenge the organizing pastor in a letter, saying in part, "It is with utter dismay that I have heard of your plans to have a joint celebration of Good Friday and Easter with the Mormon Church. I wonder if you *really* understand that while the LDS Church may certainly have a Christian ethic and use Christian terminology, they do *not* have an *orthodox* Christian theology."[14]

After few tense conversations, the Mormons pulled out. This is just one example of what motivated Christians who understand the issues can do to stop the Mormon infiltration into orthodoxy.

In another recent development, Mormon leaders in eastern Idaho asked to be part of the National Day of Prayer gathering. Not only were they invited, but one evangelical pastor, speaking not for men but for God, asked for forgiveness, not for doctrine, but for "not responding to the LDS people in Christian character." Dr. Rulon Robison, LDS Regional Representative for the area, welcomed the call for fence-mending, saying, "We have long desired to break down these walls and build bridges of friendship and understanding and love."[15]

To the general public, these episodes might slip by with an "Oh, well, how could it hurt to have them praying with a crowd of Christians?" But it is highly significant to ex-Mormons who have spent years in the LDS Church listening to speakers lifting up the Mormon Church as God's only true voice among the "whores of all the earth."[16]

One writer, trying to explain the deep quagmire into which this kind of logic has placed the Mormon Church, states:

> Mormons believe Christian churches are apostate, but the LDS church is Christian, therefore the LDS [church] is apostate. . . . Mormons say Christian churches are apostate, [and] the LDS church is not apostate, therefore the LDS church is not Christian. Mormonism assumes that the LDS church is Christian, while at the same time assuming that Christianity is apostate; the only way out of this dilemma is for Mormonism to either discard the untenable theory of a total apostasy, or cease to claim to be Christian.[17]

Mormons have already shown their hand at political and religious integration on many fronts. One Associated Press article recently explained their approach:

> In 1986, Mormons became part of the Religious Alliance Against Pornography, a wide ecumenical cross-section. In 1984, they affiliated with Religion in American Life, involving most major US denominations in seeking to stimulate weekly worship. Also, in the mid-80's Mormons entered into interreligious relief work, including aid to the homeless. They contributed about $5 million to relief efforts in famine-ravaged central Africa, much of it through Catholic Relief Services and the American Red Cross.[18]

We know that these are very worthwhile social efforts and should be applauded as such, but it is important to recognize that this is all part of a conditioning process that the Mormons have implemented in their efforts to become an acceptable part of the ecumenical body of general Christianity. In this same article some other points are clearly laid out:

> Mormons, who generally have kept aloof from other Christian communities, are gradually—and in

expanding ways—moving into working association with them. . . . "Some Mormons don't want it," said Mormon theologian Roger R. Keller of Brigham Young University in Provo, Utah. "Some of the others are suspicious of Mormons. But we've begun to break through the shell of isolation."

As misconceptions and scurrilous notions about each other are diminished, "more interchange becomes possible," he said. "I hope we are standing at the crossroads of genuine dialogue."

Let us break in here to say that Roger Keller, who was just quoted, is the Presbyterian minister we told you about earlier in this chapter who was seduced away from his church congregation in Mesa, Arizona through the efforts of Darl Anderson.

Such dialogue has flourished for years among Protestant, Roman Catholic, Anglican, Eastern Orthodox and Jewish groups, reducing old prejudices and distortions. But Mormons who were denounced, persecuted and driven westward in their early years, generally have stayed apart from that interreligious companionship and teamwork until recently. Dallin Oaks, a member of the church's ruling Council of 12, said . . . "I think the outlook for our being involved with others is good. . . . And I think other groups need us, and we need other groups."[19]

We would rejoice to see every Mormon come to Christ; however, Christians don't need the ungodly beliefs and practices of Mormonism. But Mormonism does need the credibility and blessing of Christianity. It is very frustrating to see Mormons work so hard to appear to be what they are not. They can start a friendship with every Christian pastor in the world, but it will not make their doctrines Christian. If only they could see the futility of their errors and repent corporately. *In one day* they could shed these doctrines of error and be set free in Christ. What a day of rejoicing that would be to see people who are trying so hard to look like Christians actually become *the real thing!*

The Only True Jews

The Mormons aren't just interested in stepping into mainstream Christianity; they have their *other* eye on Israel. It is the Mormons' secret claim to be the "true Israel." Even now the Mormon Church is reaching out for what it believes is its inheritance in Israel.

Chuck Sackett is the former Mormon who authored the book *What's Going On in There?* which details the actual LDS Temple ritual. Chuck was visiting in Jerusalem at the same time Jeremiah Films was there and agreed to an interview at the site of the extremely controversial BYU Extension on Mount Scopus.

Ed had been invited to Israel several years earlier during the Extension's construction to explain the LDS doctrines to leaders of the Knesset. These secular leaders were shocked to find out that the god of Mormonism was an exalted man. It was equally shocking to the religious leaders of Israel. But political expediency overcame the very vocal objections of the conservative minority, and the Mormons were able to complete the project. Former Mormon Chuck Sackett described the current situation for us:

> I'm standing here in beautiful Jerusalem. This impressive structure is built on the sacred site of Mount Scopus by the Church of Jesus Christ of Latter-day Saints, as an extension to Brigham Young University. I believe that it's very important for the Jewish people to know about the deception and misrepresentation that was employed in building this Mormon edifice. Mormons used political intrigue and great sums of money in order to cover up their true intent to proselytize Jews and convert them to Mormonism. Most of the religious Jews of Jerusalem consider this Mormon structure an abomination and sacrilege of holy ground, and are outraged by its presence.

These clothes that I'm wearing are the authentic Mormon Temple attire, which Mormons believe are copied from the actual attire that the priesthood wore in the Temple of Solomon that stood on this site behind me. Mormons believe that there has been an apostasy in Judaism, and that they hold the only true authority to administer in the rituals of the Temple that will be performed here in Jerusalem.[20]

As Chuck explained, Mormons believe that they are the only true Jews on earth today. They also believe they come from the tribes of Ephraim and Manasseh, and that they have the true blood of Israel. Mormon males are ordained into what they call the Melchizedek priesthood, and believe that when they are baptized, their blood actually changes from Gentile blood to the blood of Israel.

Mormons believe that they will build the new Jerusalem near Independence, Missouri, and it will be the primary capital of the kingdom of God on the earth. And in Jerusalem will be the secondary capital, which will be administered by Jews.

The Church of Jesus Christ of Latter-day Saints came here to Jerusalem under the banner of Christianity to establish this edifice and to establish their presence here when they are no more true Christians than they are true Jews.[21]

5

Astonishing Changes in the Unchangeable Temple

IF YOU BELIEVE THE PREMISE that the Mormon Church is true, *or even possibly true*, the LDS Temple ritual has to be at the center of your faith. It is only through the sacred Temple that you have *any* hope of personal exaltation or godhood. The path to Mormon godhood will be explained in detail in a later chapter. For now it is important to know that without the ritual and the keys the Temple provides, there can be no entrance into Mormon godhood. To an active Mormon, the Temple is like the doorway to heaven. It is so holy that Mormons, even those who have carpooled to the Temple, remain absolutely silent on *anything* regarding the rituals in which they have just participated once they step outside the Temple doors.

Prelude to Change

When the film *The God Makers* was released in 1982, it had a monumental impact that went far beyond the film itself or any expectations of its makers. For the first time ever on film, the heresies of Mormonism were revealed and the world was exposed to the darkest secrets and doctrines of the Latter-day Saints.

While the film was difficult enough for Mormons to deal with in its entirety, the parts that showed LDS Temple ordinances struck so deeply that many Temple Mormons felt a deep violation of their privacy.

Suddenly, rituals performed in solemn sanctity within the Mormon Temples under the most consecrated conditions were being shown on movie screens in as many as a thousand Christian churches each month. The secret ceremonies became the subject of numerous radio and television shows, bringing the things Temple Mormons had done in secret into the glaring light of day. In the movie, the reenactments of the rituals were displayed in full, authorized Temple costume, and were performed and supervised by former longtime Temple worker Chuck Sackett and his wife, Dolly.

The movie not only displayed the Mormons' deepest secrets to the world but gave sound evidence that they were occult in every respect, with large portions of their ceremony taken from Blue Lodge Freemasonry. In fact, one "secret" about the film is that the LDS Temple scenes were filmed in an actual Masonic lodge room that was rented for the purpose because of its similar ambiance.

No one dared challenge the accuracy of the Temple ritual reenactment. First, Mormons were bound by Temple oath to never speak of it outside the Temple. Second, the word from the LDS pulpits was that Mormons who wanted to stay in good standing in the Church had better stay away from showings of *The God Makers*. Third, the people reenacting the ceremonies in the film were working from a script containing the actual, *verbatim* rituals.

Going Public

While still officiating in the Los Angeles Temple, Chuck Sackett covertly took a small tape recorder into the Temple with him and recorded the secret rituals. The next business day, Chuck notified the Temple president of what he had done and said that he intended to publish the ritual. He let the president know that he was making himself available for both Church and legal action. He was willing to risk everything to let the world see the real LDS Temple ritual. When Chuck made the material available to other ministries to Mormons, The LDS response was to deny that there was anything more to the rumblings than a few dissidents playing at what they *thought* they knew.

When another tape recording appeared with excerpts from two other Temple ceremonies, we made the decision to create a film that would center on this critical element of the Latter-day heresy. *The Temple of the God Makers* was born. Its swift and wide distribution was credited to the great success of the first film and the tremendous interest the public had in seeing the inner darkness of Mormonism revealed. The film showed in detail that what really went on behind closed Temple doors was not bringing Mormons into a closer walk with God, but actually driving them away from God into a bizarre, occult ritual of self-glorification.

At this time, Chuck and Dolly Sackett published the full rituals,[1] and thousands of copies of their book spread across the United States and many foreign countries. *The Mormon Temple secrets were secret no longer.* They were also hardly sacred. Their cultic, anti-Christian mockery stood open and indefensible.

At that time, Ed's ministry, Saints Alive, was broadcasting daily radio programming in much of Utah, Idaho, and Arizona. One week it ran a series of programs detailing the heresies within the Temple, showing significant parallels with Freemasonry, the occult, and Luciferianism. The programs compared the rituals to the biblical warnings against such practices. The station broadcasting the programs to the Salt Lake City area was darkly warned to take the show off the air. After the second segment played, the station's broadcast tower facility was burned to the ground, and the station was unable to operate for nearly six months. These were no idle threats.

Meanwhile, the Sacketts took their presentation on the road, teaching and calling Mormons to repentance in hundreds of communities. They appeared on radio and television programs nationwide, boldly proclaiming the truth about Mormonism to potential audiences of millions.

Looking at Mormonism from a different angle, Idaho pastor Jim Spencer, a former Mormon and author of several books on Mormonism, coauthored a work with Bill Schnoebelen, ex-Mormon and ex-Satanist, which showed the parallels between

Mormonism, witchcraft, and Freemasonry. The book, *Mormonism's Temple of Doom*, was publicly endorsed by the great Christian apologist Dr. Walter Martin. Its volatile charges caused an explosive reaction within Mormonism and a great deal of controversy among the less confrontational ministries to Mormons, such that the wedge between the more intellectual ministries and the more evangelical ones widened further. Even Walter Martin's ministry pulled away from endorsing the book following Martin's death. Yet the book is a powerful tool in understanding the deep occult bedrock of Mormonism, the Mormon Temple.[2]

In the fall and winter of 1989, a revived flurry of radio programs seemed to reopen the bleeding wounds of the Mormons about their Temple. Perhaps the straw that broke the camel's back was a two-day presentation of the rituals on Christian Research Institute's nationwide radio program, "The Bible Answer Man." Broadcasting live across the country on hundreds of stations, Chuck and Dolly Sackett laid the ceremonies out once again, playing segments of the actual rituals from Chuck's original tape recording and answering callers' questions from all parts of the country.

While all of this intense activity was going on, faithful Mormons were becoming extremely unhappy over the Church's silence against the charges of heresy and occultism. To make matters even more cumbersome, some of the women in the Church were getting tired of being treated like chattel in the Temple ritual and were starting to become vocal about their feelings.

A Remarkable Event

We have no way of knowing exactly what caused The Brethren to act. We suspect it was the culmination of the many attacks, not only from the former Mormons but increasingly from within the Mormon Church. What we do know is that several months later, the LDS Church closed its U.S. Temples for what everyone believed were normal renovations and repairs. On April 10, 1990, immediately after the General Conference (the Church's largest ecclesiastical gathering of the year), the doors were once again opened to those Mormons with Temple recommends, except this time something besides the carpeting had changed. Major revisions had been made *to the rituals themselves*. As Chuck Sackett remarked in his detailed report of the changes:

> No announcement was made of a new revelation, nor was a sustaining vote taken, as church rules require. Mormons have been taught that the temple rituals were a direct revelation from God to Joseph Smith, Jr., the founder of Mormonism. Such drastic changes should only be made through another revelation to Ezra Taft Benson, the current Mormon Prophet. Mormons have been taught that such revelations must be reported at General Conference [in early April] and a sustaining vote taken to give the revelation official approval and sanction of the membership.[3]

It was apparent that the Mormon Church chose to wait until immediately after the semiannual General Conference to effect the changes and sidestep embarrassing member concern over it at the leadership meetings. Mormons, as we noted earlier, are under solemn oath not to discuss things of the Temple outside its doors. By the time of the next General Conference in October, The Brethren had the membership under control, and the drastic changes never became an issue.

What is most fascinating about the changes is that the Church had literally ripped out almost everything in the Temple ceremony that the many ministries to Mormons had been exposing since Chuck Sackett walked out of the Los Angeles Temple with that tape recording in his pocket. The parts that were removed were the *very* things being declared as grievous to God across the nation on radio and television, and in newsletters and books. The sections that were expunged were primarily those that Chuck and Dolly Sackett reenacted in both *The God Makers* and *The Temple of the God Makers!*

Mormon leaders took the only road out of the swamp. They radically changed a ritual that had supposedly been *restored to its original form* when it was given to Joseph Smith *from the very mouth of God.* We will deal with the new Mormon doctrine of progressive revelation more fully in another chapter, but as briefly noted earlier, it is the quasi-doctrine of concession that states that the revelations of any living prophet can supersede the revelations of any former prophet. What an open door to heresies within heresies!

The Details

When news of the Temple changes came, the specifics of the reformation were sketchy. The very first week, a number of calls came from far and wide about the changes. The exact details surfaced when a friend of a friend passed the details to a Mormon ministry in Salt Lake City.[4]

This material clearly confirmed the changes Chuck Sackett reported in an April 1990 report, which received wide circulation when it was duplicated in full in the September 1990 edition of the *Evangel*, a monthly newspaper produced by the ministry of John L. Smith, Utah Missions, Inc., in Marlow, Oklahoma.

The Sackett report detailed a number of significant changes, and with his permission we will quote his description of the changes at length:

> 1. The execution of the penalties have been removed from the Priesthood Signs. No longer will every initiate be required to perform the three morbid gestures associated with having their lives taken if they reveal any of the temple secrets. These gestures were:
>
>   A. Running the right thumb across the throat from left ear to right ear, signifying having one's throat slit from ear to ear.
>   B. Drawing the right hand across the chest from left breast to right breast, signifying having one's chest ripped open and one's heart torn out.
>   C. Running the right thumb across the abdomen, signifying having one's body cut asunder and one's vitals and bowels gush out.

What a relief this will be to thousands of civilized and sensitive Mormons who have been offended by this barbaric atrocity with each temple visit, and also to those who decline to attend the Temple because of this highly offensive aspect.

2. The most awesome spectacle of the entire series of temple rituals is gone! *The Sign of the Second Token of the Melchizedek Priesthood, the Patriarchal Grip, or Sure Sign of the Nail* has been eliminated. No longer will temple initiates be required to chant in unison the infamous *"Pay Lay Ale, Pay Lay Ale, Pay Lay Ale"* as they raise and lower their arms three times in the universal gesture of obeisance. No longer will thinking Mormons travel home wondering, as we did so often, what does *"Pay Lay Ale"* really mean?

3. The Masonically inspired *Five Points of Fellowship* through the temple veil has been eliminated. No longer will temple initiates be required to embrace "the Lord" through the veil in this mystical, highly occult configuration while they whisper in his ear the *Name of the Second Token of the Melchizedek Priesthood, the Patriarchal Grip, or Sure Sign of the Nail.*

The embrace is out, but it is likely that the incantation associated with it is still in. Apparently initiates will still be required to repeat back to "the Lord" through the veil: *"Health in the navel, marrow in the bones, strength in the loins and in the sinews. Power in the Priesthood be upon me and upon all my posterity, through all generations of time and throughout all eternity."*

4. Lucifer's hireling lackey, the Christian Minister, is out. No longer will initiates watch the devil hire a Christian pastor (representing all Christian clergymen) to teach his satanic doctrines to Adam. No longer will they watch him mock and ridicule the most basic doctrines of Christianity. No longer will they watch as this Christian hireling abandons his faith and teachings and changes altars to join Adam

and Eve in the Mormon Priesthood program of works and rituals.

The liturgical significance of this change is profound. It is through the initiate's personal identification with Adam or Eve, as they renounce and deny the basic tenets of Christianity, that the purging of all remnants of Christian commitment in the initiates is accomplished. This crucial act in the Mormon conversion process would seem to have been eliminated! What will be substituted to accomplish this vital function spiritually bonding the initiates to LDS Priesthood power?

5. Women will no longer be required to veil their faces during the prayer in the Endowment prayer circle. However, they will still wear the veil as their regular head covering. This was a vital symbol of the subservience of women in the Priesthood and the dominance of the man in all aspects of Mormonism. The veil is to be lifted only by her worthy resurrected husband in his process of resurrecting her.

6. Women (single and married) will no longer be required to swear an oath and covenant of obedience to their husband. This change may have the most radical effect of all on Mormonism! The oppressive stigma of female singleness will no longer be officially imposed by the Mormon god in the temple. Single women will be somewhat relieved of the extreme pressure to marry. The wife will no longer be reminded with each temple visit that her only channel to her god is through her husband and that his faithfulness determines her eternity. Each Mormon husband can no longer rely on his wife (or wives) to constantly prod and motivate him to do his duty to the church based upon her total dependence upon him for her eternal exaltation. What will become of the church as a result of the change? How many worthy Priesthood leaders will become indifferent or lazy due to this major doctrinal change? We will have to watch and discern the inevitable decline in vigor taking place[5] [all emphases added].

One of the more interesting asides to this story of the Temple ritual change was the removal of the words of the chant, *"Pay Lay Ale, Pay Lay Ale, Pay Lay Ale."* A number of years ago, the Sacketts showed that the words were a quick step-to-the-side from words in Hebrew that mimic, in their harshest translation, *"O Marvelous Lucifer."* In a far more conservative translation, the words read, *"O marvelous god,"* with the god being defined as that one to whom the words were spoken. Using even that approach, one can see in the ritual that the words had to refer to Lucifer, who was the one who responded when Adam called out what was supposed to be an English translation of the word.[6]

The Sackett report on *Pay Lay Ale* had been an issue of long-standing debate within a few of the more intellectual ministries to Mormons. Surely, ex-Mormon theorists could argue the points till the end of time. But in the Temple, when Adam called out those words, Lucifer was the *only god* who answered. Most importantly, the Mormon Church pulled the entire sequence containing the *Pay Lay Ale* chant from the ritual. There is no way of proving that the chant was removed because of the Sacketts' observations, but why else would such a critical portion of the original ritual be dropped?

One of the news reporters who interviewed Ed in Salt Lake City during the premier showings of the new film wanted to know why we had portrayed examples of the old Temple ritual in *The God Makers II*. We did it because we didn't want the Mormon hierarchy to get away with secretly removing key portions of what they claimed was a sacred ritual restored to the purity of its first-century order by the holy power of God. The theology of restorationism *cannot* allow you to change something that has already been restored to its original perfection.

The alterations in the Temple ceremony made headline news across the country. One report in the *Arizona Republic* particularly caught the flavor of the many facets of change involved.

> Revolutionary changes in temple ceremony . . . are
> seen as a move to bring the secret ceremony closer to
> mainstream Christianity. . . . The changes are the most

drastic revisions of the century, rivaled only by the church's removal at the turn of the century of an oath to avenge the killers of church founder Jo Smith, according to Mormon insiders. The (asking to remain anonymous) member said, "They are substantive, I would say, in the cosmetics of the thing rather than in substance." A former member said . . . "The climax has been eliminated. Removal of that part of the ritual is the equivalent of taking the Eucharist out of the Roman Catholic mass."

Not all Mormons are happy with the ceremony changes. "I have Mormon friends who will see it as a step toward apostasy and an accommodation to the world," said one practicing Mormon in Utah.[7]

Most Mormon Church members who allowed themselves to be quoted in news stories about revisions in the Church's confidential Temple ceremony have been summoned for interviews by Church officials. In additon, the sacred confidentiality of the Temples was reemphasized by the public communications office of the Church. As John Dart, a religion writer, noted in a Los Angeles *Times* news story:

When they [Mormons] leave the house of the Lord they are under obligation to be true to a sacred trust not to speak of that which is holy and sanctified, therefore, it is appropriate that church leaders visit with members when comments about the temple or other sacred matters are made public and are attributed to them in the news media." . . . Ron Priddis [one-time editor of the *Seventh East Press*] said he was reprimanded during his interview with a church authority (for talking to the press) and called the revisions . . . "the most significant change in the church since Blacks received the priesthood in 1978 . . . in a church that is so patriarchal, that's quite a step.[8]

Bringing members in for interviews with Church leaders is one way the Mormon Church controls its members. As we will see, not every member who disagrees with The Brethren gets off so easily.

6

Purging the Radicals

I N THE FALL OF 1992, MORMON-WATCHERS BEGAN to pick up rumblings of an uncharacteristic *purifying* within its ranks of members who would be an embarrassment to the new ecumenical face of Mormonism. The reverberations broke through the wall of silence toward the end of November, when local, regional, and national wire services carried the story of another one of the secret plans of The Brethren gone wrong. The *Salt Lake Tribune* released an article that was a balanced presentation of the outcry:

> The Church of Jesus Christ of Latter-day Saints is purging hundreds of Mormon dissidents who church officials say are preoccupied unduly with Armageddon. This massive housecleaning may be one of the church's largest since the 1850s, when thousands were excommunicated for everything from poor hygiene and low church attendance to disobeying the Ten Commandments. In recent months, Mormons from Utah, Nevada, Arizona and Idaho have been expelled and many others have been threatened.
>
> Those interviewed by the *Salt Lake Tribune* say they have faced church discipline for a range of transgressions—from having too much emergency food storage to adhering to the doomsday predictions of popular Mormon presidential candidate Bo Gritz, who received more than 28,000 Utah votes in the November [1992] election. . . .

LDS Church leaders from central and southern Utah complained of such "troublesome ideologies" during a Nov. 13-14 meeting at the Edgemont Stake Center in Provo. Elder Jeppson outlined a profile of dissidents. Stake presidents have used that profile to compile a list of warning signs.

The profile apparently was used to finger Elaine and Jim Harmston. "Our stake president said, 'You cannot discuss the gospel in your own home with anyone outside your own family or you will be excommunicated,'" says Elaine Harmston. "That was something we couldn't go along with."[1]

Apparently, the Harmstons were running a study group in their home that included a form of Temple prayer that was prohibited outside the Temple. Conducting any home study, especially one where some form of Temple prayer would be used, is virtually unthinkable within orthodox Mormonism. When the bishop issued a warning from the pulpit that attending the Harmstons' study group would bring the risk of discipline, however, the study group immediately *increased* in size. The *Salt Lake Tribune* article said that as the group swelled, area Church leaders began surveillance on the Harmstons' house, taking down visitors' license plate numbers. The visitors were then called in for disciplinary action.

Can you even imagine such a thing taking place in a normal Christian church? If a Christian minister behaved in this way, either the pastor would be looking for other work or the outlawed study group would break their ties. The group would probably become the nucleus of a new church, where the people would be concerned with being taught the meat of the real gospel instead of bowing before the strong-arm tactics of their pastor.

What is extremely rare in this case is that Mormons actually disobeyed the direct instruction of their bishop. What the Harmstons saw was that the people who came in spite of the threats were hungry for truth and "tired of the pablum they're getting from the church." While we don't necessarily agree with what the study group was teaching, we certainly have to admire the members' spunk in standing up to such Church pressure.

A key point is that the Mormon Church operates with such dictatorial control that the members of any particular local LDS Church cannot escape. They are forced to deal with the judgment and the discipline of *that* local bishop. It doesn't matter why they attended the study group. If the bishop said it was wrong to do it, they were wrong to go and in spiritual rebellion to do so. These people put their Mormon Church membership, their Temple recommend, and their actual salvation on the line by going.

Further, members who are in conflict with leadership can't avert their problems by going to some other Mormon church in town. Mormons *must* go to the ward (church) where they are assigned. Many Mormons have friends living a block or two away (and in some extreme cases, even across the street) with whom they would dearly love to attend church and share the many fellowship programs associated with church attendance. But the Mormon Church *assigns* members to wards they must attend, based upon geographic boundaries established in a clerk's office somewhere in the system.

Censured Mormons must either conform quickly and quietly or face swift expulsion from what most of them consider to be the only true church. What is so strange about the recent purge is that the very things that Mormons were encouraged to do just a few years ago, like food storage and home schooling, are now putting those same people in danger of Mormon Church discipline.

Checklist for Apostasy

Sometimes it pays dividends to have a friend in Utah who is also an active Mormon, privy to certain things not readily available to the average non-Mormon. Our friend sent us two sheets of data that are significant to our story. The first sheet appears to have come from the *General Handbook of Instruction*, in use at the ward level. It has the heading "Dealing with Apostate and Splinter Groups," and under the subheading below it lists 14 things Mormon leaders should watch for:

A. Inappropriate and Questionable Activities

1. Teaching false doctrines.

2. Teaching against the direction of local or general leaders.

3. Being in sympathy with apostate individuals or groups, including studying with them.

4. Teaching sacred doctrines and ordinances of the temple in one's home or elsewhere.

5. Practicing, teaching, studying or sympathizing with polygamists or others who have been excommunicated from the Church.

6. Conducting temple-like prayer circles or other unauthorized rituals outside the temple.

7. Following and teaching the words of dead prophets as being more authoritative than those of the living prophets.

8. Inappropriate interpretation or teaching of the scriptures or statements of the Brethren.

9. Claiming to have special divine authority or callings outside of established priesthood channels.

10. Refusing to follow priesthood leaders' specific counsel and instruction in Church-related matters.

11. Divorces among splinter group members which may result in plural marriages with other group members.

12. "Proselytizing" members into special groups who teach questionable doctrine and practices.

13. Receiving so called "inspiration" or direction for others.

14. Teaching that individuals receive inspiration or have a higher knowledge or level of spirituality which gives them greater insights or abilities than ordained Church leaders.

When The Brethren began the recent purging of radical members who might be an embarrassment, some standards were set for what constituted LDS radicalism. These standards were presented at the Edgemont Stake Center in Provo on November 13 and 14 by Elder Jeppson, who outlined a profile of dissidents. This profile was used to implicate Elaine and Jim Harmston, the couple who started the home study group we discussed earlier. The undated document is as follows:

Profile of the Splinter Group Members or Others with Troublesome Ideologies

- They follow the practice of home school.
- There is a preoccupation with the end of the world and the events preceding the coming of the Savior.
- Many have John Birch membership or leanings.
- Many do not work and have no jobs.
- They study the mysteries, feeling that what is provided in our meetings today is superficial.
- They meet in study groups.
- They listen to tapes such as the "Bo Gritz" tapes and others about such topics as Armageddon.
- They are inordinately preoccupied with food storage.
- They feel and teach that there is a great conspiracy, that the government is corrupt and that you can trust few people.
- They feel many of the members and Church leaders have gone astray.
- They feel that President [of the Mormon Church] Benson's counselors have muzzled the prophet so that he cannot tell us the things he would like to tell us, especially about the last days.
- They staunchly profess that they sustain the prophet and local leaders, but when asked to stop doing certain things,

like meeting in groups to study the mysteries, they tell you straight out they will have to take the matter to the Lord to see what He tells them before they will agree.

- Some have met or are meeting with leaders of the Church of the Firstborn.
- They believe we must be super spiritual to know the will of God or even our leaders may lead us astray.
- They read the books of Avraham Gileadi and other materials which are unapproved by the Church.
- Many of these folk are on state welfare and others try to obtain Church welfare.
- We observe that many of these people reportedly have visions and dreams which they share with group members but not priesthood leaders.
- The element of plural marriage, though seldom spoken of outside this group, continues to surface as a part of the belief structure of many.
- Some have held prayer circles in full temple clothing outside the temple.
- While this practice has now been stopped, some of these folks would linger in the celestial room of the Manti [Utah] Temple for hours to teach one another.

True Gritz

Seen as one of the key agitators who has stirred the pot, resulting in the purge of radicals from the ranks of Mormonism, is Bo Gritz, a highly decorated former Green Beret. He is the ultraconservative Mormon who made an unsuccessful third-party bid for president in the 1992 elections, but actually made a strong showing in high-Mormon-population areas.

The press reported that Gritz was warned by Mormon Church leaders to be careful of what he teaches. He was told that some of his views were out of line with the Church. Gritz was the first member of his family to convert to Mormonism, in 1984, and remains active. Still, the report said, Gritz quickly acknowledges that he doesn't agree with everything the Church teaches. "I don't personally believe we will be gods," says Gritz. "I don't think God was ever like we are, very frankly. I don't know whether Joseph Smith was a prophet a little bit, a long time, or always or never. It doesn't make any difference to me."[2]

In a related story, Gritz added, "A lot of folks, they would die if their bishop were to criticize them or if their membership were threatened. To me, it's more important what my personal relationship is with the savior."[3]

Reversing the LDS Pro-Life Stand

When Ed was in Utah premiering the new film, one of the TV stations did a news report on Church disciplinary action that was being taken against some people who were pro-lifers. In an unbelievable turn of events, the LDS Church has *reversed its almost militant pro-life position*, and LDS bishops are now counseling young women to have abortions. Twenty years ago, such counseling would have caused a bishop to be immediately excommunicated from the Church! Here is the complete transcript of the report:

Anchor:
The LDS Church says it has consistently opposed elective abortions, but some Mormons claim they are being disciplined for preaching the Pro-Life message. Paul Murphy has this exclusive report.

Murphy:
They say they are faithful Latter-day Saints, but claim they are being disciplined for their anti-abortion views.

Sharp:
It is murder—the shedding of innocent blood, for which there is no forgiveness.

Murphy:
Sharp says he was excommunicated in July only over abortion. His stake president says it was only one of four issues

leading to the discipline. John Abney was a ward clerk until he expressed his views against abortion. Now he and his wife are scheduled for a church disciplinary court.

Abney:
We do not want to have the blood and the sins of this generation to come upon our garments, either in or out of the church.

Murphy:
Roxanne Abney said she couldn't believe the conversation she recently had with her stake president.

Mrs. Abney:
One of the Lord's representatives, discussing abortion, me being against it, him being for it, and I'm on the wrong side of the fence.

Murphy:
The LDS General Handbook now says that abortion is not murder, and is permissible in cases of rape, incest or when the life or health of the woman is in danger, or the fetus is not likely to survive birth. But as recently as 1975, the LDS President said abortion is wrong, even in cases of rape. And Utah's Right-to-Life Director says she has received a lot of calls from girls who say their Bishops counsel them to have abortions.

Director:
So it wasn't for rape and it wasn't for incest and it wasn't for fetal deformity . . .

Murphy:
And the Bishop still counseled these girls to have an abortion?

Director:
The Bishop is still advising them to have an abortion.

Murphy:
These are confusing times for Sharp and the Abneys. They thought they were in line with Mormon doctrine. Now they

find themselves on the way out. Paul Murphy, KTVX 4 News.

Anchor:
Tomorrow night, a group of Pro-Life Mormons will be meeting at the Copper View Community Center in Midvale to discuss their future in the LDS church.

Reporter: Paul Murphy

Anchor: Randall Carlyle

1st LDS: William Sharp

LDS Couple: John and Roxanne Abney

Director of Utah Pro-Life group: Rosa Goodnight

Prophet quoted is Spencer W. Kimball, 1975

Video showed page of Bishop's handbook to show new rules.[4]

Freedom of Thought at BYU

In a subtler way, other members of the Church of Jesus Christ of Latter-day Saints are also feeling the heat. LDS historian D. Michael Quinn, once a highly esteemed educator, has published some things about the history of Mormonism that have not brought joy to The Brethren.

First there was his research about Church-condoned polygamy after 1890, when the Mormon Church had publicly ended the practice. Quinn says several apostles secretly tried to have him disciplined for that in 1985. Then there was the book about the occult beginnings of the Church, *Early Mormonism and the Magic World View*, which caused quite a stir. Then came his contributions about women in the Church, and finally an article titled "150 Years of Truth and Consequences About Mormon History," in which Mr. Quinn "described the punitive actions taken against those who write about controversial aspects of Mormon history."[5]

The *Salt Lake Tribune* reported that Quinn, still an active, believing Mormon, is now under investigation for apostasy.

> Mormon historian D. Michael Quinn has been on the lam for five years. Ever since three apostles encouraged his stake president to start excommunication proceedings against him when he was teaching at Brigham Young University, Mr. Quinn has managed to stay one step ahead of the Church of Jesus Christ of Latter-day Saints ecclesiastical process servers. Until last weekend.
>
> Mr. Quinn's first encounter with his local LDS leaders since moving back to Salt Lake last summer was a request to defend himself in an apostasy investigation. "No welcome visit, no home teachers, no invitations to attend ward meetings, just a summons to defend myself," says Mr. Quinn.
>
> Quinn isn't playing the game, however. "I vowed I would never again participate in a process which was designed to punish me for being the messenger of unwanted historical evidence," he wrote in a letter of response....In his letter, Mr. Quinn reiterated his belief in the core doctrines of Mormon theology.[6]

It is obvious that the Church has a loose cannon on its hands when a Mormon historian is caught between reporting actual Church history or rewriting Church history in a manner that fits the image The Brethren want to project. Michael Quinn is obviously no longer associated with BYU, but he *is* a highly esteemed, visible scholar, and his excommunication would bring a wave of negative response from the large body of more liberal-minded intellectuals within the Church. The Brethren are between a rock and a hard place of their own making.

Some of the students at BYU aren't quite as visible or lucky as D. Michael Quinn. In what we consider to be a major step back from the LDS race to ecumenicalism, BYU officials have ordered the immediate expulsion of students who quit the LDS Church. Associated Press writer Vern Anderson reports on this strong action against students who leave the faith while attending BYU:

Policy Says Rebaptism is Only Route to Gaining Reinstatement. Mormon students at Brigham Young University who leave the faith or affiliate with another religion will be barred permanently from the school under a new written policy governing such cases. Only rebaptism in the Church of Jesus Christ of Latter-day Saints will allow a student to return to the Mormon Church-owned school, according to the policy approved by BYU's Board of Trustees.

To attend BYU, a student must complete an annual Continuing Ecclesiastical Endorsement form promising to adhere to the school's strict honor code. It must be signed by an ecclesiastical leader after an interview to determine if the student is "worthy" to continue. Mormon students must be interviewed by their ward bishops, while the 1.5% to 2% of non-Mormons among the student body of 27,000 can see their own clergy. As part of the written policy, BYU officials expanded a section of the endorsement to include a question asking if a student has been excommunicated or disfellowshipped, requested that their name be removed from church rolls or "formally joined another church."[7]

Cookie-Cutter Saints

The recent purges and continuing clamp-down on individual freedom of thought should concern all Mormons greatly:

Salt Lake attorney (Paul Toscano) presiding over the Mormon Alliance, a group formed last summer to investigate cases of Mormons who believe they've been unjustly disciplined . . . says, "It is very much in the interest of world-sphere Mormonism or visitor-center Mormonism to eliminate anybody who thinks." Brigham Young called it the "iron bed of conformity." Disciplining of conservative Mormons and stepped-up

pressure on liberal and intellectual Mormons portrays
a leadership concerned that all members be cut from
the same moderate mold. Worldwide Mormons need
to be like Utah Mormons and Utah Mormons need to
be more cookie-cutter.

The Mormon Church may want cookie-cutter Saints, but it just
isn't going to happen that easily. The Church will have to enlarge
its court system before it is able to censure all thinking members,
even if they are victims of LDS control games.

7

The Birth of Heresy

B EFORE WE CONTINUE OUR PROBE of the rocking scandals and
intrigue of the Mormon Church of the 1990's, we need to
take some time out to answer the question, *Where did it all begin?*
How did this major religion ever get such a foothold in the American mind? To find out, we have to go back almost 200 years.

The early nineteenth century was a time of great religious
excitement in the northeastern United States. New York State
rocked with spiritual renewal from every direction. While mighty
men of God such as Charles Finney, sparked by the power of the
Holy Spirit, led thousands of people to the cross of Calvary, there
also arose leaders who captivated the few with the fruits of their
own vanity and drew them away into the doctrines of a different
gospel.

One such man was Joseph Smith, born into a struggling rural
farm family in 1805. The Smith family was given to dabbling in
the mysteries of divination. His father, Joseph Sr., had a special
gift of visions, through powers from the unseen world.

Joseph Smith, Jr. was to set his own mark in the world in a
series of bold and visionary declarations. He was to claim that in
the spring of 1820 he retired to a grove of trees near his home in
Manchester, New York. There he sought the word of the Lord
concerning which church he should join of all those experiencing
revival. He later testified that both God the Father and Jesus
Christ appeared *physically* before him in a pillar of light, above
the brightness of the sun.

He said that they instructed him to join none of the churches because they were all wrong; all their creeds were an abomination in God's sight, and those who professed these creeds were corrupt. According to Joseph's declarations, the true gospel of Jesus Christ was lost to the world. The power and authority of God was taken from the earth in the first century A.D., and only now was it about to be restored.[1]

Joseph later reported that on the evening of September 23, 1823, while in his bedroom and in an act of prayer and supplication, seeking divine direction regarding the next step in God's plan for his life, God moved again. Another being, who identified himself as the angel Moroni, descended in a brilliant pillar of light and repeatedly instructed Joseph in the next steps of the restoration of the true gospel through Joseph's holy calling to that purpose.

Moroni told him of a stone chest he had buried in the nearby Hill Cumorah in the beginning of the fifth century. It held a book of scripture written on gold plates, containing the "fullness of the everlasting gospel," as delivered by the Savior to the ancient inhabitants of the American continent, who were actually the descendants of Jewish settlers led there from Jerusalem by God 600 years before Christ. The chest also contained the Urim, Thummim, and Breastplate of Jewish antiquity for the purpose of translation.

Led to the site by Moroni, Joseph was instructed not to remove the items until given permission. He visited the location annually for four years, until he was told the time was ready for these scriptures to be translated. And so came the Book of Mormon, which Joseph Smith purportedly translated from "Reformed" Egyptian characters inscribed on the gold plates.[2]

Joseph later described the return of John the Baptist, who descended in a cloud of light on May 15, 1829, and ordained Joseph and his scribe, Oliver Cowdery, to the Levitical priesthood of Aaron, and gave them the authority to baptize. A short time later Peter, James, and John were to descend and confer the holy Melchizedek priesthood, which would hold the keys to all the spiritual power of Christ. Other visitors, such as Moses,

Elias, and Elijah would later appear with their special messages and keys of "restoration."

With revelation and prophecy abounding, Joseph began the building of his church. The era of Joseph Smith reached its peak when, after moving often and seeking Zion, the true gathering place of the Lamb, Smith and his followers settled in Nauvoo, Illinois.

With over 20,000 members, the Church had become a force to be reckoned with. It had political power and influence, as well as its own small army of 2500 armed men under the charge of "General" Smith, who now often wore the uniform of that position.

Always fearful of attack from without, the final chapter of Joseph's life came through "the conspiracy of traitors and wicked men." On June 27, 1844, Joseph Smith died a martyr at the hands of a mob in the jail at Carthage, Illinois, thus sealing his testimony of the Book of Mormon with his own blood, as Mormon Church history relates.[3]

While the Mormon Church split in several directions at his death, the main body of the resolute believers trekked to a Rocky Mountain retreat—the New Zion, which they named Deseret. It is now known as Utah. Through hard work and a special brand of zeal, they carved an empire out of the desert under the powerful direction of Brigham Young.

Today, Mormonism is one of the fastest-growing religions in the United States and many countries. If Mormonism were truly a Christian work, drawing people to the cross of Calvary, we could only cheer at the sidelines! *But the doctrines of Mormonism are not the doctrines of the Christian faith.* Let's examine this brief history of Mormonism in the light of Christian Scripture. In 2 Corinthians 13:1, we are warned that in the mouth of two or three witnesses shall every word be established, and we will put Mormonism to that test!

The Plumb Line of Mormon Heresy

In 2 Corinthians 11:13, Paul warns us that if people come and preach another gospel, another Jesus, another spirit, such are false apostles—deceitful workers, having the appearance of ministers of righteousness, but whose end shall be according to their works (not Christ's mercy). We are warned that Satan himself is transformed into an angel of light.

If Joseph Smith really did see what he claimed, two personages appeared to him in a pillar of light. They claimed to be God the Father and Jesus, His Son.

The first clue that something was wrong was that a physical man appeared in the role of God the Father. We are told that "God is not a man that he should lie, neither the son of man that he should repent" (Numbers 23:19). John 4:24 says, "God is a spirit, and they that worship him must worship him in spirit and in truth." Jesus specifically taught that a spirit does not have flesh and bones (Luke 24:39). In Matthew 16:17 Jesus declares that His father in heaven is not of "flesh and blood." John 1:18 states that no man has seen God at *any* time. It seems to be pretty clear.

"Someone who says, I saw the Father," says well-known Christian speaker David Breese, "is dealing presumptuously, short-circuiting good Christian theology. It is the Son who alone reveals the Father" (John 1:18; Colossians 1:15).

This is no small matter, and it is the very plumb line of Mormon heresy. Mormons believe that God is a resurrected man, a created being, and that we can become just like Him. Dr. Breese's response to this blasphemy is:

> God cannot be made. God cannot be created. The definition of the eternal God is that He is eternal, immortal, invisible (1 Timothy 1:17; 6:16; Revelation 1:18; 2 Peter 3:8). That is who the God of the universe is, and there is none other. A man is a created being and as a created being it will always be the case with him that in God he lives, and moves, and has his being. He is dependent upon the Fountainhead of life, God Himself. He cannot move by his own volition, or anybody else's, to the level of godhood—although that [concept] is very appealing to certain individuals.
>
> There is a question before the house in Christianity in our time that really is, Can a man become God?

That question is answered in the affirmative by many of the cults, like the Mormons, like the New Age movement. I assure you, it is totally presumptuous.[4]

This concept of godhood does not appeal to Mormonism alone; it is an ancient philosophy underlying much of pagan thought which proliferates through the New Age movement today.

Did Jesus Fail?

Even if the appearance of God the Father as a man did not alert Joseph Smith to the deception, the first words out of the mouth of Joseph's Jesus should have brought loud, clanging warning bells. He declared that the creeds of all the churches were an abomination to Him—that all those who professed those creeds were corrupt. The Christian pastors were deceivers. There was no authority of God left on earth!

What was the Christian confession in that day? The same as it was at the time of Christ. The same as it is today! The same zeal for souls seen in the life of Paul is the same zeal we read about in the life of Charles Finney in Joseph Smith's day—and it is the very same zeal we see in the Christian body this very hour. That is the zeal these two personages claimed was filthy in their eyes.

Can we believe that the power of God, as it was established by Christ and carried forth by His apostles and followers, was lost to mankind? Did the world become void of the authority of God? Did Jesus fail? Don't you believe it!

Isaiah 9:7 claims that there will be no end to the increase of Christ's government and peace. His kingdom shall be established forever! Why? Because the zeal of the Lord of Hosts will perform it. We are promised that Christ will reign forever, and there shall be no end of His kingdom (Luke 1:33). Jesus, being the Petra—the bedrock itself—proclaimed that upon that rock (Petra) He would build His church and the gates of hell would not prevail against it (Matthew 16:18).

One need only skim through *Foxe's Book of Martyrs* and read some of the many testimonies of the Christian martyrs throughout the centuries to know without a doubt that the zeal of the Lord of Hosts has never stopped performing the establishing of His kingdom.

And what about the Holy Spirit? Was He so much less a power of God that He could not fulfill His divine function? Jesus said the Spirit would abide with us forever, to dwell with us and in us (John 14:16,17). He promised that the Holy Spirit would teach us, being a testimony of Christ, bringing all the things of Jesus to our remembrance (John 14:26). *To receive the message of Joseph Smith's first vision would be to call God a liar, Jesus a failure, the Holy Spirit powerless, and the Bible of no merit or truth!*

Gold Plates and Angels

The next episode in the Mormon Restoration centers around the angel Moroni, who prepared Joseph Smith to succeed where Jesus had failed. Moroni, appearing as an angel of light, brings Joseph word of the gold plates and the Book of Mormon, which were to contain the fullness of the everlasting gospel.

Paul gave clear warning about anyone, even an angel from heaven, preaching any other gospel. He said that they should be accursed (Galatians 1:8). Here again, the warning flag waves frantically.

The Book of Mormon claims to contain the sacred writings of the Jewish people who relocated from Jerusalem to the western shores of the Americas in 600 B.C. The first warning sign that something is terribly amiss is that this passage was written in Egyptian, a cursed language to the Jews. There has never been a verse of Hebrew Scripture written by Jews for Jews in Egyptian. It would be blasphemous! Nehemiah makes that clear. He cursed those who had traffic with Egypt, smote them, and pulled out the hair of the offenders (Nehemiah 13:23-27).

Secondly, the Book of Mormon speaks of a great civilization, with 38 major cities and Temples as great as Solomon's—built from 600 B.C. to A.D. 400. Yet there is not so much as a stone tablet or a stick that the Mormon archaeologists can identify as Book of Mormon archaeology. This is in spite of thousands of discoveries of other cultures in the supposed Book of Mormon "locations."

The Hill Cumorah, where Joseph unearthed the gold plates, was said to have been host to a great battle in A.D. 385, where approximately a half-million people died with all manner of weapons of war. The site would have to hold a mountain of archaeological evidence, yet not a single piece of evidence has been produced in proof of the greatest battle in this hemisphere in the history of all mankind.

Joseph's later claim that John the Baptist descended and restored the Levitical priesthood of Aaron can only lead one to believe that he had little or no knowledge of the Bible or Jewish tradition at the time.

John the Baptist never held the Levitical priesthood, and could not restore something he never had, even in Mormon theology. John wore the skins of an animal and ate food that was considered unclean to the Levitical priesthood. He functioned by proclaiming Jesus Christ, calling people to repent and be baptized. The priesthood functioned within the temple at the altar. It doesn't match up.

If he were a member of the priesthood of his day, its leaders knew nothing of it. When challenged by Christ regarding this very subject, they were ignorant of John's authority (Matthew 21:23-27). Further, the Mormon priesthood that Joseph Smith claimed was a "restoration" does not deal with the key functions of the early Aaronic priesthood, which was the offering of gifts according to the law (Hebrews 8:4).

Jesus has given us a *better* covenant, established upon *better* promises, and has made the old vanish (Hebrews 8:6,7,13). Why would Jesus want to restore what He had come to end?

Joseph Smith claimed that Peter, James, and John came and restored the Melchizedek priesthood. This declaration, like each before it, cannot meet the test of Scripture or logic.

In Mormonism, no man can hold the Melchizedek priesthood without first holding the Aaronic priesthood. Those great apostles of the Lord most obviously were not operating as Levitical priests. Everything they did within the record of the Word of God places them totally outside that dead priesthood.

The true Melchizedek priesthood was always a priesthood of only one! It existed *before* the law was given (Genesis 14:18) and *after* the law was ended (Hebrews 7:11-17). It sprang forth with the first offering of bread and wine (Genesis 14:18). It reappeared only when the final offering of the broken body of Christ and His shed blood ended the penalty of the law as He became our sin offering by the sacrifice of Himself (Hebrews 9:12-14).

The final irony of Joseph Smith's life comes in the story of his death. The Mormon Church pronounces him a martyr, sealing the testimony of the Book of Mormon with his blood. Yet truth, and Mormon history, tell another story.

By 1844, Joseph already claimed 27 "celestial" wives, by Church count, and 48 by historian Fawn Brodie's count.[5] Always on the lookout for more, he finally provoked several leading men within the Church to take action. Austin Cowles, first counselor to the Church at Nauvoo, and William Law, Smith's second counselor, published charges of heresy, adultery, and fornication against Joseph Smith in the Nauvoo Expositor.[6]

Joseph destroyed the press, and charges were filed against him in Carthage, Illinois, the nearest community having non-Mormon officials. At first, Joseph fled and hid, but was convinced to return, at his wife's pleading, by Orrin Porter Rockwell, his bodyguard. Upon his return, Smith was arrested.

An Ignominious Death

Joseph was on the second floor of the jail, with visitors and an unlocked door. After members of his own militia retired to their homes for the night, a mob formed outside, shouting insults. As some of the mob came up the narrow stairwell, Joseph discharged his pistol into their midst, killing two men and wounding a third. He and his brother, Hyrum, were killed in the exchange of gunfire.[7]

Under no circumstance can Joseph Smith be described as a martyr, sealing his testimony of the Book of Mormon with blood. He died in a gunfight, in a tragic ending caused by his own carnal, sinful use of other men's wives. The biblical account of a martyr is seen in the death of Stephen. Stephen was stoned to death for his testimony of Christ as the Messiah. He knelt down as he was killed, crying, "Father, lay not this sin to their charge!" (Acts 7:60).

Whom should we follow—Jesus Christ, the Alpha and Omega, who said, "Before Abraham was, I AM" (John 8:58), or Joseph Smith, the man who said, "I have more to boast of than any man had—neither Paul, John, Peter, nor Jesus ever did it. I boast that no man ever did such a work as I"?[8]

By every test of a prophet, Joseph Smith failed. By every test of man, he was a fully debauched heretic. Yet today over 8 million people follow his teachings in spiritual blindness, and the numbers are climbing.

8

False Prophecies of Joseph Smith

THE VERY EXISTENCE OF MORMONISM hinges on its central tenet that it was founded by Joseph Smith, who claimed that he was called of God to reestablish Christ's true church on the earth. In the last chapter we showed that this could not possibly be true. However, Mormons revere Joseph Smith as a true prophet of God and the holy man upon whom God Himself laid the authority to oversee God's people and usher in the last dispensation of time. If Smith's claims to having seen God and Christ and to having received his prophethood and authority from them were really true, two very important things would follow for the Christian church.

First, the Christian world would have to recognize that the "New Testament" era was over and that a new era had begun. To understand this concept one needs to understand the place of the "office" of prophet. The calling of the Old Testament prophet was "one to whom and through whom God spoke.... Their messages were very largely the proclamation of the Divine purposes of salvation and glory to be accomplished in the future."[1] The prophets and their messages were the pointers to Jesus!

In Luke 16:16, the Lord clearly states, "The law and the prophets were until John; since that time the kingdom of God is preached, and every man presseth into it." The time for declaring the forthcoming of the kingdom was over; the kingdom itself was now to be declared by the Son Himself!

Hebrews 1:1,2 makes it even clearer: "God, who at sundry times and in diverse manners spake unto the fathers by the prophets, hath in these last days spoken unto us by his Son, whom he hath appointed heir of all things, by whom also he made the worlds." This was said *after* Christ had risen and the church was in operation. No prophet was appointed to be the head of the church and spokesman for God. Christ had fulfilled that empty office in His own right when He said, "It is finished." Yet as we read in 1 Corinthians, the *gift of prophecy* was active in the body of the church . . . but not anywhere in the headship of the church (see 1 Corinthians 14).

So if Joseph Smith was the spokesman through whom God would now issue His orders, then the established order of New Testament government would have to be ended, and the church would have to step into a new covenant that was *not* foretold by Christ, by whom God was to speak to us in New Testament times.

Second, if Smith's claims to have restored Christ's true church on earth *were* true, then we could step back from the responsibility of "every man presseth into it" and simply listen to the instruction and counsel of the Mormon prophet and trust and obey the words from his mouth as though they came directly from God. However, in order for us to take that step of obedience, it would be wise for us to check the biblical tests of a prophet, as given in the Bible, and put this new-era prophet to the same tests by which every Old Testament prophet was judged. We need to do that with Joseph Smith. After all, over 300 exact prophecies of the Old Testament were fulfilled by Christ in His birth, life, death, and resurrection. Some of these prophecies were foretold over 900 years before His birth. *Prophets can be checked out for accuracy.*

One would think that any member of a "restoration" church that bases its very existence on its own latter-day prophet would be able to give any willing listener a long litany of "true prophecies." At least the earnest seeker would expect to find dusty volumes of such prophecies abounding in church libraries throughout the new kingdom. Yet in Mormonism *they don't exist in mind or matter*. While some people who claim both scholarship and membership have written books on the subject, they are not received by the Church in any official capacity, especially since much of the work is contrived.

If you doubt that the true Mormon avoids such discovery, just ask a Mormon to extemporaneously recite five or six favorite Joseph Smith prophecies. You will rarely get past one or two of the most commonly used "faith promoting" stories, which are hardly kingdom-shaking.

One such story that really did come true (if Joseph actually gave it) was a "word" given to Orrin "Porter" Rockwell, Joseph Smith's bodyguard and Church assassin for apostates of the early Mormon Church. Smith promised Rockwell a quiet death in bed if he never cut his hair. Porter killed a lot of men through the years, and we are told he died in bed.

It is amazing that when the LDS missionaries share the joys of having a church led by a living prophet and are asked to produce a list of the prophecies of their living prophet or any of their deceased prophets, including Joseph Smith, they cannot produce any such list. You would expect that any reasonable, thinking person would flee from such foolishness. Yet millions of people testify that they "know" by personal revelation that Joseph Smith is a prophet of God.

It is our position that he meets the test of Scripture as one of the foretold *false prophets* who would come in the last days. We have gathered a number of the prophecies of Joseph Smith, some of which we had to dig out of the LDS closet. Judge them for yourself.

Remember, as you read the following list, that according to Deuteronomy 18:20-22, *it takes only one false prophecy to make a prophet false,* just as it takes only one murder to make a person a murderer. As you read the many false prophecies of Joseph Smith, keep this biblical teaching in mind.

The Abridgment of *Doctrine and Covenants* 137

Although there are actually dozens of false prophecies we could begin with, we chose one which has come to newfound prominence in recent years. In 1976, Section 137 of *Doctrine and*

Covenants was submitted to the General Conference of the Church of Jesus Christ of Latter-day Saints for a vote to be "sustained" as scripture. It is a narrative of a vision supposedly seen by Joseph Smith in Kirtland, Ohio, in 1836.

What the members who voted on this new addition to scripture were not told by The Brethren is that whole paragraphs (216 words) of the actual revelation as recorded in the *History of the Church* had been conveniently left out of the version to be included in *Doctrine and Covenants*. The reason for these omissions was that four false prophecies were contained in the part of the revelation which was censored out. These prophecies were so obviously false that even the average Mormon reader would notice their falsity. Therefore they went down the "black hole" of Mormon history.

What exactly did these missing parts contain? If you go to the official *History of the Church* published by the Church's own publishing company, you will easily be able to find the missing prophecies.[2] Here is what is *not* in the new Section 137:

> [Joseph Smith:] I saw *the Twelve Apostles of the Lamb, who are now upon the earth, who hold the keys of this last ministry* in foreign lands, standing together in a circle, much fatigued, with their clothes tattered and their feet swollen, with their eyes cast downward, and Jesus standing in their midst, and they did not behold him. The Saviour looked upon them and wept.
>
> *I also beheld Elder M'Lellin in the south,* standing upon a hill, surrounded by a vast multitude, preaching to them, and a lame man standing before him supported by his crutches; he threw them down at his word and leaped as a hart, by the mighty power of God.
>
> Also, *I saw Elder Brigham Young standing in a strange land,* in the far south and west, in a desert place, upon a rock in the midst of about a dozen men of color, who appeared hostile. He was preaching to

them in their own tongue, and the angel of God standing above his head with a drawn sword in his hand, protecting him, but he did not see it.

And I finally saw the Twelve in the celestial kingdom of God. I also beheld the redemption of Zion and many things which the tongue of man cannot describe in full [all emphases added].

If this prophecy were true, it would have been a truly inspiring and wonderful declaration! Unfortunately, for the Mormon faithful, a short look at these missing parts reveals the false prophecies they contain.

The most striking of these is that Smith claimed to see his original "twelve apostles" all in the celestial kingdom. This is difficult to imagine, since there was already division between Smith and the majority of the apostles, beginning with discord in Kirtland, Ohio. The first portion of the missing parts shows his less-than-subtle rebuke of their resistance to his will in words like "fatigued ... tattered ... eyes cast downward. ... The Saviour looked upon them and wept." Smith was calling them to get into line and submit themselves to his full authority. That's the carrot offered in the last portion, "I finally saw the Twelve in the celestial kingdom of God."[3]

However, his "thus saith the Lord" must have had little effect on these men, because at least seven of the 12 were soon excommunicated or apostatized from the Church: John F. Boynton and Luke S. Johnson (1837),[4] Lyman Johnson (1838),[5] William E. M'Lellin (c. 1838),[6] Thomas B. Marsh and Orson Hyde (1838),[7] and William Smith (1845).[8]

How could they ever have attained the celestial kingdom under those conditions? They couldn't! They were not only accursed by their very acts of apostasy or excommunication, but fell victim to the LDS Church's own scriptural denunciation. *Doctrine and Covenants* 84:40,41 clearly states:

Therefore, all those who receive the priesthood, receive this oath and covenant of my father, which he

cannot break, neither can it be moved. But whoso
breaketh this covenant after he hath received it, and
altogether turneth there-from, shall not have forgiveness of sins in this world nor in the world to come.

Although a few of these men later returned to the Mormon
Church, none of them were even close to the standards necessary
for attainment of that highest degree of glory. The majority
remained apart for life. Therefore the prophetic utterance, "I
finally saw the Twelve in the celestial kingdom of God," could
not be true. It would have been false even if only one apostle
remained outside the fold.

In addition, the vision of M'Lellin preaching and working mir-
acles in the south never came true because he apostatized from
the church without ever doing it!

Brigham Young did bring the Mormons west and was a great
colonizer and orator, but the vision of Brigham Young preaching
to "men of color" in their own language, in some strange and
faraway place in the Southwest, never took place either—or at
least there is no trace of it in the very detailed records and diaries
concerning his reign as prophet.

Finally, "Zion" (Independence, Missouri) was never redeemed,
and has never been redeemed in the more than 150 years since
the prophecy was made. Is it any wonder that The Brethren chose
to remove whole chunks of this "inspired" revelation?

Was Emma Smith "Destroyed"?

One of the most significant sections of the *Doctrine and Covenants* is Section 132, which deals with the plural marriage (polygamy) revelation. However, it also contains many false prophecies:

> And as pertaining to the new and *everlasting* cove-
> nant [i.e., polygamy or plural marriage], it was in-
> stituted for the fulness of my glory; and he that
> receiveth a fulness thereof must and shall abide the
> law, *or he shall be damned, saith the Lord God* (v. 6).

> Let mine handmaid, Emma Smith [Joseph's first wife] receive all those [wives] that have been given unto my servant Joseph, and who are virtuous and pure before me; and those who are not pure and have said they were pure shall be destroyed, saith the Lord God. . . . And I give unto my servant Joseph that he shall be ruler over many things; for he hath been faithful over a few things, and from henceforth I will strengthen him. And I command my handmaid, Emma Smith, to abide and cleave unto my servant Joseph, and to none else. But *if she will not abide this commandment [of plural marriage] she shall be destroyed, saith the Lord; for I am the Lord thy God, and will destroy her if she abide not in my law* (vv. 52-54).

> And if he *have ten virgins given unto him by this law*, he cannot commit adultery, for they belong to him, and they are given unto him; therefore he is justified (v. 62) [all emphases added].

Where do we begin? First of all, plural marriage was an "everlasting covenant" that *lasted only about 50 years*. It was officially done away with in 1890.[9] How can something that is ordained by God as "everlasting" stop? Second, according to verse 6, everyone who is not living in plural marriage in the LDS Church is damned. That means that *almost all Mormons*, except for 20,000 or so Fundamentalists today who still keep the original commandments of plural marriage, are damned!

Verse 53 says that Joseph Smith would be strengthened henceforth. Whether he was depends on one's definition of "henceforth," as he was shot dead by his enemies less than a year later!

Verse 54 threatens Emma Smith with destruction if she doesn't let Joseph have all of his wives without complaint and acknowledge the divine origins of plural marriage. Emma *never* did these things. She fought against the plural marriage doctrine, yet she lived to a ripe old age while Joseph was shot just months later. Emma was so opposed to polygamy that she went off with Joseph's son, Joseph Smith III, and started the Reorganized Church of Jesus Christ of Latter-day Saints, which denies that Smith *ever* taught polygamy.

The Civil War Prophecy

This one is a little longer, but it should be looked at closely because the Mormons like to claim this prophecy as one of Joseph Smith's *true* prophecies. Yet it just doesn't bear close scrutiny. In *Doctrine and Covenants* 87:1-8 we read:

> *Verily, thus saith the Lord* concerning the wars that will shortly come to pass, beginning at the rebellion of South Carolina, which will eventually terminate in the death and misery of many souls; And the time will come that war will be poured out upon all nations, beginning at this place. For behold, the Southern States shall be divided against the Northern States, and the Southern States will call on other nations, even the nation of Great Britain . . . and they shall also call upon other nations, in order to defend themselves against other nations; *and then* war shall be poured out upon all nations.
>
> And it shall come to pass, after many days, slaves shall rise up against their masters, who shall be marshalled and disciplined for war. And it shall come to pass also that the remnants who are left of the land will marshal themselves, and shall become exceedingly angry, and shall vex the Gentiles with a sore vexation.
>
> And thus, with the sword and by bloodshed the inhabitants of the earth shall mourn; and with famine, and plague, and earthquake, and the thunder of heaven, and the fierce and vivid lightning also, shall the inhabitants of the earth be made to feel the wrath and indignation, and chastening hand of an Almighty God until the consumption decreed hath made a full end of all nations.

> That the cry of the saints, and the blood of the
> saints, shall cease to come up into the ears of the Lord
> of Sabaoth, from the earth, to be avenged of their
> enemies. Wherefore, stand ye in holy places, and be
> not moved, until the day of the Lord come; for behold
> it cometh quickly, saith the Lord. Amen [all em-
> phases added].

This prophecy was given on Christmas Day, 1832, almost 30 years before the Civil War. Although the prophecy looks good on the surface, it must be realized that at the time it was given, South Carolina was already involved in many rebellious acts, and this fact was widely published in the papers of the time.[10] Congress had passed a tariff in July of 1832 that South Carolina had declared unacceptable.

It was during that Christmas season that the nation's press expected and wrote about the impending outbreak of civil war, beginning with this rebellion in South Carolina. Even the U.S. Army was on alert. With this knowledge at hand, it didn't take much of a seer to predict the unfolding events. Even a paper published by the Mormons themselves contained such news.[11]

However, *the war did not come to pass*. Added to the dating problems, the scope of the prophecy is not in balance. In just one item, the prophecy states that war would begin locally and pour out upon all nations and would be the direct cause of an international global war. Even World War I did not encompass all nations, and it was *50 years* after the Civil War and had no possible relationship to it!

After being given, this entire prophecy was shelved and never appeared again during Joseph Smith's lifetime. In fact, the first two editions of the *History of the Church* did not include it even though it was in the original manuscript. It reappeared in 1852 when the war again seemed imminent.

One former Mormon has pointed out that there are at least 20 elements in this prophecy, and for it to be a true prophecy all of those elements would have to have come to pass.[12] In human terms, those odds are 1 in 1,048,576—a truly remarkable achievement, had Smith pulled it off. Obviously, he did not.

In another example of failure in this prophecy, verses 4 through 6 state that the slaves will rise up, the remnants left in the land will rise up against the Gentiles (non-Mormons), and the bloodshed, famines, and plagues (caused by the great war) will bring with God's wrath and "a full end of all nations." This did not happen. In fact, Smith got only two elements out of 20 right, and those were based on current events and common sense.

Pestilence and Earthquakes in the USA?

Here is an explicit false prophecy (given in 1833) from official Church history:[13]

> And now I am prepared to say *by the authority of Jesus Christ*, that not many years shall pass away before the United States shall present such a scene of bloodshed as has not a parallel in the history of our nation; pestilence, hail, famine, and earthquake shall sweep the wicked of *this generation* from off the face of the land ... flee to Zion before the overflowing scourge overtake you, *for there are those now living upon the earth whose eyes shall not be closed in death until they see all these things*, which I had spoken, fulfilled [all emphases added].

Obviously, none of these dire predictions have come to pass, and it has been over 150 years since they were given. No one is now left alive from that generation. The scope of the warning was centered on the *generation* in which the Mormons were still calling on their converts to leave their homes, cities, and countries to "come to Zion." They have long since stopped this mandatory migration to the center of Mormonism. That generation had passed before the end of the nineteenth century.

Jesus' Return

Joseph Smith made this reference to the second coming of Jesus:

Were I going to prophesy, I would say the end [of the world] would not come in 1844, 5 or 6, or in forty years. There are those of the rising generation *who shall not taste death* till Christ comes.

I was once praying earnestly upon this subject, and a voice said unto me, "My son, if thou livest until thou art eighty-five years of age, thou shalt see the face of the Son of Man." I was left to draw my own conclusions concerning this, and I took the liberty to conclude that if I did live to that time, He would make His appearance. But I do not say whether He will make His appearance or I shall go where He is. *I prophesy in the name of the Lord God, and let it be written—the Son of Man will not come in the clouds of heaven till I am eighty-five years old (48 years hence or about 1890)* [all emphases added].[14]

Interestingly, this passage is taken from Smith's diary, and modern LDS "historians" have removed the phrase "48 years hence or about 1890" because it so clearly demonstrated the falsity of the prophecy.

None of the "rising generation" ever saw Jesus' coming. Jesus certainly did not come in "about 1890." A century has passed since that date, and Smith's prophecy lies dead and buried along with that rising generation.

The Potsherd Prophecy

Although Mormons like to exhibit their patriotism, Joseph Smith was not overly fond of the U.S. Government. In 1843 he declared:

If the government, which received into its coffers the money of citizens for its public treasury, cannot protect such citizens in their lives and property, it is an old granny anyhow; and *I prophesy in the name of the Lord God of Israel*, unless the United States redress the wrongs committed upon the Saints in the state of

Missouri and punish the crimes committed by her officers, that *in a few years the government will be utterly overthrown and wasted, and there will not be so much as a potsherd left* [emphases added].[15]

Congress failed to comply with Smith's demands. It did not protect the Mormons, and did not redress the wrongs done against them. In spite of this, the Congress was never overthrown, and the U.S. Government has never been destroyed, overthrown, or wasted. After more than 140 years, the United States is the most powerful country in the world!

Remember Oliver Granger?

Another personal prophecy of Smith's which fell to the ground was *Doctrine and Covenants* 117:12-15, which says in part:

I say unto you, I remember my servant Oliver Granger; behold, verily I say unto him that his name shall be *had in sacred remembrance from generation to generation, forever and ever*, saith the Lord [emphasis added].

Ask 100 Mormons who Oliver Granger is and 99 will give you a blank look. His name is supposed to be in everlasting remembrance from generation to generation, and yet most Mormons have never heard of him, nor can they give any reason why he should be held in sacred remembrance.

Did Joseph Smith Triumph over His Foes?

The section of *Doctrine and Covenants* where this prophecy is given, Section 121, is prefaced in the LDS Church introduction as "Prayers and Prophecies written by Joseph Smith the Prophet, while he was a prisoner in jail in Liberty." Note what is said in verses 5-15:

My son, peace be unto thy soul; thine adversity and thine afflictions shall be but a small moment; And then, if thou endure it well, God shall exalt thee on high; *thou shalt triumph over all thy foes.* . . . And also that God hath set his hand and seal to *change the times and seasons, and to blind their minds,* that they might not understand his marvelous workings; and take them in their own craftiness. . . . And not many years hence, *that they and their posterity shall be swept from under heaven, saith God,* that not one of them is left to stand by the wall [all emphases added].

This prophecy promises that Smith and his Church would triumph over all their foes. This never happened. They had just been driven out of their "Zion" in Independence, Missouri. Smith was to die by the hands of his foes about five years later. The entire Mormon Church was run out of the state about eight years later and had to flee to Utah! Can this be triumphing over your enemies?

Even in Utah, the power of the Mormon Church was ultimately broken by the federal government, which forced the Church leaders to submit to government authority and to do away with their cherished doctrine of plural marriage. More recently, the Church was forced to succumb to outside pressure again, either changing its racist position on blacks or losing its tax-exempt status. Is this triumph?

We need to ask: When did God change the times and seasons on us? When did He blind the minds of Smith's enemies? When were every one of Smith's enemies "swept from under heaven"? In fact, most of them long outlived him!

Boastful Prophets

In *Doctrine and Covenants* 3:4 (given in 1828), we find this:

For although a man may have many revelations, and have power to do many mighty works, *yet if he boasts in his own strength, and sets at naught the counsels of God,* and follows after the dictates of his own will and carnal desires, *he must fall and incur the vengeance of a just God upon him* [all emphases added].

Bear this prophecy in mind as we move ahead several years to 1844. In May of that year, Smith proclaimed:

> *I have more to boast of than any man ever had.* I am the only man that has ever been able to keep a church together since the days of Adam....Neither Paul, John, Peter, nor Jesus ever did it. *I boast* that no man ever did such a work as I. The followers of Jesus ran away from him; but the Latter-day Saints never ran away from me yet [all emphases added].[16]

Just 30 days from making that boast, on June 27, 1844, Joseph Smith was murdered by a mob in the Carthage, Illinois jail.[17] It would seem that he fell and incurred the vengeance of a just God upon himself. This is not how Mormons see it, but at least this time Joseph's prophetic word was true.

A Prophet Without Error?

Near the end of his life, Joseph Smith insisted, "There is no error in the revelations which I have taught."[18] Joseph Smith also said, "I am learned and know more than all the world put together."[19] Subsequent Mormon leaders have affirmed that once the prophet has spoken, the Mormon Church has its marching orders. In one Ward Teachers' message (a monthly message sent by The Brethren to the homes of the Mormons), members were told:

> He [Satan] wins a great victory when he can get members of the Church to speak against their leaders and do their own thinking....When our leaders speak, the thinking has been done. When they propose a plan—it is God's plan. When they point the way, there is no other which is safe. When they give direction, it should mark the end of controversy. God works

in no other way. To think otherwise, without immediate repentance, may cost one his faith, may destroy
his testimony and leave him a stranger to the kingdom
of God.[20]

Having made such a strong affirmation, one would think that
the die had been cast and the words of Joseph Smith would live on
in the hearts and minds of the Mormon people for eternity, but it
isn't so. When the Mormon Church changed the doctrine on
blacks being allowed to hold the priesthood and go to the Temple,
the bedrock doctrines of Joseph Smith and Brigham Young were
shattered and a new theology emerged.

The Brethren had already been at work, preparing the Saints
for several decades of enormous change. At a BYU Stake meeting on May 5, 1974, General Authority S. Dilworth Young had
warned the students about modern revelation. He said, "Modern
revelation is what President Joseph Smith said, unless [then]
President Spencer W. Kimball says differently."[21]

After the shock waves settled down following the blacks receiving the priesthood and being allowed in the Temple, more
revelation knowledge was given to the people. On February 26,
1980, a landmark speech was given before the student body of
Brigham Young University by Ezra Taft Benson, who was at that
time the president of the Council of Twelve and next in line to
ascend to the presidency of the Church upon the death of Spencer
W. Kimball. (Benson is the present prophet of the Church as we
write this.) His message, "The 14 Fundamentals of Following
the Prophet," listed those things that set the LDS prophet apart
from the rest of mankind. Among the things he listed were:

> *Second*, the living prophet is more vital to us than
> the standard works [the scriptures]. . . .
>
> *Third*, the living prophet is more important to us
> than a dead prophet.
>
> *Fourth*, the prophet will never lead the church
> astray. . . .

Sixth, the prophet does not have to say, thus saith the Lord, to give us scripture.[22]

The door was now opened wide to begin the changes to the LDS doctrines that separate it from the mainstream of Christianity. The trick is to be able to change just enough to slip in the side door of the ecumenical body of believers without giving up some of those *special* things that make their faith so much more to them. One of the problems is that the Mormons adore their prophet, seer, and revelator. He is their door into the throne room of God and the instructor of their fate. How can they ever give him up?

LDS General Authorities can only acclaim the prophet with unmasked adulation:

> We can all be blessed by the words of the prophets of the Lord—if we will only listen and follow their counsel. How fortunate we are that "the living God" has restored his "living Church" with "living prophets" and additional "living scriptures."[23]
>
> Having a living prophet on the earth today is evidence that God loves us and is interested in us. When we speak of the prophet of the Church, we mean the President of the Church who is president of the High Priesthood. He is sustained by the membership of the Church as "prophet, seer, and revelator." He holds the "keys of the kingdom" (see D & C [*Doctrine and Covenants*] 107:91-92). The prophet and his counselors constitute the First Presidency of the Church. We sustain the First Presidency and the Council of the Twelve as prophets, seers, and revelators.
>
> As Elder Bruce R. McConkie explains, "Those called to preside over quorums, wards, stakes, or other organizations in the Church should be prophets to those over whom they preside." He points out that the First Presidency presides over all the presidencies in the Church and that they do so because of their

> apostolic authority, holding "both the fulness of the priesthood and all of the keys of the kingdom of God on earth. The President of the Church serves in that high and exalted position because he is the senior apostle of God on earth. . . . (He) is the presiding prophet on earth and as such is the one through whom revelation is sent forth to the world."[24]

The prophet is so vital to Mormonism that his writings and speeches are considered by the Church as direct revelation from God. The only problem is that by the time a man works his way through the tangled hierarchy of the Mormon Church to the top spot, he is often too old to be more than a figurehead prophet. For the last several years, up to and including 1993, Ezra Taft Benson has been so frail that he is nonfunctional:

> Ezra Taft Benson, the 93-year-old president of the Church of Jesus Christ of Latter-Day Saints, broke ground on the gleaming, $24 million San Diego Temple in 1988, but is too sick to attend its open house, which begins today. It is an irony that has not gone unnoticed by some Mormons, who fear Benson is no longer able to receive divine inspiration to lead the 8.5 million member, worldwide church.
>
> Mormon historian D. Michael Quinn, who is under investigation by church leaders for apostasy, has described Benson as "mentally diminished." . . . Mario De Pillis . . . incoming president of the Mormon History Association, has gone so far as to say Benson is senile.[25]

During the time it takes for President Benson to pass away and a new prophet to be chosen, Gordon B. Hinckley, counselor to President Benson, continues to function as the acting president of the Mormon Church. Elder Hinckley filled this same function for the then-ailing Spencer W. Kimball during the last years of his office.

It is interesting to note that the next in line to take the presidency and become the Church's prophet upon the death of Benson is Howard W. Hunter, president of the Council of Twelve Apostles, who is already so frail that he must use a walker.[26]

Revelations... of God or Man?

Hugh B. Brown, a high-ranking member of the Mormon hierarchy for 22 years, up to his death in 1975, is recorded in recent memoirs as saying that many Church decisions called "revelations" were actually decisions first "thrashed out" thoroughly by the top authorities. Those decisions "are no less revelatory, but it is simplistic to think that it [revelation] comes as a bolt out of the blue," said the memoirs' editor, Edwin B. Firmate, a grandson of Brown and a law professor at the University of Utah.

The decision-making procedure, Brown explained, generally worked like this:

> An idea is submitted to the First Presidency and Twelve, thrashed out, discussed and rediscussed until it seems right. Then, kneeling together in a circle in the temple, they seek divine guidance and the president says, "I feel led to say this is the will of the Lord." That becomes a revelation. It is usually not thought necessary to publish or proclaim it as such, but this is the way it happens.[27]

9

A Tangled Tale of Scripture

T RYING TO SORT OUT THE MASSIVE COMPLEXITIES of the Mormon scriptures is somewhat akin to the frustration one might feel in trying to rewind a pickup load of tangled fishing line. Every time you feel like you have made some headway, another mess pops up. It would be easy to cut the line and clear up little sections at a time, but that doesn't solve the basic problem!

Mormon scripture is comprised of four documents: The Bible, the Book of Mormon, the *Doctrine and Covenants*, and the *Pearl of Great Price*. However, the Mormons have never really had to confront their scriptures as individual units within a full set of integrated documents that can be measured by simple "scriptural test" procedures. The average Mormon sees LDS scripture only in the inflexible context of classroom references within the rigid teaching structure imposed by the LDS instruction manuals. It is *never* looked at from a critical, scholarly perspective.

The Mormon is taught to unequivocally accept the LDS scriptures as the pure word of God, without error or inconsistency—except, ironically, for the Bible, which is in fact the only *real* standard by which any doctrine can be tested. By discrediting the authority of the Bible, Mormons thereby cut loose the other three LDS scriptures from any biblical accountability. *The only acceptable measurement for LDS scripture is the LDS scripture itself*, and that has already been given the fullest approval of an "infallible" latter-day prophet. There is no room for the application of generally accepted biblical scholarship.

The Eighth Article of the LDS "Articles of Faith" states, "We believe the Bible to be the word of God *as far as it is translated correctly*; we also believe the Book of Mormon to be the word of God"[1] (emphasis added).

Mormonism teaches that there are several problems with the Bible. First, many of its books are missing, so it is only an incomplete compilation at best. Second, we are told that many plain and precious things were taken away from the Bible by that "great and abominable church," as recorded in 1 Nephi 13:25-28 in the Book of Mormon. The very document that requires biblical testing discredits its only credible witness!

The final severance from biblical accountability is the continued LDS teaching that what was left of the Scriptures has been so often and badly translated that our present Bible is of almost no "stand alone" value. Apostle Orson Pratt, an early Mormon theologian, summed up the LDS position when he stated:

> Who, in his right mind, could for one moment, suppose the Bible in its present form to be a perfect guide? Who knows that even one verse of the whole Bible has escaped pollution, so as to convey the same sense now that it did in the original?[2]

Joseph Smith said, "I believe the Bible as it read when it came from the pen of the original writers. Ignorant translators, careless transcribers, or designing and corrupt priests have committed many errors."[3]

What they are saying is that the Bible, which at best represents only 25 percent of the LDS scriptures, is the weak link. Yet Mormons are winning people to their biblically unfounded faith by carrying the Bible under their arms as though they read and believe it. It's just the ticket into the Christian's door for most Mormons.

What the Mormons end up with is a set of spiritual laws that force them to judge their scripture as perfect by their own measure of faith and not by any objective criteria. If there is an obvious contradiction with the LDS scripture and what is being taught by the present prophet, the Mormon cannot judge or test the prophet by the scripture. According to President and Prophet of the Church Ezra Taft Benson, the current LDS doctrine is that *the living prophet is above scripture.* There is absolutely no way out.

Burning in the Bosom

The finality of the Mormon theology is not based upon evaluation by scriptural evidence, but is based entirely upon a "burning in the bosom." Again, LDS scripture demands this final proof of itself and tells its members that this experience is what they must seek. Oliver Cowdery was the second elder to Joseph Smith in the founding of the Church and in the translation of the Book of Mormon. In a word of admonition to him during the translation of the Book of Mormon, the Mormon god declared through Joseph Smith:

> I say unto you that you must study it out in your own mind; then you must ask me if it is right, and if it is right I will cause that your *bosom shall burn within you;* therefore you shall feel that it is right. But if it be not right you shall have no such feelings, but you shall have a stupor of thought that shall cause you to forget the thing which is wrong.[4]

When Mormon missionaries come into a home, they will talk about their first prophet, Joseph Smith, and the Book of Mormon and will instruct the investigator to read the Book of Mormon and to pray about it. They will encourage the reader to seek that divine *burning in the bosom* which will prove that Joseph Smith is a prophet of God and the Book of Mormon is really scripture. Moroni 10:4 will be quoted:

> And when you have received these things, I would exhort you that ye would ask God, the eternal father, in the name of Christ, if these things are not true; and if ye ask with a sincere heart, with real intent, having

faith in Christ, he will manifest the truth of it unto you
by the power of the Holy Ghost.

Missionaries use this quote to put the burden of proof on the
investigator's sincere heart, his real intent, and his level of personal faith, rather than *on fact.*

Actually, the investigator *will* feel good about it. It all becomes
a subjective evaluation. The LDS scriptures and prophet are not
to be tested. The LDS doctrines are not to be tested. The biblical
knowledge and Book of Mormon knowledge of the investigator
are not to be tested. They are to *just pray sincerely* and this divine
burning in the bosom will be the proof that the missionaries are
delivering divine truth directly from God.

A Personal Experience

I (Ed) vividly recall my own experience with the burning in
the bosom.

I can vividly remember lying on my bed for the better part of a
whole night crying out to God for a burning in my bosom so that I
would know the Mormon Church was true. Hour after hour I lay
there, with my breast lifted upward, as though it were on an altar
of sacrifice, pleading for the evidence of this eternal truth. I knew
that my heart was sincere, and yet the guilt of my not experiencing the manifestation was almost more than I could bear.

Finally, many hours into my vigil, that burning came. I felt an
actual, physical burning sensation in my breast. I would later
testify that it was as though I had a rise of seven or eight degrees in
body heat. My chest was at a high fever temperature. I rejoiced in
the certainty of my faith. I *knew* that the Church was true, that
Joseph Smith was a *true* prophet and that the Book of Mormon
was the pure, *true* word of God. Yet in retrospect, I never checked
one single teaching of the missionaries against the Holy Bible to
see if it matched up.

It is interesting that when, as a born-again believer, my wife,
Carol, prayed the prayer of Moroni 10:4 as she read the Book of
Mormon, seeking to know of its truth, she would fall asleep and

experience that stupor Oliver Cowdery was told would be the evidence of untruth. Perhaps she was praying to the wrong God. When I prayed, not being born again, I prayed as instructed by the missionaries. I received one answer, and she received a totally different one. Yet we were both sincere. What was the difference?

An Inspired Version?

Mormons use only the King James Version of the Bible. Any others are apostate translations. It is also interesting to note that the LDS Church publishes its own edition of the King James Bible. An article, "Church Publishes First LDS Edition of the Bible," by Lavina F. Anderson appeared in the October 1979 edition of the LDS *Ensign* magazine and described the enormous project and the intense commitment of the project workers to cross-reference this edition to the other standard works of the Church.

Aside from the very obvious question of why the prophet did not add back all the plain and precious missing parts and correct the translation errors plaguing the Bible all these years, one comment regarding the project almost flew off the page. In the last paragraph of the article, the writer reported:

> Brother Rasmussen added, "Sometimes Brother Patch and I would be discussing a matter of linguistics, and, as we concluded, one of us would remark, 'That feels good.' I suppose to some people this might seem like a slipshod way to be scholars, but we could tell when we were moving in the proper direction and we could certainly identify the stupor that came over us when we weren't. ... In some ways, scholarship was the least important part of our work."[5]

As a by-product of referencing the new edition, one long-debated topic among the diverse subgroupings within the various branches of Mormonism including Josephite or Restorationist

churches was clarified. It dealt with the authenticity of a manuscript called the *Inspired Version of the Bible*, written by Joseph
Smith prior to his death. The copyrighted property of the Reorganized Church of Jesus Christ of Latter-day Saints, the *Inspired
Version* was never given full credentials by the Utah branch—
until the release of the new LDS Edition of the King James Bible.

It is quite significant that this new edition firmly places the
Inspired Version in the position of a Standard Work or a *fifth item*
of approved Mormon scripture, albeit integrated into the fourth.
The title page classifies the new edition as the "Authorized King
James Version with Explanatory Notes and Cross References to
the Standard Works of the Church of Jesus Christ of Latter-day
Saints." In the "Explanation Concerning Footnotes," on page vi,
it identifies JST as the code for the *Joseph Smith Translation*. The
Joseph Smith Translation (the *Inspired Version*) is referenced by
footnotes throughout the new LDS Edition in clarification of
some of the errors in the King James Edition.

The Problem with Inventing Scripture

During the question-and-answer time following an early showing of *The God Makers* film in Colorado Springs, Colorado, Ed
made the point that all the extrabiblical scripture that Mormons
used was out of order with God's Word. Among the several
references he gave was Revelation 22:18,19, which he said stated
that anyone who would add to the Bible or subtract from it in any
way was in deep trouble with God.

A Mormon woman in the group challenged him on this statement and emphatically declared that this was only in reference to
the book of Revelation in its *single* content and had no bearing
upon any other book of Scripture, including any Latter-day Saint
scripture. Ed asked her if these curses would be in effect if anyone
had dared to alter *just* the book of Revelation in any way. She
replied that this was obviously so.

Ed then showed her that in the *Joseph Smith Translation* Smith
had added to or subtracted from the book of Revelation over 85
times.[6] "Even in the smallest context of the warning, Joseph

Smith stands condemned as a false prophet," he declared. She stared in shock. Later, a local LDS leader came up to Ed after the meeting and quietly whispered, "It doesn't matter; he was just adjusting the incorrect parts. I know that he is a true prophet!"

The Jesus of the Book of Mormon

Is the Book of Mormon "Another Testament of Jesus Christ," as the Mormons claim? Or is it "A Testament of *Another* Jesus Christ"? Let's check it with one simple test, comparing what happened when Jesus went to Calvary in the Bible and in the Book of Mormon. If they are testifying of the same Jesus Christ, the *testament* should be the same!

The various New Testament writers in the Bible describe the events this way:

> Jesus, when he had cried again with a loud voice, yielded up the ghost. And, behold, *the veil of the temple was rent in twain from the top to the bottom*; and the earth did quake, and the rocks rent; and the graves were opened; and many bodies of the saints which slept arose, and came out of the graves after his resurrection, and went into the holy city, and appeared unto many. Now when the centurion, and they that were with him, watching Jesus, saw the earthquake, and those things that were done, they feared greatly, saying, Truly this was the Son of God (Matthew 27:50-54, emphasis added).

> And Jesus cried with a loud voice, and gave up the ghost. And the veil of the temple was rent in twain from the top to the bottom. And when the centurion, which stood over against him, saw that he so cried out, and gave up the ghost, he said, Truly this man was the Son of God (Mark 15:37).

> And it was about the sixth hour, and there was a darkness over all the earth until the ninth hour. And the sun was darkened, and the veil of the temple was

> rent in the midst. And when Jesus had cried with a
> loud voice, he said, Father, into thy hands I commend
> my spirit; and having said thus, he gave up the ghost.
> Now when the centurion saw what was done, he glori-
> fied God, saying, Certainly this was a righteous man
> (Luke 23:44-47).

> When Jesus therefore had received the vinegar, he
> said, It is finished; and he bowed his head, and gave
> up the ghost (John 19:30).

The word "earthquake" is used in the verses from Matthew 27 to state that the earth shook. It must not have been severe, since John doesn't even mention it. Luke indicates that people stood by as the earth shook and the sun went into eclipse for three hours. One thing is clear: *No one died from the earthquake.* At His resurrection on the third day, graves were opened and some people who had died in earlier times were resurrected to walk into the city.

> In the end of the Sabbath, as it began to dawn
> toward the first day of the week, came Mary Mag-
> dalene and the other Mary to see the sepulchre. And,
> behold, there was a great earthquake; for the angel of
> the Lord descended from heaven, and came and rolled
> back the stone from the door, and sat upon it. His
> countenance was like lightning, and his raiment white
> as snow; and for fear of him the keepers did shake,
> and became as dead men. And the angel answered
> and said unto the women, Fear not ye, for I know that
> ye seek Jesus, which was crucified. He is not here, for
> he is risen, as he said. Come, see the place where the
> Lord lay (Matthew 28:1-6).

Again, the word "earthquake" is not used in the destructive sense. The earth shook and the stone rolled away from the door. People were not killed.

It's Not Quite the Same in
the Book of Mormon

The Book of Mormon describes a supposed migration of Jews to Meso-America hundreds of years before Christ was born. There is no archaeological evidence of this ever occurring; however, Mormons are taught to believe the truthfulness of the tale in spite of the facts.

In the Book of Mormon, the Mormon Jesus brought death and destruction with him to the cross. In 3 Nephi, chapters 8 and 9, the Book of Mormon details the events surrounding Christ's crucifixion as they were experienced by the people of the new-world, Book-of-Mormon lands. Judge for yourself if it is the same Jesus.

These chapters describe the desolation at Christ's death of the great city of *Zarahemla* by fire. It states that the city of Moroni—

> did sink into the sea and the inhabitants thereof were drowned . . . the earth was carried up upon the city of *Moronihah*. . . . There was great and terrible destruction in the land southward. . . . Terrible destruction in the land northward. . . . The highways were broken up. . . . Many great and noble cities were sunk and many burned and many shaken till the buildings thereof had fallen to the earth. . . . All these great and terrible things were done in the space of three hours (3 Nephi 8:9-19).

Third Nephi 9 tells of further wrath as the Lord also destroyed the cities and inhabitants of Gigal, Onihah, Mocum, Jerusalem, Gadiandi, Gadiomnah, Jacob, Gimgimno, Jacobugath, Laman, Josh, Gad, and Kishkumen (a total of 16 major cities).

Who did all this killing to testify of the Lord's atonement on Calvary? Third Nephi 9:15 reveals the murderer of approximately 2 million innocent inhabitants of the Book of Mormon lands: "Behold, I am Jesus Christ the son of God. I created the heavens and the earth and all things that in them are." He adds,

"Behold, I have come unto the world to bring redemption unto the world to save the world from sin" (v. 21).

It appears that the easiest way to bring redemption was to kill the vast majority of people in those lands—the very people Mormons believe are Jesus' "other sheep . . . which are not of this fold," referred to in John 10:16. This Mormon Jesus was a god of wrath, exercising some form of pagan judgment. Could this truly be the act of the One who was supposed to be the end of the law (Romans 10:4)?

Compare that Mormon Christ to the biblical Jesus who compassionately cried out to His Father, "Father, forgive them, for they do not know what they are doing."

Simply put, there are two different Jesuses at work here. The Christ of Mormonism is not the Christ of the Bible. Second Corinthians 11:1-5 tells us there will be those who will teach a *different* Christ. Paul says of them, "Such men are false apostles, deceitful workmen, masquerading as apostles of Christ" (2 Corinthians 11:13). So there is a biblical warning about those who bring the doctrine of another Jesus, plus a simple test. Do the Mormons and the Book of Mormon pass that test? No, they do not and never will.

Power in the Blood?

The Mormons have a difficult time understanding what actually happened at Calvary. In the LDS pamphlet "What the Mormons Think of Christ," we see the problem. In the section "The Blood of Christ" (page 22 in the 1976 edition), we read:

> Christians speak often of the blood of Christ and its cleansing power. Much that is believed and taught on this subject, however, is such utter nonsense and so palpably false that to believe it is to lose one's salvation. For instance, many believe or pretend to believe that if we confess Christ with our lips and avow that we accept him as our personal savior, we are thereby saved. They say that his blood, without any other act than mere belief, makes us clean.

What is the true doctrine of the blood of Christ? Salvation comes because of the atonement, and the atonement was wrought through the shedding of the blood of Christ. In Gethsemane Christ sweat great drops of blood from every pore when he conditionally took upon himself the sins of the world, and then the shedding of his blood was completed upon the cross.

The Mormon Church teaches, and professes in Article 3 of its Articles of Faith:

We believe that through the atonement of Christ, all mankind may be saved, *by obedience to the laws and ordinances of the gospel* [that is, the laws and ordinance of the gospel according to the LDS prophet—emphasis added].

The Bible clearly teaches another Christ . . . and another gospel:

And you, being dead in your sins and the uncircumcision of your flesh, hath he quickened together with him, having forgiven you all trespasses; blotting out the handwriting of ordinances that was against us, which was contrary to us, and took it out of the way, nailing it to his cross; and having spoiled principalities and powers, he made a show of them openly, triumphing over them in it (Colossians 2:13-15).

But now in Christ Jesus ye who sometimes were far off are made nigh by the blood of Christ. For he is our peace, who hath made both one, and hath broken down the middle wall of partition between us; having abolished in his flesh the enmity, even the law of commandments contained in ordinances; for to make in himself of twain one new man, so making peace; and that he might reconcile both unto God in one body by the cross, having slain the enmity thereby; and

came and preached peace to you which were afar off,
and to them that were nigh (Ephesians 2:13-17).

In the early Mormon Church, a more orthodox Christ was
preached. But when Joseph began to teach the strange doctrines
of this different Christ, the Church could no longer embrace the
reality of the blood of Calvary and its full redemptive work. That
was when the Church removed the red wine from the communion
table and began using water. This act literally washed away the
reality of the blood from its Christian converts. The same holds
true today. The cross and the blood have become strangers to the
Mormons. The cross of Christ is absent from every single one of
the thousands of Mormon churches. And so is the Christ who
went to it willingly for us all. (For a comprehensive overview of
the many historical and archaeological problems in the Book of
Mormon, see appendix: Testing the Book of Mormon.)

The Pearl of Great Price

Throughout this book we have quoted many references from
Doctrine and Covenants, which is a compilation of doctrines put
forth by the Church's prophets. No discussion of LDS scripture
would be complete, however, without touching upon the *Pearl of
Great Price*, and in particular, that part known as the book of
Abraham. The book of Abraham was supposedly translated by
Joseph Smith from some papyrus fragments that the Smiths had
purchased from a man claiming to be an Egyptologist traveling
through the area in which the Smiths lived with several mummies on display.

Using several of the facsimiles (Egyptian pictures found with
the mummies) from the papyri, Joseph Smith demonstrated that
they were representations of Father Abraham in Egypt and then
proceeded to "translate" the papyri fragments into their English
meanings. This was done prior to the time of general understanding of the Rosetta stone decoding of the ancient Egyptian language.

In a recent comparison of the papyri to Joseph's notes, it was
apparent that the thirteenth and fourteenth verses of Abraham 1

were translated from one single character resembling a backward E. Joseph Smith translated this one character into 76 words, with nine proper names and eight other nouns! The character for the Egyptian god Khonso was translated by Joseph Smith into 177 words in Abraham 1:16-19.

Dealing with this issue has been a major test of faith for Mormon scholars. Three major non-LDS Egyptologists, Klaus Baer, Richard A. Parker, and the late John A. Wilson, reviewed the fragments and all concluded that Joseph's translation was totally incorrect and his restorations of the facsimiles were a *gross injustice to the art of Egyptology*. What the Egyptians had inscribed on the papyri and what Smith had described them as were not even remotely comparable.

Parker describes Facsimile 1, an Egyptian picture found facing page 1 of the book of Abraham as a—

> well-known scene from the Osiris mysteries, with Anubis, the jackal-headed god on the left, ministering to the dead Osiris on the bier. The penciled restoration (by Smith) is incorrect. Anubis should be jackal-headed. The left arm of Osiris is in reality lying at his side under him. The apparent upper hand is part of a second bird which is hovering over the erect phallus of Osiris (now broken away). The second bird is Isis and she is magically impregnated by the dead Osiris and then later gives birth to Horus who avenges his father and takes over his inheritance.[7]

Klaus Baer basically repeats the same description in his translation of the papyri as the "Breathing Permit of Hor." He states:

> The vignette of P. JS I [Joseph Smith papyri] is unusual, but parallels exist on the walls of the Ptolemaic temples of Egypt, the closest being the scenes in the Osiris chapels on the roof of the Temple of Dendera.

He specifically describes Facsimile 1:

There are some problems about [Smith] restoring
the missing parts of the body of Osiris. He was almost
certainly represented as ithyphallic, ready to beget
Horus, as in many of the scenes at Dendera.[8]

In other words, the picture was a *known* pagan image. It *meant*
something. It wasn't even remotely close to what Joseph Smith
claimed in his Father Abraham fraud. All three Egyptologists
confirm that the Joseph Smith papyri dealt exclusively with
pagan rituals, pagan gods, and the Breathing Permit of Hor.
Again, the Mormons are free to cling to their unfounded delu-
sions, which certainly fit the occult background of the founder of
Mormonism!

One of the most revealing and honest "in-house" appraisals of
this document was published by Dr. Edward H. Ashment, an
LDS Egyptologist working with the translation department of
the LDS Church. Throughout Ashment's appraisal of the facsimiles, he deals with pagan rituals and pagan gods. At no time does
he make a connection to Abraham, Abraham's God, or Abraham's religion—just paganism. While Ashment went far out
of his way to soften any blows against Mormonism's founding
prophet, no one can read his work and not see the totally inaccu-
rate definitions given the pagan works by Joseph Smith.[9]

How can any intelligent Mormon hold these pornographic
drawings in the *Pearl of Great Price* as the sacred Word of God?
This is blasphemy and blindness at its highest.

Previously, we described the Mormon scriptures as similar to a
pickup truck filled with tangled fishing line. We are still standing
in that pickup truck, up to our waists, almost incomprehensibly
looking all about us at the unbelievable mess. Where do we go
from here? We have hardly begun to clear up the twisted ends.

Our God is not the author of such confusion. We have taken
you far enough so that you may never doubt what Proverbs 30:6
means when it says, "Add thou not unto his words, lest he reprove
thee, and thou be found a liar." You have seen only the beginning
of an endless series of lies built upon lies, so compounded that it is
an impossible task to work your way back to the truth.

10

Present-Day Polygamy and Blood Atonement

JOSEPH SMITH, THE SELF-PROCLAIMED PROPHET OF GOD and founder of the Mormon Church, used the doctrine of divine revelation to legitimize his polygamous marriages to many wives at the same time. He spiritualized the immorality of his plural marriages and declared polygamy to be "a New and everlasting Covenant; and if ye abide not that covenant then are ye damned; for no one can reject this covenant and be permitted to enter into my glory."[1]

Polygamy was an essential doctrine of the young Mormon religion and a requirement for godhood. The promise of eternal increase and glory awaited true believers:

> They shall pass by the angels, and the gods, which are set there, to their exaltation and glory in all things, as hath been sealed upon their heads, which glory shall be a fulness and a continuation of the seeds forever and ever. Then shall they be gods, because they have no end; therefore shall they be from everlasting to everlasting, because they continue; then shall they be above all, because all things are subject unto them. Then shall they be gods, because they have all power, and the angels are subject to them. Verily, verily, I say unto you, except ye abide my law ye cannot attain this glory.[2]

In addition to his first wife, Emma, Joseph Smith appears to

141

have actively enjoyed numerous other wives, ranging in age from 15-year-old Helen Mar Kimball to 59-year-old Rhoda Richards. Writer Fawn Brodie counted 49 women, most of whom he married during 1843 and 1844. Of that list, at least 12 were married women with living husbands.[3] His first plural wife was Fannie Alger, a barely pubescent teenager who was living in their home at the time.[4]

Brigham Young, successor to Joseph Smith, and second prophet of the Mormon Church, vigorously proclaimed that "the only men who become gods, even the sons of God, are those who enter into polygamy."[5] Brigham Young took his own words enthusiastically to heart and maintained a polygamous household of several dozen wives.

The God of Judeo-Christianity is clearly opposed to the taking of more than one wife. Yet today's social climate is inclining more and more toward permitting groups of different cultural and religious persuasions to have freedom to exercise their various beliefs. Laws restricting plural marriage today may soon change if they are challenged in our liberal courts, thereby accommodating the multinational influx of polygamous religions and cultures that currently exist in America.

In Utah, numerous polygamous offshoots of the LDS Church still live what is known as "The Principle" (of plural marriage) with impunity. Mormons aren't the only group with this kind of doctrine. There are now over 7 million Muslims living in America alone, many of whom currently consider plural marriage as an orthodox right of their faith.

In 1890, under orthodox Christian and government pressure, the Mormon Church was forced to reevaluate the divine commandment of polygamy. Fighting for statehood, Utah was confronted with the need to shed this doctrine, which the rest of the country viewed on a par with white slavery. Confusion and anger resulted when the "new and everlasting" commandment spoken by God's first two latter-day prophets was revoked by then President and Prophet Wilford Woodruff.[6]

Many Mormons who had embraced this eternal promise of glory rebelled. To deny "The Principle" would be to reject the very structure and function of their family units and their spiritual lives. After all, Brother Joseph warned them that if they did not live the Covenant, they would be damned. Many of the polygamists fled to Mexico and Canada. Others, less affluent, removed themselves to the outer edges of the Mormon kingdom, settling in such places as southern Utah and northern Arizona. Many others considered President Woodruff's action such an evil act of political expediency that it caused the anointing of God to be lifted from the Church. They defected, forming their own offshoots of Mormonism. They would not be drawn away from the true faith by false leaders.

Today's Fundamentalists

Generally known as Fundamentalists, many of these groups function today, still believing that the doctrines taught by Joseph Smith and Brigham Young were divine truth, still holding to the Book of Mormon, the Melchizedek priesthood, Temple garments, and other evidences of their faith. They stand convinced that the LDS Church is lost in total apostasy and that their particular group now holds the divine keys to this last dispensation of time.

While the actual number of people involved is hard to pinpoint because of the clandestine nature of such groups, it is generally thought that there are more than 20,000 polygamists in and around Utah. Group sizes vary from small family units to entire rural communities. Most of the plural wives come from within the ranks of the polygamous groups themselves. There are always young girls available from the many large families that the practice of plural marriage seems to produce.

Polygamy in Utah is an embarrassment to the Mormon Church, especially at a time when they want to quietly step into the general ranks of ecumenical Christianity. However, the Mormon Church won't officially recognize it as a *Mormon* problem and deal with it as such. We are convinced that unless the LDS Church openly confronts the issue as a product of its past and pulls back the curtain of silence in the matter, it will *never* be dealt with appropriately. It is a strong branch of the family tree which will not go away without some very serious pruning.

Margaretta Spencer is a former Mormon and the wife of Jim Spencer. Jim is also a former Mormon and was a pastor in Idaho before he founded Through The Maze, a full-time ministry to the Mormons. He is the author of a number of excellent books on the subjects of Mormonism and evangelism. Margaretta told us about having to deal with polygamy in her childhood:

> I was born and raised in the Mormon Church, and I can remember, because of my heritage, going to my cousin's family reunion, and we had to wear name tags with the wife's name on them, so that we could recognize which family we were descended from.[7]

Jim Spencer summed up the core of the issue for us when he said:

> Those who take their religion most seriously return to polygamy, because it has not been expunged from Mormon scripture. In fact, if a Mormon is very honest, he probably needs to be a polygamist. However, polygamy is a horror. *The history of polygamy is a history of women who shared their men.* And it's a history of power and manipulation.[8]

Thelma "Granny" Geer is an ex-Mormon who has an LDS family tree that goes back to the pioneer days of Utah. She is a descendant of John D. Lee, a Mormon bishop who was involved in the infamous Mountain Meadow Massacre near St. George, Utah in 1857, "in which more than 120 emigrants were ambushed and slain."[9]

Lee was eventually executed for his part in it. Granny is the author of the best-selling book *Mormonism, Mama and Me* and a dedicated Christian witness to untold thousands of Mormons. She shared her thoughts about polygamy in an interview for *The God Makers II* film:

My great grandfather, John D. Lee, was a polygamist. He served under Joseph Smith and Brigham
Young. He had 19 wives and 64 children, so that he
could become a god as God is now. He really believed
that God and Jesus are polygamists, and that every
Mormon man would have to have a lot of wives. There
is also the warning that any person who will not believe this, and enter into the polygamist temple marriages, they shall be destroyed.[10]

When we were in Utah doing some of the shooting for *The God
Makers II* film, Pat Matrisciana, president of Jeremiah Films,
struck up a conversation near Temple Square with Art Buella, a
bystander who turned out to be a Mormon Fundamentalist and a
practicing polygamist with a "calling as a prophet." Art volunteered to be interviewed for the film and told us:

I was in the Mormon Church for 11 years, never
missed my tithing once; I had a Temple recommend.
And then the [Mormon] Lord showed me that they
[the Mormons] had departed from the original track
that Joseph and Brigham had set out. They passed a
law that a man could only have one wife, and actually
it is the order of heaven for man to have more than one
wife.[11]

Lillian's Story

To see the fruit which this early and supposedly irrevocable
doctrine continues to bear to this present day, we need look no
farther than the story of Lillian Chynoweth. Lillian, an attrac-
tive, tall, dark-haired woman, cautiously approached Jeremiah
Films late in the summer of 1988. Following the recent murder of
her husband, Mark, she had been in hiding from her Fundamentalist family group in fear for her own life and the lives of her
children. She told Pat and Caryl Matrisciana that she didn't know
how long she could stay out of harm's way, but before something

did happen to her, she wanted to tell her story on camera. She wanted the world to see what was really going on behind the secret curtain of Mormon Fundamentalism. It was obvious to both Pat and Caryl that she did not expect to escape detection much longer.

From firsthand experience Lillian wished to reveal the horrors of the fruits of this branch of hard-core Mormonism. She knew the depths of its poison because she had lived in the midst of its tenets all her life. She was witness to the murders, the cheating and stealing and lying, and the degradation that its women and children went through every day of their lives, all justified in the name of their polygamous, vengeful god and declared through the mouth of his prophet, Ervil LeBaron, Lillian's own father.

Lillian's story centered on her psychotic father, who had ordered her husband killed, and on the intrigue surrounding the deaths and suicides of 27 members of her family unit since 1972. Her father was the prophet and leader of a large Fundamentalist group called The Church of the Lamb of God. The LeBaron family had been polygamists for a number of generations.

After the 1890 Mormon manifesto which outlawed polygamy, Lillian's grandparents left the state of Utah for Mexico to continue to practice their beliefs. Her grandfather, Alma Dayer LeBaron, founded the town of Colonia LeBaron, where Lillian was born in 1955 as the fourth daughter of Ervil M. LeBaron.

Lillian was raised in this small colony in Mexico, tucked away in a beautiful valley setting in the Sierra Madre Hills. The people she grew up with were mostly the LeBaron brothers (her father and her uncles) and her cousins, but the town grew as people were converted. Lillian confided that the group today has the most sophisticated forms of weapons available and that all the group members are trained to kill.[12]

Lillian remembers her father as someone who studied biblical law and Mormon doctrine and who wrote many pamphlets. She was his secretary for ten years and worked closely with him until she realized that, in her own words, he was not only a "pervert" but "demon possessed." She recollects in her earliest childhood memories "of secret meetings" and "a lot of things going on behind closed doors, including wife swapping."

As a child Lillian "was groomed to marry very young." She says that she "was taken aside and told that it was the Lord's will that we marry such men [polygamists], that we would gain our crown of exaltation, and that we would be priestesses unto the most high god." She explained that among the men there was a network of trading daughters; they would pick and choose and try to gain favor to get the wives of their choice.

Lillian sadly recalls the sorrow and suffering that polygamy caused her mother, who "wanted to do what was right . . . all the wives tried to do what was right, but there were problems, jealousy being the primary one." Lillian promised herself while still a child, and after hearing her mother weep many a night, that she would never get involved with polygamy.

She had a curious childhood bathed in the "Law of Consecration," which is the sacrifice of all things:

> The right to our own husband exclusively, the right to have property, or money, all of it belonged to the kingdom. My father taught us that the means justifies the end for the cause of the kingdom of God. There was a lot of auto theft; everyone was involved in shoplifting and stealing food and clothing. We all worked and we gave a hundred percent of everything to my father for his cause. Even when he was in prison he required all of our money to pay for his attorneys. We usually subsisted on very little. We ate out of dumpsters, we took clothes out of the goodwill collection boxes to cover ourselves. As a child, a very young child in the cult, I was subjected to a lot of suffering because we were sometimes undernourished, we didn't always have the proper clothing, or shoes.

Because of her promise to herself, Lillian chose her own husband, Mark Chynoweth, and they were married. However, after their marriage Lillian's father was continually after Mark to take on more wives because, Lillian contends—

that was one way that he, my father, could control
men, but my husband never took the bait. My father
offered him a lot of my sisters, over and over. He told
him to just sleep with them; finally he offered him my
11-year-old sister to wife, at that age. That's when I
stood up and said, "No, that is sick!"

Lillian and her husband firmly believed that—

the Lord, in His mercy, showed us the deception that
we had been involved in. We knelt, at the time that we
found out that we had been deceived, and we committed our lives to the Lord, and asked Him to please
purge out the old wrong beliefs that we had, yet to fill
us with His Truth. And above all, we asked Him
please not to let us be deceived again, because we
wanted to serve Him. And we purposed to draw as
many of my father's family out of my father's cult and
introduce them to the true gospel, the gospel of redemption and the New Testament.

Lillian and her husband left her father's group when they refused
to bring another wife into the marriage. They left the area and
started a new life for themselves, hoping and praying that her
father would not seek retribution for their so-called apostasy
under the Fundamentalist doctrine of "blood atonement."

Lillian and Mark had a very loving relationship for 15 years
until he was murdered, in Lillian's words by "one of my half-
brothers and one of my half-sisters" in the process known as
"blood atonement."

A Bloody Doctrine

This doctrine is the second side of the grotesque Fundamentalist coin. It teaches that there are certain sins for which the blood
of Christ cannot cover the sinner. The sinner must have his or her
own blood shed to atone for that sin. In Fundamentalist groups,
those sins were as many and as varied as the warped imagina-
tions of the leaders would allow.

When Lillian and her husband found the real Christ, they dreamed about spreading the Christian gospel together. They attended seminary to study the Bible and had a desire to enter a pastoral ministry one day. They hoped to start a home school to further the teaching of biblical principles. However, their hopes and aspirations were short-lived. On June 27, 1988, their dreams ended in a bloody explosion of horror. That was the date assassins from The Church of the Lamb of God paid a visit at their place of business in Houston, Texas and executed Lillian's husband. The slaying of Lillian's husband, Mark, in Houston, coincided with the murders of three other so-called traitors to the cult in Irving, Texas. They were Lillian's brother-in-law, Duane Chynoweth, his young ten-year-old daughter, Jennifer, and Eddie Marston, 32, one of Ervil's stepsons. [13]

Little Jenny's only crime was that she was with her father and therefore was an eyewitness to the brutal execution. We had seen the news coverage on TV, and our eyes had been riveted to the sneaker sticking out from under the blanket covering her small body on the coroner's gurney. A life of promise and happiness had been wiped out to satisfy some wicked, shameful doctrine of darkness.

The execution date of June 27 was no accident. The significance of the date and time of the shootings (4:00 P.M.) was that they fell on the one-hundred-forty-fourth anniversary of the martyrdom of Prophet Joseph Smith. The importance of the murders taking place on the very hour and date of the anniversary of Joseph Smith's killing is part and parcel of the bizarre ritual of blood atonement. All the premeditated ceremony surrounding these consecrated killings was part of the offering, a sweet-smelling sacrifice to the god of Mormonism, a plea bargain for the unwashed sins of mortal men. Early Mormon prophets and leaders set the tone for these murders more than a hundred years ago, their voices still echoing across the decades to take yet more innocent life:

You who have committed sins that cannot be forgiven by baptism, let your blood be shed, and let the smoke ascend, that the incense thereof may come up before God as an atonement for your sins and that the sinners in Zion may be afraid.[14]

I could refer you to plenty of instances where men have been righteously slain in order to atone for their sins. . . . I have known a great many men who have left this church for whom there is no chance whatever for exaltation, but if their blood had been spilled, it would have been better for them. . . . This is loving our neighbours as ourselves; if he needs help, help him; and if he wants salvation and it is necessary to spill his blood on the earth in order that he may be saved, spill it.[15]

These are not radical Fundamentalist prophets like Ervil LeBaron speaking. These words come from the mouths of two of Mormonism's leaders: J.M. Grant and Brigham Young. How can Mormon Church leaders pretend to be separate from the evils of blood atonement? How can they deny it? It is all around them. Until recently, even the death penalty in Utah was by firing squad so a murderer's blood would be spilled and the sin atoned for properly.

Mormon Church officials are concerned that the concept of blood atonement is perceived by many Utahns as official church doctrine, an anti-capital punishment activist says. . . . Noting that the church's stance on blood atonement and capital punishment has changed over the years, Buckley Jensen said, "Church officials did promote blood atonement as late as 1961. And in 1978, the church stood behind capital punishment, but not blood atonement. Now, the church is neither for nor against the death penalty and is definitely opposed to the idea of blood atonement."

In a 1954 writing, the late Mormon Church President, Joseph Fielding Smith, stated, "If then he would be saved he must make sacrifice of his own life to atone—so far as in his power lies for that sin, for the blood of Christ alone under certain circumstances will not avail."

However, in a 1978 letter, Bruce R. McConkie stated that blood atonement "was advocated by the church only within the setting of a theocracy."[16]

Of course, McConkie knew that the goal of Mormonism is that someday this country will become a Mormon theocracy, operating under a Mormon prophet. Then, all these *spiritual laws* such as polygamy and blood atonement will be openly reinstated for the good of the "kingdom." Do you wonder now where these strange, brutal doctrines of the LeBarons come from?

During our videotaped interview, Lillian's face radiated with joy in her relationship with a God whom she knew and loved. She spoke with enthusiasm of future expectations, her longings for her children, and her aspirations to lead her entire extended family to the truth of real Christianity.

The cameras were rolling as Lillian recounted shocking stories of the past, and a thrilling story of the present. She had now found a precious relationship with the real Lord Jesus Christ and was learning daily from God's true Word, the Holy Bible. She had a passionate zeal to spread her new message of hope to all her family and particularly hoped her words would reach those many other innocent victims still trapped in her now dead father's cult. However, she was not naive about the malevolent physical and spiritual dangers that surrounded her mission. She spoke openly about the arsenal of sophisticated weapons that were stashed away in the cult she had fled:

> They do a lot of trading with the Mexican government. They steal vehicles from the U.S. and trade them for weapons and protection in Mexico, to the Mexican government. Even the nine-year-olds are trained to kill. They are to be feared. . . . They are fearless.

At that point Lillian looked into the camera intently and said:

> I would just like you to know that if anything hap-
> pens to me . . . ever, or to my children, I believe that
> the Mormon Church, in general, will be responsible.
> Because the very doctrine of blood atonement, the
> doctrine that requires that our blood might be shed, so
> that we might obtain salvation in the hereafter, stems
> from Mormonism.

It was sobering to think that there really were people *some-where out there* convinced that they were bound by blood oath to execute the holy orders of a dead man, to kill that man's own flesh, his own daughter. Yet our own thoughts on that balmy summer day could not focus on that reality; we could not comprehend the seriousness of Lillian's anticipation of their brutal retribution. The story of Lillian, gleaned from the Jeremiah Films interview, is one of horror, intrigue, and shocking murder. It illustrates results of a family gone wild, fatally poisoned by the fruits of Mormonism.

Sidestepping Responsibility

It may be easy for critics to dismiss the accusations of Lillian, who placed the general responsibility for all of the death and destruction in her family at the door of the Mormon Church. Critics and Mormons alike may claim that Mormonism no longer officially practices such atrocities. But, while the Mormon Church may no longer sanction or approve Joseph Smith's original commandment to practice plural marriage, they do still hold him, and his successor Brigham Young, in high and worshipful regard. They still consider these men to have been the mouthpieces of God. The very section of *Doctrine and Covenants* that lays out the literal requirement to enter into plural marriage or be damned *is still there today* and received as holy scripture by every Mormon believer.[17]

In fact, LDS Priesthood Quorums are still being taught that Joseph Smith holds the full authority and all spiritual keys to this last dispensation of times.[18] It goes without saying that there are hundreds of thousands of people out there who believe this with all the fibers of their being. There are obviously some who will not let later Church leaders wash out his eternal commands for what was obvious political expediency.

On June 27, 1988, the day Mark Chynoweth and the others were executed, Sharon Fryer of Houston's Channel 13 Eyewitness News interviewed the local Mormon stake president, Bervin Blake, who offered his condolences to the family, and then said that "a connection between the LeBaron group and Mormonism does not exist." The TV reporter added, "The teachings of the splinter group is completely foreign to those of the Mormon Church."[19]

Once again, the Mormons had been swift to cast off the child of sin that was birthed in the inner rooms of their past. Bervin Blake's words were a betrayal of truth and came straight out of the dark pit of Mormonism's inner belly. Lillian's story shows that the Fundamentalist connection to the Mormon Church still exists. Mormonism birthed these offshoots whose followers number in the tens of thousands and who look to Joseph Smith, Brigham Young, and the Book of Mormon as their standards of truth.

The thousands of people caught up in polygamy and Mormon Fundamentalism still esteem the original teachings of Joseph Smith and Brigham Young. They still use the Book of Mormon and the speeches and writings of early Church leaders as their rod of truth, and they still wear the old-style Temple garments that were worn in Brigham Young's day instead of the fashionable, shorter style of modern-day Mormonism.

Instead of dismissing their relationship with these groups, Mormons should recognize that the fruits of Mormon teaching at its purest level logically lead to these consequences. These sins stem from the hard-line doctrines of Mormonism that were considered God's inviolable word to man before the repackaging of Mormonism began and the Mormon public relations department stepped in to help The Brethren clean up the Church's image. The Mormon hierarchy should be challenged to confront the errors of the teachings of their prophets and get involved in being part of the solution to the problem. Mormonism needs repentance and restoration to orthodoxy, not continual revision.

Lillian talked about the bedrock LDS doctrines that controlled the LeBaron clan:

> We were raised with the basic tenets of Mormonism, including polygamy, which was openly and freely practiced in our community. My father had a total of 11 wives, my mother being the first. We were very sincere about all the aspects of Mormonism. We used the Book of Mormon as one of our main sources of knowledge. It is a requirement in Section 132 of the *Doctrine and Covenants*; it is clearly stated that if we are to attain the highest degree of glory, we must do the works of Abraham. Therefore we were taught that in order to attain the celestial glory, a man must take more than one wife.

But for the LeBarons, spiritual guidance didn't stop with the LDS standard works. It extended to whatever Ervil LeBaron wanted, whenever he wanted it.

> My father constantly claimed revelation for every last thing that we did, and controlled everything that we did, as much as he could. And I came to find out what a perverted thing he was really involved in. He would actually take several of his wives to bed at once. And he was very involved in marrying other men's wives. So the pressure was on always for men to marry several women.
>
> The youngest girls were reserved exclusively for the older men, who would have a harder time securing more wives, so that's how they worked it. My father got most of his wives by bribing other men with his daughters. I was one of the ones who refused to fall into that, and I chose my own husband, and married, and had a very loving relationship for 15 years—until I lost him through this blood atonement process.

When we finished with the videotaping, we knew that we had been in the presence of someone who was truly living in the center of Psalm 23. There was an anointing on Lillian's life and a strength she demonstrated that came from knowing that she was willing to lay down her life.

Shocking News

Not long after that, we were told that Lillian had returned to her home in Houston, to pick up the pieces and get on with her life. She returned her children to what she hoped would be a normal life again. Things quieted down.

Then four months later came the shocking news. On January 28, 1989, Lillian Chynoweth was found dead. One of the children found their mother lying dead on the floor of the den, a revolver at her side. The official police report said it was suicide. Others deeply question that, knowing that Lillian felt she had work to do before her family caught up with her, knowing it would have been a small matter for her brothers to gain access to her home and execute her in a way made to look like suicide.

Did several of her brothers come to the house, and did she let them in? Or did Lillian commit suicide? Only the Lord can answer those questions. We will never know until heaven, unless some LeBaron clan member claims responsibility for it.

What we do know is that Lillian is dead, her children left without a mother or father. A sparkling light has been extinguished. The intrigue and police investigations that surround that polygamous sect continue.

On January 20, 1993, three members of the LeBaron clan were convicted in the slayings of Mark Chenowyth and the others on the testimony of a fourth member who turned State's evidence:

> Three members of a polygamist sect were convicted of civil rights violations in the slayings of a child and three former adherents who prosecutors said were shot for leaving the church. The jury was to

continue deliberating today on conspiracy and murder for hire charges. The verdict Wednesday means the defendants—William Heber LeBaron, 28, Patricia LeBaron, 27, and Douglas Lee Barlow, 31—could receive life in prison without parole, plus 25 years.[20]

Deeper into Dark Pit of Blood Atonement

This doctrine of blood atonement sounds just too strange to be true. Could people really kill family members under some delusion that God was blessing it as an act of spiritual love? It is impossible for reasonable people to comprehend, yet it was true with the LeBarons.

Lillian gave us a special insight into the underbelly of blood atonement:

> At the same time [she and Mark left the cult], our names were on the list to be atoned for. My father believed that we were traitors to God's cause and that our blood must be shed to atone for the sin of turning against light and knowledge, as he supposed. And so he set about having many killed. Twenty-seven, mostly our family, have been killed since 1972. Yet I don't regret it all. My hope and prayer is that many will come to the true knowledge of the Lord's goodness, and will not be deceived; that this [*God Makers II* film] will be used primarily to help the Mormon people to realize the deception that they have fallen into—because my father's teachings are directly connected with what Mormons believe.

As a child Lillian knew of secret goings-on in meetings because the meetings took place in her home. Sometimes she was allowed to come into meetings and listen. She knew that the vows taken were—

> considered to be very sacred, namely the covenant of blood atonement, which is a ritual they go through if

someone "turns against the light and knowledge" of the gospel that Joseph Smith taught. They make specific signs, and ask that their blood might be shed, that they may have salvation in the hereafter.

We asked Lillian to describe her experiences with the doctrine of blood atonement, and it was as though we had opened a dark door to the past.

My father was the patriarch of the church of the First Born of the Fullness of Times, and my uncle Joel was the prophet and grand head of that same church. In 1972, my father had my uncle Joel murdered because my father, who had started taking other men's wives, was released of office. In a vengeful sense, my father arranged for the murder of his own brother.

During her interview Lillian was convinced that—

this blood atonement process is still going on in the Mormon Church, and my father practiced it openly. He felt that the Mormons were real hypocrites. He exposed Mormons all the time for being hypocrites because they hid the true beliefs of Mormonism. I am convinced beyond a shadow of doubt that my father was murdered in the Utah state prison [in 1981] by the Mormon Church. He was a very charismatic man, and had control of his cell block. He had most people working for him, and the Mormons feared him greatly, so I believe that they killed him.

Did the Mormon Church have a vendetta against the LeBarons? Lillian's brother Isaac paid his tithes to the LDS Church and attempted to "redeem his generation" by returning to the true Church, but the Mormon Church wouldn't allow him to repent— it wouldn't even show him forgiveness. In Lillian's words:

My brother Isaac LeBaron was a devout Mormon.
. . . He very much wanted to have the priesthood. He
did everything he could to qualify to receive his ordinances. He went before the bishop in Houston, Texas
to try to gain his qualifications. There was a list of
things he had to do and accomplish before he could
receive the ordinances of the priesthood. The last
time, they said that they could not give him the priesthood because he was Ervil LeBaron's son. Shortly
thereafter, on June 18, 1983, he committed suicide in
my home. My brother felt like his life was worthless
and hopeless because he couldn't obtain the priesthood. He had everything in the world to live for, yet
he felt like his life was over because he could not
obtain what he most wanted, and that was the priesthood that the Mormons talk about and preach about.

Some people say that blood atonement is a direct
murder, but I think that it's carried out oftentimes in a
different way. Where the Mormons will make some-
body feel so bad, and reject the priesthood to them,
and they know that they will commit suicide because
if the priesthood is not granted to them, their life is
not worth living.

Lillian looked away for a few moments, a sorrowful look fixed
upon her face. Then she turned back to the camera:

The ones that murdered my husband and my family, my brother and my sister, I forgive them entirely. I
love them; they are my own family. And they truly,
sincerely feel like they are doing what is right. I am
praying that somehow, through all of this, that I get
the opportunity to witness to them, and to show them
how the Lord has worked in my life. Because, but for
the grace of God, I could still be involved in that too.

And so, there is nothing but compassion in my
heart for them, and we are not bitter, and we are not

vengeful, and we do not seek to condemn them, but to bring them to the knowledge of the redeeming power. When they realize what they have done, I pray that they will repent, and I know there can be forgiveness for them.

Although this has been such a big tragedy and loss to our family, and to many people, there has been a lot of good come out of it. It has drawn myself and my family close to the Lord; my life is in His Hands. And through all this tragedy that's one thing I have gained, an abiding love for the truth. And my children have also been able to go through this, knowing that all things work together for good, to those of us who love the Lord—*and we love the Lord.*

What a tragedy! What a waste of precious life! What a mockery of Christ and His redemptive act of sacrificial love at Calvary! Mormonism will never shake the fruit of this vine. This doctrine is still so entwined in their theology that they will never escape its tentacles. They may deny it loudly in one breath, but in the very next, breathe it back into their corporate soul.

For example, the late Mormon apostle Bruce R. McConkie, in his definitive book on LDS theology, *Mormon Doctrine*, denied that the Church ever practiced or taught blood atonement. Yet on the same page he stated that because the blood of Christ is not sufficient to forgive certain sins, the Mormon god requires man to have his own blood spilled.[21]

Art, the polygamist/Fundamentalist leader we interviewed in Salt Lake City, explained it this way:

Blood atonement is, that if you have charity enough for someone to save them, the shedding of their blood is the only way that they can atone for certain sins. Jesus shed His blood as an infinite sacrifice, but there are some sins that the blood of Jesus cannot atone for, and therefore it requires the shedding of that man's blood to atone.[22]

Adds Thelma "Granny" Geer:

> Adultery, apostasy, marriage to a Negro, for not
> receiving the gospel, for lying, for any of the other
> offenses, they would have to have their own blood
> shed to have forgiveness of sins. People really thought
> they were doing a favor, in my great grandfather's day,
> to shed the blood and save their soul, and it's still
> taking place today. My great grandfather, John D.
> Lee, was one of the Mormon men who were called the
> Avenging Angels, or Destroying Angels. It was their
> duty, their obligation, to cut the throats, shed the
> blood of people who are apostate Mormons, who
> were guilty of speaking against the authorities.[23]

Meanwhile, back on Temple Square, in our interview with the
man who claimed to be a polygamist, Art continued to justify his
theology based on the teachings of Joseph Smith:

> The original doctrine that Joseph Smith and Brig-
> ham Young taught is exactly what I believe. I am now,
> at present, baptizing people, and I have five apostles
> now, and we are out teaching and preaching the gos-
> pel, trying to get the Mormons into the original doc-
> trine that Brigham and Joseph had the Church set on.
> And I refuse to give it up, so I have been cast out of the
> Mormon Church because of it.[24]

There is the rub. Polygamy and blood atonement, the arcane
curse of early Mormonism, has never been far below the thin
layer of makeup that covers the pretty face of the "families are
forever" Mormon Church. It was standing right there on Temple
Square.

11

The Satanic Connection

O N OCTOBER 25, 1991, JUST IN TIME to spoil Halloween, a secret internal report from the Presiding Bishopric of the LDS Church surfaced. It alleged that satanic ritual child abuse (known as SRA) was being perpetrated by both members and leaders of the Mormon Church in Utah, Idaho, California, Mexico, and elsewhere.

SRA is defined as abusive acts of either emotional, psychological, sexual, or physical battering which are done in a religious or occult context. These acts are designed to subjugate the children involved and brainwash them into a satanic mindset. SRA is usually done by parents, grandparents, or other adults who have access to the children and perform these evil deeds in the sadly misguided hope of gaining occult power from Satan.

According to the *Salt Lake Tribune*, the report by LDS Bishop Glenn L. Pace stated that such abuse was being done by members and officials of the Church. Even Temple workers and Tabernacle choir members stood implicated of SRA in Church meeting-houses and possibly even in the Temples. At least 45 of the victims claimed they were forced to observe or participate in human sacrifice.

In the report, Pace testified:

> I have met with sixty victims. That number could be twice or three times as many if I did not discipline myself to only one meeting per week. . . . I don't pretend to know how prevalent the problem is. . . . Assuming

each [victim] comes from a coven of 13, we are talking about the involvement of 800 or so right here in the Wasatch Front [an area of southeast Idaho and north and central Utah]. Obviously, I have seen only those coming forth to get help.[1]

Saints Alive had received a copy of the report in late summer. The organization opted to refrain from publishing it without further substantiation, since it would have been difficult to believe on its own merit. (Saints Alive had been accused, in the past, of publishing sensationalistic or occult information about the LDS Church and wished to be careful in the matter.) However, while similar information had been emerging for years about this kind of practice within the Church, this was the first time the Church itself had in any way acknowledged its existence.

At the 1990 Capstone Conference in Salt Lake City, Jeremiah Films showed video preview clips of some of the footage they had taken for the film *The God Makers II*. These clips included an interview with one man who testified that he was involved with others in satanic rituals within the LDS Church and on LDS property. The stories we had been gathering closely matched those reported by Bishop Pace a year later. In fact, we suspect that the Church interviewed several of the same people.

That was not the first time we had reported on the diabolical core of the LDS theology. Ed had exposed the Church's satanic roots three years earlier when he spoke on "The Sure Sign of the Nail" in Salt Lake City in 1987.[2] Dr. Walter Martin (now deceased) happened to be ministering with Ed that night, and he commented that Ed had better be prepared for the heat he was going to take from all sides for opening up that bag of demons. It was a prophetic word.

Even before the 1987 meeting, Saints Alive had published information from a former Satanist and Temple Mormon, Bill Schnoebelen, who had joined the staff at Saints Alive. Bill testified that he had converted to the LDS Church under the direction of his occult leader and had compared the numerous parallels between witchcraft and LDS Temple rituals.

His testimony later evolved into the books *Mormonism's Temple of Doom* and *Whited Sepulchers: The Hidden Language of the Mormon Temple,*[3] which he coauthored with Jim Spencer, Idaho pastor and former Mormon. This information chronicled the precise corollaries between LDS Temple practices, Freemasonry, and witchcraft, both past and present.

Even before that, former Temple veil worker Chuck Sackett produced material in *What's Going On in There?* in 1982 which showed that the mysterious Temple chant, "Pay Lay Ale" (removed from the Temple rites in 1990), was most likely a rough translation from the Hebrew language which suggested that the chant could easily mean *"Marvelous Lucifer!"* or *"Marvelous (false) god!"*[4] Thus the satanic connections in Mormonism were by no means news to those who monitor the cults. However, we were heartbroken to find that the problem within the Mormon Church was apparently more widespread than even we had imagined.

A Different Spin on the Story

However, we were disturbed by the strange spin put on the story by the media. Essentially, the LDS Church was portrayed by some as being *victimized* by evil Satanists who had infiltrated its ranks and defiled its children.

Additionally, the LDS Church issued the following official statement:

> Satanic worship and ritualistic abuse are problems that have been around for centuries and are international in scope. While they are, numerically, not a problem of major proportions among members of the Church of Jesus Christ of Latter-day Saints, for those who may be involved they are serious.

That could receive an award as the bland understatement of the year! If a high-level LDS leader reported over 800 Satanists

who are "active Mormons" in just the Wasatch Front and between 60 to 180 victims, that *is* a problem of "major propor-
tions," at least anywhere but in Mormon Utah.

We have prayed with and counseled dozens of people who are
survivors of one sort of occult activity or another. Each of them is
a precious human being who has had incalculable damage done to
him or her by this sort of evil. Without the power of the blood of
Jesus Christ, such people would have little hope at all. Their
personal plights *cannot* be trivialized.

Beyond that, it is historically difficult to characterize the LDS
Church as an innocent church which just happened to be *victimized* by invading satanic perversion. Certainly, many churches
have had this sort of problem come up in the past few years—
though none to the spectacular degree indicated in Bishop Pace's
report. However, there are some deeper issues that touch on theology and spirituality, and they must be addressed.

Fruit Doesn't Fall Far from the Tree

Most reports of the LDS Church's problems with satanic abuse
don't mention that Mormonism was originally brewed in a seeth-
ing caldron of occultism, sorcery, and blood sacrifice. Contrary
to the charming, Church-approved tale of the "First Vision," in
which Joseph Smith was supposedly visited by two gleaming
Personages, the actual beginnings of Joseph Smith's spirituality
were steeped in witchcraft.

First, Joseph Smith, Sr. and his entire family were casting
magic circles and practiced the "faculty of Abrac," according to
Joseph Smith, Jr.'s own mother, Lucy Mack Smith![5] Abrac is
short for Abracadabra and was a common, old-fashioned way of
saying that they practiced *folk magic*.

Joseph Smith himself practiced "glass-looking," a nineteenth-
century term for crystal-ball gazing. He was convicted of this in a
Bainbridge, New York court.[6] In fact, Joseph's annual meetings
(on a witchcraft holiday) with the angel "Moroni" on the Hill
Cumorah were actually attempts to conjure up a demon spirit
through magic and necromancy.[7] There is strong evidence that in

1824 he actually had to dig up the body of his dead brother, Alvin, and bring part of that body with him to the hill to gain the gold plates from which he translated the Book of Mormon![8]

Joseph Smith was also well-known in his community for using blood sacrifices in his magic rituals to find hidden treasure. According to one report of the period:

> Jo [sic] Smith, the prophet, told my uncle, William Stafford, he wanted a fat black sheep. He said he wanted to cut its throat and make it walk in a circle three times around and it would prevent a pot of money from leaving.[9]

Smith's participation in this kind of occult ritual is borne out by several other testimonies.[10] Additionally, after his death, Smith was found to be carrying a magic talisman on his person which was sacred to Jupiter and designed to bring him power and success in seducing women.[11]

With unbiblical practices like that at its roots, how could the tree of Mormonism be anything else but sinful and occult? As has been frequently shown, the sacred Temple rituals of the LDS Church are grounded in practices familiar to those involved in both Freemasonry and witchcraft. Even many of the icons on the outside walls of the older Temples are textbook examples straight from witchcraft. This demonic core of Mormonism is hardly hidden from view.[12]

Is it any wonder that Mormons get involved in these sorts of abominable practices when they are submitted to a priesthood that flows right out of the very jaws of demonism? When their founding prophet and his family were sorcerers, how could Mormons resist the allure of the occult or Satanism?

Where Is the Revelation Power?

If the LDS Church is truly the Church of Jesus Christ and run by a "living prophet," how could such atrocities as satanic ritual abuse even get to first base? LDS doctrine teaches that all bishops and stake presidents have "keys of discernment" with which they can tell if Church members are lying or living unworthy lives. Yet many of these Satanists are also card-carrying "Temple Mormons," who must pass the annual muster of stringent questioning from both their bishop and their stake president. *In fact, Bishop Pace reported that some of the Satanists were bishops and stake presidents themselves!* Again, quoting from Pace's report:

> They [the victims] have told me the positions in the church of members who are perpetrators. Among others, there are Young Women leaders, Young Man [sic] leaders, bishops, a patriarch, a stake president, temple workers, and members of the Tabernacle Choir. These accusations are not coming from individuals who think they recognized someone, but from those who have been abused by people they know, in many cases their own family members. . . . We are disturbed to receive reports that a scoutmaster has abused the boys in his troop. . . . Not only do some of the perpetrators represent a cross section of the Mormon culture, but sometimes the abuse has taken place in our own meetinghouses.[13]

Additionally, Mormons believe that their Temples are watched by angels, and that no unworthy person (even if he or she holds a valid Temple recommend) can enter. If such a person were to try, either the human Temple worker at the gate would be "told by the Holy Ghost" to refuse that person entry, or the angel would stop him or her. How much more so would these sentinels stand against the entry of those involved in actual evil rituals, unless they themselves were evil angels? Remember, Pace said that some of the perpetrators were actually Temple workers.

In speaking of these Satanists, we are talking about *people who torture children and kill people*! If such perverted people can pass undetected by all the protective power of the priesthood authority of the LDS Church and participate in their sacred Temple rites, what good is there in the blind and toothless Mormon priesthood?

Mormons often quote Amos 3:7, "Surely the Lord God will do nothing, but he revealeth his secret unto his servants the prophets," to prove the truthfulness of the Church and the sure need for a living prophet. However, if even a tenth of Bishop Pace's accusations are true, not only has the Lord been doing things without revealing them to the LDS "prophets," but Satan has also been sliding a lot of evil by them.

Since virtually all the testimonies Pace has gathered are from adult survivors of SRA, these practices have gone on in the LDS Church for at least a generation, if not multiple generations! Yet where were the "prophetic" warnings of these practices 20 years ago? The truth is that these are prophets who do not prophecy in the name of the true God.

Preaching the Devil's Sermons

Another issue which has emerged through the publication of the Pace report is that many of the victims Pace interviewed became aware of the atrocities done to them through their attendance at the Temple. Participation in its rites triggered flashbacks of rites they took part in as children. This was only possible because the LDS Temple rituals were *virtually identical* to those rites being done by the Satanists! As Pace notes:

> I'm sorry to say that many of the victims have had their first flashbacks while attending the temple for the first time. *The occult along the Wasatch front uses the doctrine of the Church to their advantage.* For example, the verbiage and gestures are used in a ritualistic ceremony in a very debased and often bloody manner. *When the victim goes to the temple and hears the exact words, horrible memories are triggered* [emphases added].[14]

But the theory now presented by the Mormons and their supporting media is that Satanists infiltrated the LDS Church. These Satanists stole the rituals of the Temple and deliberately used them in a satanic, blasphemous fashion. Bishop Pace says:

> The perpetrators are also living a dual life. Many
> are Temple recommend holders. This leads to why the
> Church needs to consider the seriousness of these
> problems. In effect, the Church is being used.[15]

However, it seems to us that it is difficult for Mormons to say
that their most sacred rituals have been blasphemed when they
are already so blasphemous that the exact words used in these
ceremonies can be used, word for word, by Satanists!

It has long been known that the LDS Temple rituals were full
of occult and satanic symbolism. Many of those portions shown
in the *God Makers* and *Temple of the God Makers* movies are the
very same portions subsequently quietly removed from the Temple
ritual. Some of those elements had been present in witchcraft and
Freemasonry long before Joseph Smith was born!

Whether these modern Satanists and witches stole the rites
from the LDS Temple (as the Pace report and others suggest) or
whether portions of the ceremonies were being used by both the
Satanists and the Mormons separately cannot be proven. The
same core of spiritual evil permeates both. However, along the
Wasatch Front, most likely the numerous LDS Temple-recom-
mend holders who have been among the perpetrators brought
much of the Temple ritual into the more enlightened liturgy of the
dark arts. If this is the case, as Pace suggests, and the LDS
Temple ceremonies can be so easily and effortlessly adapted to
witchcraft and Satanism that the victim "goes to the temple and
hears the exact words," it plainly shows that the Temple rituals
are already replete with pagan and antibiblical elements. According to what we read into the Pace report, the rituals apparently
need only minor tinkering to be completely compatible with
diabolical theology! As our friend Jim Spencer has said, "When
the devil starts preaching my sermons, I'd better start asking
myself where I am getting my material."

Do You Think We'll Get an Apology?

Since Jeremiah Films and Saints Alive began speaking out on
these issues of the occult and satanic core elements in Mormonism,

we have been the target of steady and severe criticism, not only from Mormons, but also from several other ministries. Ed has been accused of being psychotic or out of touch with reality for speaking out about the satanic roots of Temple Mormonism.[16]

Jim Spencer and Bill Schnoebelen have had their reputations slandered and their ministries attacked. Bill, as a former Satanist and Temple Mormon, was singled out. Everything possible was done to destroy his testimony of having been a witch who was told to join the LDS Church by high-level witches because it was essentially a safe organization for witches. As early as 1986, Bill warned about the strong correlations between the Temple rites and occult ceremonials.[17]

These attacks have cost us a great deal. Many people chose to believe what was being said and no longer supported the ministry of Saints Alive. Yet Ed chose not to respond publicly, because he felt the Lord did not call him to fight publicly with other ministries. Ed and Bill did respond with answers, but that only fueled the fires of criticism, and the attacks continued.[18]

We have quietly but firmly held to our position. Now LDS leaders and the news media are speaking openly of the satanic conspiracy within Mormonism, and we wonder if we will hear any apologies from those who attacked us. Ironically, one ministry that was at the forefront of the attacks over our penchant for seeing devils everywhere was the one to publish the Pace report, and for that we are grateful. Certainly, these reports have vindicated our position in the strongest possible way on the satanic strongholds within Mormonism.

Ultimately, whether Satanism abused the safe haven of Mormonism or Joseph Smith borrowed freely from Freemasonry, the occult, and witchcraft (or Abrac), the larger point is that *all of these religions are tributaries of the same satanic river*.

It should be a cause of deep concern to every Mormon that witches and Satanists can blend so seamlessly and effortlessly into their Church! It should cause their hair to stand on end to realize that Joseph Smith was openly involved in Freemasonry and witchcraft *at the very same time he revealed the Temple rituals*. It should be even more alarming that Satanists have been freely moving about in the most sacred precincts of its Temples all these years. Since there has been no statement from The Brethren concerning a purge of these pagans, it should terrify the Mormons that these evil people are still moving freely among the faithful, watching over the Saints with the evil, roaming eyes of hungry wolves.

The Brethren would do well to spend a little more time using their revelatory powers and openly casting out the satanic element in the Church and a little less time worrying about the home schoolers and Bo Gritz groupies. But the sad truth is that they won't because they can't.

The Juggernaut of Sin

The alleged multigenerational character of these satanic groups within Mormonism brings into stark relief the broader problem in the LDS Church—the sin problem.

Mormonism denies the biblical doctrine of original sin. Mormons do not believe the Bible when it says, "All have sinned, and come short of the glory of God" (Romans 3:23) and "There is none righteous, no, not one" (Romans 3:10). They refuse to accept the words of the psalmist when he declares, "Behold, I was shapen in iniquity, and in sin did my mother conceive me" (Psalm 51:5).

Mormons, in keeping with today's prevalent New Age worldview, would prefer to think that humanity is essentially good. This same philosophy is the foundation of all Eastern mysticism. They do not believe the Word of God which teaches us the painful truth that "the heart is deceitful above all things, and desperately wicked: who can know it?"(Jeremiah 17:9). They have departed from the revealed truth of God. Therefore they cannot understand or appreciate the enormity of the deep sin in their own lives, or in the lives of their fellow men and women.

Because of this, the Mormons begin with a faulty premise. They believe that they can, through an effort of personal human will, achieve victory over the sin in their lives—without the blood or the cross of Jesus Christ.

Dr. David Breese is the president of Christian Destiny and the author of many books, including the best-selling *Know the Marks of a Cult*. In his interview with Jeremiah Films, he responded to this type of antibiblical teaching:

> The Bible says, "Not by works of righteousness which we have done, but according to His mercy He saves us." How then are we saved? On what basis do we go to heaven? When you believe that Jesus Christ is the Son of God, that He died for your sins on Calvary's cross, and that sacrifice is the sufficient payment for your sins, you are instantly and eternally saved by the grace of God. [19]

Mormons turn their backs on the only solution to sin which God provides. They do not understand that in their lives, as in the lives of all unregenerate people (people who have not been born again), there is a spiritual *entropy* at work.

Entropy is the thermodynamic law which states that all elements tend to break down and degenerate over time. If anything, this is even truer in the spiritual sense than in the natural. Sin nature, whether in a person, family, or institution, just doesn't get better. Over the years it tends to get worse, unless the completed work of the cross and the blood of Jesus Christ are applied. As the drug addict needs more and more of a dose each time to reach that *power edge* of the experience, so also does the sinner need to reach deeper into sin to attain that same power edge of the sin nature.

Anyone formerly trapped in sin, whether drugs, drunkenness, fornication, pornography, or false religion, will readily testify to the implacable power of that particular sin over his or her life! It is a downward spiral of evil that can spread even to their children and grandchildren. It is a spiral from which they were powerless to escape without the grace of Jesus Christ.

The sin problem in the LDS Church and in the lives of individual Mormons cannot *ever* get better until the Church corporately and Mormons individually repent of their idolatry and come to the cross.

Mormons involved in the occult practices found in the standard LDS Temple rites are dabbling in true occult rituals. No wonder they can be drawn in such numbers into the deeper, darker practices described in the Pace report!

We can look back a century-and-a-half and see Joseph Smith practicing necromancy and fornicating with underage girls, committing wholesale adultery. We should not then be surprised to find his spiritual descendants trapped in the same and even worse forms of sin. If Joseph practiced sorcery and animal sacrifice, why should we be shocked if some Mormons today practice sorcery and human sacrifice, as the Pace report documented?

Only people who have come to terms with their own sin nature could be apologetic about the growing momentum of evil we are witnessing within the LDS Church. The response of The Brethren, however, has been to turn Bishop Pace into an invisible man and act like nothing was out of balance in having hundreds of Satanists running around the heart of Utah and the Church.

The Mormons are simply following in the footsteps of their "prophets." It is a path of destruction from which they must flee for their very lives. The Bible leaps out in this matter: "For the leaders of this people cause them to err, and they that are led of them are destroyed" (Isaiah 9:16).

In the words of Jeremiah, "For my people have committed two evils: they have forsaken me the fountain of living waters, and hewed them out cisterns, broken cisterns, that can hold no water" (Jeremiah 2:13).

As Mormon As the Tabernacle Choir

These sins that are coming to light are the logical progression of the chain of events started by Joseph Smith and Brigham Young. Many LDS apologists and even a few in ministries to the Mormons want to portray these alleged crimes as a bizarre aberration. They present it as the result of evil devil worshipers sneaking in and infiltrating the LDS Church. Yet the spiritual reality is that the Mormon people are hopelessly trapped in an increasingly tangled web of occultism and sin.

Looking at the historic precedents set by Joseph the adulterer and sorcerer and Brigham the murderous "Blood Atoner," one can say that such crimes are as typically Mormon as the Tabernacle Choir. They are just a side of Mormonism which has been hidden from public view until the story broke through the veil of secrecy. It is a side that, until now, very few people could see, and which will, if The Brethren have their way, soon be hidden again as though it never existed. This ostrich approach has worked repeatedly, and it will probably work again. The Scriptures tell us that—

> If our gospel be hid, it is hid to them that are lost, in whom the god of this world hath blinded the minds of them which believe not, lest the light of the glorious gospel of Christ, who is the image of God, should shine unto them (2 Corinthians 4:3,4).

There is no doubt in our minds that the god of the Mormon Temple ritual, the god that requires the swearing of bloody oaths, the god whose most sacred rituals are done in secret, the god whose solemn rites are clearly tied to the occult, is that same god who has blinded the minds of the unbelievers who enter those Temple doors.

The only hope for Mormonism is Jesus Christ, God come in the flesh. We praise God that thousands of Mormons are being set free from the power of the priestcraft that controls the Mormon Church and its downward spiral of evil. We praise God that these things of darkness have been exposed to the light of truth. We need to pray that these new revelations will cause many more sincere LDS people to begin to question the roots of their faith and look to Christ instead of Joseph Smith!

Ed said it clearly and boldly in Salt Lake City in 1987. Let us say it clearly again! The god of Mormonism is Lucifer, the elder brother of the Mormon Jesus, the instructor of eternal truth for Adam and Eve in the LDS Temple ritual itself. *Dear, dear Mormon people, flee for your very lives from this evil thing!*

12

Secrets of a Wealthy Kingdom

T WO OF THE MOST CLOSELY GUARDED MYSTERIES about the LDS Church are its finances and its involvement in businesses. Though it is not well-known, the fact is that the Mormon Church is among the wealthiest institutions in America.

Just how wealthy was a matter of conjecture until the 1985 publication of *The Mormon Corporate Empire* by John Heinerman, a Mormon, and Anson Shupe. The book's information was staggering, and has recently been updated by a series of four major articles in the *Arizona Republic* newspaper.

The series' development was heavily opposed by Mormon Church leaders, who have not willingly released any financial data about the Church's finances in decades. It is our understanding that as thorough as the articles are, they were still censored by pressure from The Brethren, and even the paper admits that there may be a great deal more to learn about some aspects of this ecclesiastical empire.

The series, "Mormon, Inc., Finances and Faith," provides a new and very comprehensive breakdown of the Church's finances and acquisitions.

A Fortune 500 Church?

The articles conservatively estimate that the LDS Church collects about $4.3 billion a year through tithing, plus $400 million from its many ecclesiastical (Church-related) enterprises. In tithing receipts alone that comes to $11,780,822 per day!

A comparison of the Church's $4.7 billion income with the sales of publicly traded companies would place it 110th on the Fortune 500 list. Its revenues are larger than Maytag, Hershey Foods, or Avon, and the Church has a much lower "cost of sales" than any of the regular businesses: It is selling personal exaltation and godhood.

The Church's *business* subsidiaries generate an additional $4 billion a year in sales which, if included in the total, would make the LDS Church an $8.7 billion corporation, between 54th and 55th place on the Fortune 500 and larger than Honeywell, General Mills, or Campbell Soup.

Its income exceeds donations to the United Way, the largest U.S. charity, and surpasses the national incomes of the YMCA, the Salvation Army, and the Red Cross. Although not as wealthy as the much larger Catholic Church, the articles note that the LDS Church has a much better bottom line. Most American Catholic dioceses are awash in red ink, while the Mormon Church operates with no debt load at all.

The LDS Church released a response to the articles, which, as might be expected, gave no specific corrections, but said that the articles' estimates of Mormon wealth were "grossly overstated."

The *Arizona Republic* reported that LDS officials refused its reporters' requests for access to tax returns. They released the information only when the paper stood firmly on IRS regulations that permit public inspection of such documents. The *Republic* admits that it was not able to get a complete, up-to-date listing, but it concluded that the LDS Church—

- controls at least 100 companies that generate about $400 million a year for the Church through contributions, dividends, or trusts.

- never borrows money to finance its acquisitions. It pays cash, using portions of its members' tithing and its business income.

- has become one of the nation's largest landowners.

- has investments in excess of $1 billion.[1]

The articles served to squelch one of the most common rumors, even among Mormons. The paper claimed that it could find no record of the Church having ever owned part of Coca-Cola. The closest it could come was the apparent fact that Mormons sold sugar to Coke for use in its soft drinks at one time.

In pursuing the facts about Mormon Church finances, it is important to note two things: 1) This information is certainly incomplete; and 2) there is a difference between businesses or corporations owned by the LDS Church and businesses owned by individual Mormons.

For example, the Marriott enterprises are Mormon-owned, yet not by the LDS Church, but rather by the LDS Marriott family. Even in this case, much of the Marriott stocks and bonds are out there in other hands. Yet it is helpful to know if such concerns are run by Mormons, because if they are, you can assume that at least 10 cents of every dollar they earn *individually* is probably given as a tithe on their income.

According to the article, the Church owns at least 699,000 acres of land in the United States and Canada, almost half of which is located in Florida near Orlando. In fact, the Church may be Florida's largest single owner of undeveloped real estate. Other states with LDS-owned farmland are Iowa, Illinois, Nebraska, Indiana, Missouri, and Oklahoma, plus an 88,000-acre ranch in Alberta, Canada.

This does not include other commercial properties, which amount to over $204 million worth of properties in Utah and California. The Church has amassed farm, ranch, and real estate holdings that today exceed $1 billion, including the $18 million Security Pacific Bank Plaza in Tucson and a $10 million shopping mall in Orange County, California.

Closely Held Assets

In the midst of this dizzying array of millions, it is startling to realize that the LDS Church *technically* owns nothing. Rather, all of the assets are owned by one of two holding companies: The

Corporation of the Presiding Bishopric, which is in charge of the Church's "ecclesiastical" assets (like Beehive Clothing, which makes the Temple garments) and its parent holding company, the Corporation of the President of the Church of Jesus Christ of Latter-day Saints (CPC).

The CPC is essentially the president of the Church and his counselors! Thus a handful of men have total control of this huge amount of economic power! A complete listing of the companies they control would be longer and more brain-numbing than this book would permit. But by way of example, the CPC runs such large conglomerates (with a total value of about $1.6 billion) of secular industry as:

- Deseret Management ($1.3 billion in known assets)
- Deseret Trust of California ($17.8 million in assets managed)
- ZCMI department stores ($124 million in assets)
- Property Reserve of Arizona ($117 million)
- Columbia (Washington) Ridge Farms ($26.7 million)

The paper stated that the Church appears to spend about $2 billion a year to maintain its Temples and its 16,000 local church buildings. Putting more than 40,000 missionaries in the field costs the Church $550 million dollars a year!

We would be remiss if we did not mention some of the extraordinary inroads the LDS Church has made into the media. The LDS Church's media arm is the Bonneville International Corporation, which owns the following radio and TV affiliates around the nation:

KAAM-AM, KZPS-FM Radio (Dallas)

KBIG-FM (Los Angeles)

Keystone Communications (sales, $25 million)

KIRO, Inc. (Seattle) (sales, $32 million)

KMBZ-AM, KMBR-FM (Kansas City) (sales, $1.1 million)

KMEO-AM/FM Radio (Phoenix) (sales, $2.3 million)

KOIT-AM/FM Radio (San Francisco)

KSL (Salt Lake City)

KTMX-FM Radio (Chicago)

WNSR-FM (New York City) (sales, $1.1 million)

Additionally, the LDS Church owns its own newspaper, the *Deseret News*, and its own publishing company, Deseret Books. The *News* can be counted on to virtually ignore any story which shows any unpleasant truths about the LDS Church. Deseret Books owns a chain of 24 stores which sell $97 million in books each year. Among religious publishers, only the Sunday School Board of the Southern Baptist Convention sells more.

You can imagine that with this sort of media influence, when the Church talks (or forbids others from talking), the networks listen. We have at times run into frightening opposition in the media toward running any stories on the Church that place it in a negative light.

The casual visitor to Salt Lake City, Utah, cannot help but be overpowered by the granite-like strength and power of the Mormon empire. Standing among the towering fountains and gardens in front of the Church office building and looking down to Temple Square, you have to think that this is the way God's home office would look if "Thy Kingdom Come" were listed on the New York Stock Exchange.

The details of this vast financial side of the LDS kingdom are known within the LDS Church only by a select few leaders, and even then only on a need-to-know basis. The complex network of corporations within corporations has spread out the controls and lines of authority so that even most of the Church's business managers see only what The Brethren want them to see. Most employees within the LDS business empire would need a road map to get to the top. The Brethren want it that way.

No Accountability

Although elevated to the office of spiritual leaders, the majority of The Brethren were successful businessmen before they were called by "revelation" to join the ranks of the LDS hierarchy.

Unlike members of other churches, Latter-day Saints, including those in lower levels of leadership (such as bishops and stake presidents) who have faithfully and sacrificially contributed their tithes and offerings, their time and energies, and given their whole identities to the Church, are powerless to call for an accounting or to participate in any regular corporate decision. They must faithfully submit to every decision from the top.

For a Mormon to ask for a financial accounting by The Brethren would be an incomprehensible act. Mormons are taught that God has called these Brethren. In their minds it would be a lack of faith in God to even question their divine judgment. To do so would be ruinous to an individual's testimony of the truthfulness of the Mormon Church and a fatal first step into the downhill spiral to apostasy.

We asked John Heinerman, Mormon author of the book *The Mormon Corporate Empire*, what he thought of the wealth and power base of Mormonism. His response was quite revealing:

> I have always been fascinated with the great wealth and power the Church of Jesus Christ of Latter-day Saints wields nationally and internationally. The Mormon corporate empire, in terms of dollars and cents, is rather impressive for several reasons. Number one, in the book [*Mormon Corporate Empire*], we take a conservative figure of about 8½ billion dollars that the empire is worth, and we of course have footnotes in the back of the book showing how we arrived at those figures. But really, with all the research that we have done, the figure is closer to 11½ to 12 billion dollars, worldwide, [for] all of their investments and holdings.

Now these investments and holdings primarily fall into real estate, such as Temples, meeting houses, seminaries, religious institutes, which comprise close to half of the assets of the Church. Another percentage of about 25 percent would be in business holdings, agribusiness, their ranches, their business real estate holdings, their investment portfolios. Through the research that we obtained . . . some of it came from computer printouts from the Church Finance Department, that was given to me in 1982 and '83, which formed the heart and core of the book.[2]

As we listened to this man pour out this immense storehouse of data regarding the affluence and might of his church, there was no doubt in our minds that in John Heinerman we had tapped into a wellspring of hidden knowledge and enthusiasm.

The one thing I was amazed at was that the . . . LDS Church rolls over every year between 1½ and 2½ billion dollars just in its investment portfolios. They're into everything from agricultural futures like soybeans and pork bellies to cattle. They've invested heavily in power companies. They have one portfolio called the Bond Substitute Portfolio. And they have a little over a quarter of a billion dollars just in that.

Some of these investment portfolios bring huge dividends and returns, and others lose millions of dollars. For instance, in the Bond Substitute Portfolio, which has investments in a number of power companies around the country, in that two or three hundred thousand shares here and there, many of these power companies have been involved in nuclear reactors, nuclear facilities that have drained the power companies to where now the power companies have invested in basically white dinosaurs. The result is, the stocks of many of these power companies have plummeted. The Church has taken a pretty good beating in this direction. When there was the collapse of the stock market here last fall, someone asked me how much I thought the LDS Church had lost. And I said, just based on what I was familiar with in 1984 and '85 . . . it was probably in the neighborhood of 11 to 15 million dollars. And someone I talked with from the finance department some years ago said, "When we make investments, we don't pray to God, and we don't go by revelation, we do it just like the world does." And so of course, you win some, you lose some.

When we got down to the question of what the Mormon Church *does* with all this wealth and power, John was refreshingly candid about it.

The LDS Church uses this wealth to go and help increase its membership, to go and promote and pros-elytize the gospel that it is advocating worldwide. The Church has been fortunate to have a number of its people in prominent positions around the country in political authority: senators, congressmen, people in the Reagan cabinet, people in the CIA and the FBI. At times the Church has called upon them to go and do a favor for the Church, get the Church out of a jam, or use their political clout in behalf of the Church.

One thing I think is important to point out, most people do not realize the full extent and power of the LDS Church. Two examples very quickly. One, when I was doing research for *Mormon Corporate Empire*, I had a run-in with the LDS Church Security. To make a long story short, I was sitting in a Church office build-ing in July 1983, and . . . the Church attorneys were being located. They wanted to interview me and try to find out how I had gotten my information.

Heinerman relates his discovery of confidential police and FBI documents while waiting for his interview:

I was sitting in the office alone, and I happened to notice on a particular desk in front of me, several documents. And so I looked around, and no one was there, and I turned them around, and on the first one there was a name of an individual that I've forgotten, but it said, "Salt Lake City Police Department, Police Record." I slid the document down, and it [the second document] said, "Federal Bureau of Investigation," and the name of an individual. And these were apparently reports about these individuals and their activities.

The secretary came back into the room, took the documents, put them in the top drawer of her desk, locked it, and then proceeded to give me a mild tongue-lashing, saying, "You know, you shouldn't be snooping around in there." I said, "Well, you shouldn't be leaving documents lying around. You know," I said, "This a police report and an FBI report, and I thought those things were confidential." And she said, "Listen, we can get anything we want, on anyone we want, at any time we want."

We asked John to tell us a little more about Church Security. He smiled proudly as he said:

Now the profile of LDS Church Security! The fellow that I had first run into was with Air Force counter-intelligence for 26 years. Another fellow was with the Los Angeles County Sheriff's Department. The head of Church Security, who recently died, was a top FBI man under J. Edgar Hoover. They have retired CIA men working, they have people from the Navy counterintelligence. And so the Church has amassed an incredible amount of security personnel from different law professions, and that gives it some of the best security of any religion on the face of the earth.[3]

Why would any church require one of the largest, most highly trained security forces ever found in any portion of this country's private sector? The concept staggers the mind, except when you realize that The Brethren have the security force because it is in fact needed.

Mormonism, the Media, and Damage Control

As with any image-conscious corporation, the Mormon Church responds to public relations problems smoothly and quickly. Not only does it command an efficient and polished communications team to market Mormonism to the world, but key Mormons have been placed in powerful positions and have had the ability to control virtually all media programming.[4] The Mormon-controlled media conglomerate, Bonneville International Corporation, is one of the largest owners of radio and TV stations in the country.[5]

The power of the LDS Church in the media was confirmed during a "60 Minutes" news exposé on Mormonism. After labeling the story as sloppy journalism, the Mormons forced a rare apology from "60 Minutes" and the dismissal of the producer of the segment.[6]

Mormons in political office have been able to pressure Hollywood not to produce films that portray Mormonism in a negative way.[7] Recently even the *Washington Post* got into the action over this misuse of power. A $20 million miniseries based on the book *The Mormon Murders* was apparently kept off the air because it would have revealed the conspiratorial power of the Mormon Church in the Hoffman murder case.

> Rumors surfaced at CBS Network headquarters last week that the elders of the powerful Church of Jesus Christ of Latter-day Saints were gearing up to kill a devastatingly unflattering mini-series called "The Mormon Murders."

The article went on to state that while the book was bad enough, the miniseries was fraught with danger for the Church:

Of the two, the mini-series has generated the most fear and loathing; fear of the global consequences of a multi-million-viewer audience and loathing for the book that spawned it.[8]

John L. Smith, Director of Utah Missions, made this comment:

I'm especially concerned with the amount of influence they have over the media; you know, the people who really control our country are those in control of the media. The Mormon Church owns, not only a number of radio and television stations in Salt Lake City, but in Idaho, in Washington State, in Los Angeles, in Dallas, in Kansas City, and not only do they own a number of these radio stations and cable companies, but companies that they also own in turn own others of these.[9]

Secrecy, power, and freedom from accountability—The Brethren have it all, and they will continue to use it as long as the Mormon faithful allow them to.

13

The Hinckley Affair

N O ONE IN UTAH WILL ARGUE about the Mormon death grip on the media, especially when it comes to things that do not please The Brethren. We followed a story that is a classic example of the closed-fist power of The Brethren. It is a story that has caused us so many problems and personal attacks that in a certain sense it would have been better for us if we had never heard the name Charles Van Damm. In fact, throughout our contacts with him, our video interview, and our research on his background, there was very little we held in common with the man. But his story needed to be told.

On August 4, 1988, Charles Van Damm was interviewed on radio station KZZI in West Jordan, Utah. What he shared must have rocked the Church headquarters to its very foundation. The radio station that dared to air the interview with Charles Van Damm was subsequently bought out within days, and the talk host who featured the story was fired.[1]

Van Damm was a 52-year-old former Mormon who had been excommunicated for homosexuality. On the radio program he alleged that he had been involved in some illegal business transactions with a Mormon Church leader and some other members, and that he had a homosexual relationship with this Church leader, whom he identified as Elder Gordon B. Hinckley, a member of the First Presidency of the Church. He said that the homosexual affair with Hinckley began about 25 years ago, back in the early days of Hinckley's apostleship. Van Damm stated that he was now dying of AIDS and wanted to set the record straight before he died. As you can imagine, shock set in over Zion.

Charles Van Damm was born and raised in Utah. He was from a very prominent, multigenerational Mormon family. The Van Damm name is well-represented in the Utah business, social, and political world. His grandfather was a judge in Utah and his grandmother's brother, George Albert Smith, was the eighth president of the Mormon Church. One of his father's brothers was, at the time of our study, the president of the West Jordan Temple in Sandy, Utah. Van Damm was married with children, but, like many of his Mormon friends at the time, he was bisexual. During the day he worked as a general manager in a car business, and at night he frequented the gay bars, of which there are many in Salt Lake City. Later in life, Charles moved to Denver, Colorado, where he claims he opened and managed two gay bars. He was living in Arizona at the time of our interviews.

While still in Salt Lake City, Charles said that he was introduced to a very good friend of the Hunter brothers, owners of the bustling car business where he worked on Main Street. The man was Gordon B. Hinckley. According to Van Damm, that was to be the beginning of a "discreet" sexual relationship between "Gordy" and Van Damm, and also the beginning of a financial partnership of some sort between the two. Charles was either divorced or separated from his wife at the time and needed a house to live in, while Gordy wanted "a party pad" where he could hold his "wild parties." Van Damm claimed that they bought an expensive, five-bedroom house together. Charles oversaw the buying and furnishing of the home and eventually coordinated the parties that were to take place there. He arranged for the women, who were often prostitutes. He arranged to supply the house with alcohol and eventually drugs. Charles alleged that Gordy was bisexual and had a preference for young boys.

Charles stated that he continued to be involved sexually with Hinckley over the years, and in what he described as some shady and illegal deals. Charles was eventually excommunicated for homosexuality and went on to lead an active homosexual lifestyle. As we mentioned earlier, at the time of the radio interview

Charles was diagnosed with fully developed AIDS. Today he is dead.

A Mormon Searches for Truth

One of the people who picked up on the Charles Van Damm story was another lifetime Mormon, Bill Claudin, of Orem, Utah. Even though Van Damm's charges were more than 20 years old, it affronted Bill that one of the top spiritual leaders in his Church would have been involved in such a lifestyle and yet openly preach against it. The events surrounding the Van Damm affair and the swift action by *someone* to quickly silence the station and Van Damm's story set a fire under Bill. He personally contacted Van Damm and met with him. Bill took copious notes during his interviews and began his own investigation into Charles' allegations. At first, he expected to gain evidence that the Van Damm story was not true. Specifically, he started looking for concrete evidence and for eyewitnesses to the gross immorality that Van Damm claimed existed at such a high level in the Church.

Claudin was convinced that if the allegations were not true, he would find that out quickly enough. However, if they were true, he would soon find the hard evidence. He would then take that evidence to his bishop, who would be required to send it up the ecclesiastical ladder to the Council of Twelve. Then the Church, operating under the principles of divine authority, would take the necessary disciplinary action, in spite of Hinckley's position in the Church.

As more and more of the pieces fit during Bill Claudin's investigation, however, more and more Church doors were being closed to him. It was during one of these frustrating times that someone recommended that he contact Jeremiah Films. Bill sent copies of his discoveries to Pat and Caryl Matrisciana, and they forwarded copies of the material to Ed Decker. The final link was for Pat and Ed to fly to Utah and begin their own follow-up investigation. If what Bill Claudin had unearthed was indeed true, this was explosive evidence regarding President Gordon B. Hinckley, First Counselor to the LDS Prophet and President of the Church, Ezra Taft Benson. A monumental story was ready to break. Or so they thought.

After a long visit with Bill Claudin, going through all the data he had gathered, Ed and Pat, along with Bill and his wife, Diane, flew to Arizona, where Charles Van Damm was living out the last stage of the disease that had all but destroyed his body. Van Damm was extremely weak, and it was difficult for us to infringe upon him in his condition, but those of us who came to see him, and Charles himself, felt it was vitally important to record his story. It was to be Van Damm's last interview. He passed away shortly after.

For the Record

In this deathbed declaration recorded by Jeremiah Films, Van Damm admitted that the reason he was only now bringing this information to the public was because he no longer had anything to lose:

> I think that the public should be knowledgeable of what the Mormon Church actually does and is, because they wreck lives. That's why I'm coming out like this, because somewhere along the line these people are going to know that I'm telling the truth. What can they do to me? Can they kill me? I'm dying anyway; what difference does it make?[2]

Just the effort of those few words exhausted him. We had to wait several minutes between each set of comments for him to gather his strength for the next. On camera, he was vocal with the issues he wanted exposed, many of which go beyond relevance here. He felt wounded, angry, and hurt that the Church excommunicated him and others for being homosexual, when, as he claimed, the Church encourages such behavior with its missionary program, sending young boys out by twos to live and sleep together for two years.

> I was personally involved with the apostle Gordon Hinckley sexually. We became financially involved in

a house on Lakeline Drive. We bought the house for a party pad. And Gordon Hinckley came up there all the time, and I had to arrange women for him. I had to arrange booze for him.

He claimed that homosexuality "is rampant in the Mormon Church; there are a lot of guys in the Mormon Church right now that live a double life. They have boyfriends *and* wives." He expressed real concern for the way his friends were being treated by the Church:

> I have had some of these poor returned missionaries that I've been good friends with in the gay scene, and they come to me, and they just don't know what to do because their families walk away from them. Lots of people can't handle losing their family.

Charles says that he was saddened by Hinckley, who "was making a mockery of everything that Mormonism meant to me at one time in my life—and it did mean something to me. I was proud to be a Mormon, I'd stick my chest out." But the hypocrisy of having to hide their homosexuality was too much for some to bear. "I saw some of my best friends end up in mental hospitals, and losing their families, and losing their lives. I saw suicides that were ridiculous."

Charles Van Damm isn't the only gay Mormon to fight those kinds of battles. The authors of a 1992 *Salt Lake Tribune* article expressed the views of many when they wrote:

> If the truth were discovered, they [homosexuals] could be attacked by strangers, branded as perverts or banned from church. What these men and women are afraid to admit is that they are homosexual. "They can lose their jobs, friends and family," says Salt Lake Police Officer David Ward, who served as the city's liaison with the gay community. "They can be kicked out of their homes when the landlord finds out."

> The Church of Jesus Christ of Latter-day Saints
> has strict rules of behavior: marriage in the temple,
> children and a religious life. If obeyed, heaven is the
> reward. Unwilling to forsake their faith, many LDS
> gays and lesbians lead traditional heterosexual lives.
> Some have gay lovers and frequent gay bars—taking
> a second name for their secret lives.
>
> "You have two lives when you are gay," says a
> secondary school teacher as she sips a beer at the
> lesbian bar, Puss N' Boots. "You have to hop in and
> out very fast. You get good at it. You play the game."[3]

Van Damm was hurt because he felt that he was "chastised" by the Church only because he was an active homosexual. Sadly, he alleged that they "took away my children from me" and ruined his marriage. He claimed that some of the hierarchy were involved and are still "closet gays." He felt betrayed by the hypocrisy of those in authority, betrayed because he was denied his Mormon privileges for the very same sexual activity pursued by many who were excommunicating others for what they themselves did in secret. He admitted he was striking back at his onetime friend, Gordy, because Hinckley was sitting at the top of the world, his family and reputation still intact, while Van Damm and other Mormons like him were ruined and excommunicated at the very hands of men like Hinckley.

Verifying the Story

In order to document Van Damm's deathbed allegations, Jeremiah Films felt it important to fully verify his story through the testimonies of other people whom Bill Claudin had found during his investigation. They decided to do in-depth video interviews with three of the people who were eyewitnesses.

Before we share their stories, we would like to clear up a small point. We have been accused of validating the testimonies of what our critics call "shady people." Since the film's release, the reputations of these eyewitnesses have been destroyed because they admitted having seen Hinckley with Van Damm at some of these "low-life" parties. However, these parties didn't exactly encourage attendance by moral giants with impeccable character. What were Mormons in such good standing as Hinckley and the Hunters doing there in the first place? At least the people we interviewed had the honesty to come forward with what they knew. Their testimonies are certainly valid in any court of law, despite their backgrounds or lack of Temple recommends. We can only wish that Hinckley would be so candid.

One of the first eyewitnesses we talked to was Ben, who had been a lifelong family friend and brother figure to Charles Van Damm. He spoke highly of Charles' business aptitude and his conscientious, hard work during his business management of the Hunters' car dealership. Charles knew how to sell, and he moved a lot of cars for the Hunters. Ben said that Charles was generously paid for his work at the dealership, and was always handling special deals for the Hunters and for Hinckley. He had seen Hinckley off and on at the dealership with Van Damm and the Hunters, and also at the house where many of the parties were held. Ben was dismayed when he discovered that Charles was "AC/DC" (bisexual). It was a side of Charles that he (Charles) had kept hidden from his friend Ben for a very long time.

Ben was born, raised, and baptized a Mormon, but calls himself "a Jack-Mormon": "I don't mean hypocrite. I mean, because they [Jack-Mormons] don't attend church, and maybe they don't pay their tithing, they're still LDS! I still believe the Book of Mormon."[4]

Ben's greatest complaint during his filmed interview focused on the hypocrisy and double standards practiced by fellow Mormons. Those in authority, such as the Hunter brothers, Hinckley, and "the higher Church officials," whom Ben saw regularly at Charles' parties with "prostitutes" and "young boys," deeply prejudiced his outlook toward the Church.

Several times in the interview, Ben was questioned about his certainty on the Hinckley identification. There was no doubt that Ben knew exactly who Gordon B. Hinckley was and no doubt that he had seen him at parties, not only at the house but also several

times at a small apartment above the Hunter car dealership.
Hinckley disgusted him, not because of what he had been doing,
but because he preached one thing to the good Mormons during
the day and did things that would get anyone else excommunicated at night:

> If you say you live the Book of Mormon, then you
> should live the Book of Mormon. If you don't want to,
> you should get yourself out of the Church. If you are
> going to be a good LDS, and be up in the First Pres-
> idency of the Church, or a bishop, or whatever you
> might be—if you don't live what you preach, what in
> the devil is the use to having any religion in the first
> place?

Referring to Van Damm's excommunication, Ben commented:

> How can you condemn somebody for doing a lot
> less than you are doing? They don't have to be hypo-
> critical, and that was what got me upset about these
> three [the two Hunter brothers and Hinckley] people.
> They didn't practice what they preached. In other
> words, if they claim to read the Book [of Mormon],
> and believed in the Book [of Mormon], why were
> they in such a position that they could excommunicate
> somebody that wasn't doing nearly as bad a thing as
> they, a bunch of switchers and homosexuals, were
> doing?

We wanted to get another, independent description of the house
that Charles claimed he and Hinckley had. We asked Ben to
describe the house on the hill:

> It had four or five bedrooms, three-story job, beau-
> tiful home. We used to go up there all the time. Louie
> would bring up four or five girls at a time, bring them
> to the door. Mr. Hinckley, among other people, was

there. But they'd drink and dance, and maybe the
girls would dance for them, you know, in front of
them; then they'd gather up a man and go into the
bedroom.

Ben paused in reflection for a moment, then smiled apolo-
getically. "These parties were something else. And these are
people that are supposed to be good LDS."

New Leads

It is interesting the way facts come into an investigation and
open up other unexpected information. When Ben mentioned
the name Louie, we asked him to describe the man for us. He told
us that Louie was the car-lot man at the Hunters' business who
had supplied the "girls," or prostitutes. Not only had Bill Claudin
also heard about Louie, but he had actually found him, interviewed him, and set up an appointment for us with him.

The Louie whom Ben had mentioned was waiting for us at his
home that evening. Louie worked for Walter Hunter, the Mormon bishop who was the co-owner of the car lot on Main Street.
He worked for Charles Van Damm at the Hunters for five or six
years, and admitted that he knew there were several LDS men
who were high up in the Church who used to come around to see
the Hunters and Charlie Van Damm and who partied at Van
Damm's house on Lakeline Drive. He knew exactly who Hinckley was because one time Hinckley brought in a car that Louie's
mother bought from him.

Louie kept the cars and the property at the business clean
during the day, and at night would go out to do collection work.
On request he would sometimes supply "paid" girls and deliver
them to the party house. Sometimes he would get a call to bring
more liquor. At those times he would see "important" Church
members attending. Louie certainly had the street smarts to see
things and people at the house and car lot and to keep things he
heard from the girls to himself. There were times that he made
more money on these special assignments than he made during

the day at the lot. Life wasn't exactly like the picture-perfect "family home evening" image for a black man in Utah during the sixties and the seventies.

Because of Louie's work in collections he was also privy to some illegal transactions and unethical goings-on that are associated at times with what he termed "rougher car dealerships," things you would have hoped not to see in places belonging to people of high standing within the Mormon Church.[5]

We asked Louie to describe Charles' house and what Louie did there. He described the house much as Charles and Ben had and again told us:

> I took prostitutes up in Indian Hills, which is an exclusive neighborhood in Salt Lake, and this went on for several years, and basically most of the girls they requested me to bring them were black girls. And most of them were tall and kind of lanky.

Louie didn't have much regard for some of the partygoers. Although not a Mormon himself (Louie is black, and these events were going on when being black was still a Mormon curse), Louie understood that some of the people involved were playing secret games:

> They were supposed to be important people, and supposed to be good churchgoing people and things like that. Some were bishops and counselors, and doing those various things that I actually seen, going there or leaving there. My word.

By now, we knew that we had some hard facts. We had interviewed Charles, Ben, and Louie separately. None knew what questions we were asking anyone else. None admitted to having seen or talked to the others for years. We were getting solid, confirming descriptions of the house, the participants, and the activities. All three were *resolute* about seeing Gordon B. Hinckley, the same Hinckley who was now in the Presidency of the

LDS Church. We had extended video footage of every word said. Yet we felt we needed at least one more independent confirmation. That would give us four eyewitnesses.

A Woman's View

Bill Claudin had come up with the names of certain women who had participated in some of the parties and had located several of them. These women were not prostitutes, but close friends to a few of the LDS married men who regularly attended. One was away with her husband on an older couples' mission for the LDS Church and would not return to the United States for some time, but Bill met with another woman who was willing to talk to us.

Viola had been the special girlfriend of one of the Hunter brothers back in the sixties. She confirmed that he was the co-owner of the car business on Main Street and substantiated much of Van Damm's account, and more, about the wild parties at what she called "the Hinckley and Van Damm's party pad on Lakeline Drive."[6]

She was introduced to Hinckley at one of those parties and stated that he was at most of the parties she attended. She claimed that she personally saw Hinckley participate actively in the "sexy" dancing and watched him as he went back to the bedrooms with different women on several occasions. She also said that at those parties which were attended by "paid girls," there was much switching of partners, striptease, and "dirty dancing." The alcohol and mixed drinks were always plentiful.[7]

We asked Viola to describe what usually went on at the parties:

> Mr. Hinckley and all of them were sitting there, and I remember one night when I was there he was sitting there, and he was really getting loose, you know. And he had his arm around this one girl, and pretty soon I seen everybody just taking off going this way and that way to different rooms. When you see it with your own eyes, you know what they really do,

especially high officials, like Mr. Hinckley. I said, "I can't believe this."

We asked her how she equated Hinckley's behavior with his Church position:

> I knew that Hinckley was high in the LDS Church, and I knew that Hunter was high in the Church too, a bishop, and I just couldn't believe Hinckley's behavior. I saw it with my own eyes, the drinking and carrying on. These LDS people, especially high officials, really are hypocrites.

She was an eyewitness to the close relationship between Gordy and Van Damm, and although she never saw Gordy and Charlie go off together to a bedroom, she verified Hinckley's desire for young boys, citing one example when one night, at one party, she saw Hinckley involved with two teenagers:

> There were a couple of young boys there at the party one night when I was there. And I'd say they were around 15 or 16, that I seen them talking with Hinckley, and they went off to a bedroom together, Hinckley and the two boys.

That verified exactly what Charles Van Damm had told us in Arizona:

> He'd like to have feminine-looking boys, youngsters. I'm talking about 15, 16 years old, just little youngsters, babies. He had used me sexually, myself, personally. And then excommunicated me on the homosexuality.[8]

We left Utah with hours of videotaped interviews, only part of which we have included here. Much of the material was too descriptive to incorporate and would not have added to the breadth of this story in any way. It was put away with the rest of the material that Jeremiah Films had been gathering for *The God Makers II* video, which at that time was still four years away from being completed.

If at First You Don't Succeed

At around noon on the day we interviewed Ben and Louie, we attended what Bill Claudin called an "awareness event and press conference" on the street in front of Gordon B. Hinckley's Church office. Just before we had flown to Utah for the interviews, Bill had taken all his updated material back through the Church system and even to the press without success. His bishop advised him that if he continued to pursue this line of interest, it would cost Bill his Church membership. *Bill knew that the charges were true.* He knew he was being stonewalled, and he decided that he would sooner live out his life with truth than with the Mormon Church.[9]

When we arrived at Temple Square, friends of Bill and Diane Claudin, along with some volunteers from the Utah Saints Alive chapters, were marching up and down the crowded street in front of Hinckley's office with signs exposing Hinckley's homosexuality. Needless to say, the air was electric and the situation tense. Church Security agents were everywhere with cameras and video recorders, zooming in on every protester, every sign, and every pedestrian who happened to get caught in the crossfire or accept a press release from Bill or Diane.

Ed jumped into the fray and began carrying a sign, while Pat Matrisciana turned the Jeremiah Films camera on the action. Bill Claudin finally had the attention of the press, who were gathered around him as he told his story:

> We are here to today to protest the actions of the Church in hiding the facts relating to Gordon B. Hinckley. Gordon B. Hinckley was involved in heterosexual and homosexual love affairs.[10]

Meanwhile Ed and other protesters were being interviewed by other news reporters. One lady was saying:

> They live a double standard. Their leaders are say-
> ing one thing and living another lifestyle. They ex-
> communicate bisexuals in the mainline LDS Church.
> Why are the leaders getting away with it?

Another said, "We just believe that if Gordon B. Hinckley is professing that you should be morally clean so you can sit in judgment of others, that he should be judged by the same standards."[11]

Gordon B. Hinckley has to be in a tight spot. Speaking about sexual behavior to the all-male priesthood at the Saturday night session of the April Conference, on April 4, 1987, Hinckley had said:

> Chastity before marriage and fidelity after will do
> more than anything to check the spread of AIDS.
> Prophets of God have repeatedly taught through the
> ages that practices of homosexual relations, fornica-
> tion, and adultery are grievous sins. Sexual relations
> outside the bonds of marriage are forbidden by the
> Lord. We affirm those teachings.

In his speech, he linked the spread of AIDS to "sexual adventurism, which is spreading like another plague across the world."[12]

That night we watched the local television news programs with amazement. Except for one extremely brief note about some ex-Mormons picketing the Church offices again, there was nothing to indicate anything regarding this serious charge against one of the very top leaders of the Mormon Church. The blackout was the same in the newspapers the next day. *It was unbelievable.* Had similar allegations been made against a Christian leader or rabbi, it would have received worldwide publicity. But in this case, an extraordinary media blackout stopped the hottest story of the eighties concerning one of the top Mormons in the world.

Answering the Critics

The God Makers II film has been hit from every side from the day of its release. The portion of the film focusing on the homosexuality a Mormon leader seems to be the center of the whirlwind. One would expect more noise over the satanic connection and the killing of little babies in dark rituals, or the power and wealth of the Mormon Church being used to buy a place of honor in mainstream Christianity, but that is not so. It's the issue of Hinckley's history of homosexuality.

Critics say that President Hinckley's homosexual deviances are not relevant because they took place years ago, and that the film uses reports from eyewitnesses who are less than upstanding, Temple-going Mormons. Unfortunately, we can only answer that these were the people Hinckley played his deviant games with. It scarcely cancels out the truth of their information, nor does the passing of time conflict with the sincerity of documentation.

Because a man is an active homosexual dying of AIDS does not remove his right to be heard. While Van Damm was alive, the LDS Church had as much time as we did to dig out the truth. Why didn't they file against him and the others in a legal action and get to the bottom of it legitimately? To now dismiss the use of eyewitness accounts as renegade journalism and demean it to the ranks of *National Inquirer* type hype is ludicrously prejudiced.

Highly reputable newspapers and television stations use such reporting daily. For instance, at time of this writing, *USA Today* reported on the airing of "The Secret File on J. Edgar Hoover" on the PBS "Frontline" program. It stated that PBS was a reputable TV network and said that the documentary alleged that Hoover was a homosexual and "dressed as a woman." As we watched the program the next night, J. Edgar Hoover was forever labeled a transvestite by *one single woman* who was at a "party" with Hoover. Other eyewitnesses attested to his homosexuality, gambling, and blackmailing that allowed organized crime to flourish, but his cross-dressing at a party was verified by but a single witness about whom we knew absolutely nothing.[13]

A Sad Ending

We videotaped Bill Claudin again on July 30, 1990, just before he went into his bishop's office to attend his excommunication trial. He said:

> Tonight I'm being excommunicated here at the Oak Hills First Ward for telling a story of truth about one of the high-ranking members of the LDS Church, namely Gordon B. Hinckley. There is nothing within the doctrinal procedures of the Church that allows any one member the opportunity to bring an accusation against any of the presidency of the Church. My good bishop here at the Oak Hills First Ward—as I got to know him, he's a good man—he knows the truthfulness of the story. He has talked to one of the witnesses personally, and unfortunately, working for the Church and being a bishop in this ward, he is unable to stand up for me.[14]

Bill Claudin tried to go through the proper Church channels to find the truth of this affair. The result for Bill was swift expulsion by the Church.

14

Back to Basics

T HE BASIC DOCTRINAL ERROR OF MORMONISM can be summed up in the religion's key theological position regarding God and man. It is called "The Law of Eternal Progression." This doctrine is central to the Mormon faith. It teaches that *"as Man is, God once was, and as God is, Man may become."* [1] We are going to sum it up in a very short narrative, but remember that what we are describing is *false doctrine*, totally contrary to the Word of God.

Mormonism teaches that the Mormon god, Elohim, was born on another planet, exactly as we are born—through a physical act of sex between a man and a woman. Elohim grew up to maturity on that planet, being obedient to the "Laws and Ordinances" of the god over that planet, who was also once a man with his own god above him, and so on. [2]

Elohim died and was resurrected and judged by his god. He was found to be worthy, raised to godhood, and given many righteous women as wives. He was sent with his wives to his Celestial residence near the great star Kolob, somewhere in our galaxy, where he began to procreate and beget "spirit children," without physical bodies. As his children grew in age and numbers, a patriarchal society developed and still continues there today. [3]

The Law of Eternal Progression teaches that you and we, all of the human race, were sent here from that place to gain physical bodies like the Mormon god, Elohim, did, and to go through a time of testing and learning as Elohim had before us.

As the story unfolds, when it was time for Elohim to prepare the earth for occupancy, the head of the gods called a council of the gods, and there the gods concocted the plan for earth. Elohim asked his two eldest sons—brothers (probably from Elohim's number one wife)—to prepare plans for the council to review. These brothers were Jesus and Lucifer!

Upon review of the plans, the council chose the plan of Jesus, and He was raised to the position of godhood. Apparently the vote was a close one, for Lucifer became angry over the decision. He led one-third of the children of Elohim into an open rebellion over the decision. They battled against another third of the children, who were in agreement with the council decision. The final third of Elohim's children were obedient to the council, but didn't want to get involved in the battle. They were not valiant in defending the decision.[4]

It is hard to imagine how the spirit children of a physical god fought without physical bodies, or why Elohim was unable to control his own children, but at the end of the fighting those who fought for Jesus won. Lucifer and his third of the spirit children were cast out from Kolob, and arrived here on earth as Satan and the demons.

Those who fought valiantly with Jesus would come to earth as "white and delightsome" people—the more valiant we were, the blonder our hair, the whiter our skin. The less valiant we were, the darker our complexion and hair. That third who did not want to get involved became the black race, born under the curse of Cain. There were no neutrals on Kolob.[5]

The Mormon god, Elohim, apparently forgave blacks on June 9, 1978. Now they too can become members of the Mormon Melchizedek priesthood and eventually become Mormon gods (and become white).

When it came time for Jesus to take on flesh, Elohim came to earth physically and had sexual relations with Mary, one of his daughters from Kolob, to beget Jesus. Remember, Elohim is an exalted man—totally *physical* in nature.[6]

The Mormon Jesus was married to at least three identified women: the two sisters of Lazarus, and Mary Magdalene. He converted water into wine at one of his own weddings at Cana. One Mormon apostle taught that the reason Jesus was so persecuted was because he had so many wives and concubines. Other teachers taught that Jesus was the father of many children.[7]

The Mormon Jesus died on a cross to atone for Adam's transgression, which was an actual *blessing* that allowed us to gain physical bodies and mortality. Without this transgression we could not gain the physical attributes we needed in our own journey to godhood, because it was through the transgression that we knew how to procreate and become gods. Adam's act brought mortality and physical death into the world. Jesus' death on Calvary brought only physical resurrection and immortality into existence. This atonement assured *all mankind* of only physical resurrection; after that we will each be judged according to our works and blessed for our own works or punished for our own sins.[8]

The Mormon doctrine teaches that the Christian emphasis on the cross is pagan and of the devil. There is no cross displayed in any Mormon building anywhere. Its use, even in the home or as a piece of jewelry, is forbidden! The cross as the place where Jesus became our sin offering is vehemently labeled as heresy.

Likewise, the doctrine of His shed blood is rejected. The Mormons use only bread and water in their Sacrament. The true doctrine, according to Mormonism, is that Jesus sweat blood for our sins in Gethsemane, on the condition that we are to be obedient to all the laws and ordinances of the Mormon gospel.[9]

If we are thus committed and also go through the Mormon Temple ceremony, if we are obedient to the end, and if the judgment on our personal works of obedience is sufficient to cover the personal sin in our lives, we can be judged worthy to enter into the Celestial kingdom, the highest degree of glory, and become gods and goddesses.[10]

Each man will be given many wives to take to his new kingdom, and will be sent out to some new place, even as Elohim was sent out before him. There the process will begin anew. Finally, in order to go into the Celestial glory, we must each "pass by brother Joseph" and receive his final approval![11]

While the Mormon Church teaches that we will go forth in the family unit, with all our worthy family members, the actual doctrine is that when the worthy man goes forth, only his wife will accompany him, and she only as the first wife of many. Each worthy son will go forth as a god over his own kingdom. Each worthy daughter will be given as a wife to some worthy god elsewhere.

Whatever else you may think about that neighbor, friend, or loved one who is a Mormon, you need to remember that each and every Mormon you know is committed to this great plan and is struggling somewhere on a rung of the ladder in his or her own personal progression. To challenge their belief in this doctrine only reinforces the teaching they receive that the True Faith will be persecuted. Mormons must be approached with prayer and love. Your attitude is most important. Scripture says that Jesus told the foolish and blind of His day that they would not see Him until they said, "Blessed is he that cometh in the name of the Lord" (Matthew 23:39). It is likewise true that the Mormon people will open their blinded eyes and see the Lord when they truly feel that you are there, with love, in His holy name.

The Antidote for Falsehood

The many times that Jesus was confronted with false doctrine, He spoke of the true Word of God. In every area of false doctrine with Mormonism, the true Word of God can be given as the antidote. Let's compare the Law of Eternal Progression with the Word of God.

Let's explore the doctrine that god/Elohim is a part of a multi-generation family of gods. The God of the Bible and Christianity says:

> Before me there was no God formed; neither shall there be after me (Isaiah 43:10).

> I am the first, and I am the last; and beside me there is no God (Isaiah 44:6).

> Ye are my witnesses. Is there a God beside me?
> Yea, there is no God; I know not any (Isaiah 44:8).

Our God says that He had no father or mother, or gods above Him. He has no brothers or sisters who are gods, and there will never be any god after Him. It is clear that God knew what He was talking about! When He blessed Abraham, He swore by Himself, because He knew none greater (Hebrews 6:13). The Scripture says that it is impossible for God to lie (Hebrews 6:18). Let's believe God! Who would dare take Joseph Smith's word over the very Word of God?

Our God denies that He grew up on another planet. He denies that He became a god through the judgment of some other god: He inhabits eternity (Isaiah 57:15). He does not change (Malachi 3:6). In Him there is no variableness or shadow of turning (James 1:17). He was always God, even before time existed (John 1:2).

The Mormon doctrine has turned people away from the living God to a fable of vain imagination. Their foolish hearts have been darkened. Professing themselves to be wise, they have become fools. Why?

> [They] have changed the glory of the uncorruptible God into an image made like to corruptible man. . . . [They] changed the truth of God into a lie and worshiped and served the creature more than the Creator, who is blessed forever (Romans 1:21-25).

Unlikely Brothers

Digging through the fable that men will become gods, have goddesses for wives, and propagate societies of spirit children, we pause at another startling heresy: the doctrine that Jesus and Lucifer are brothers!

We are told in Scripture that the great Son of the Morning, Lucifer, was cut to the ground and brought down to hell because he sought to exalt his throne above the stars of God (Isaiah 14:12). He was an anointed cherub or angel of God, but was a *created being* (Ezekiel 28:14,15). Yet it was Jesus who created the very angel the Mormons claim was His physical brother (Hebrews 2:9,10). Finally, Christ's position versus that of any angel is made crystal clear: Jesus was always God—far better than the angels: "Unto which of the angels said he [God] at any time, Thou art my Son; this day have I begotten Thee"? (Hebrews 1:4,5). None!

Begotten or Elected?

According to the Mormon gospel, Jesus became our Savior through a vote of a "council of gods," because He had a better plan than Lucifer. The Scripture again declares that Jesus always was God and was with God from before time existed (John 1:1-5). In the Greek, John 1:18 declares that Jesus is the "only begotten *Theos*" or the *only begotten God without beginning*. His goings forth have been from of old, from everlasting (Micah 5:2). He told the world that "before Abraham was, I AM" (John 8:58). Our Jesus is the Alpha and Omega, the beginning and the end, the first and the last (Revelation 22:13). To reduce Him to anything less is to deny His very divinity—the very reason only He could be the sin-offering to end all sin-offerings (Hebrews 9:12-14)!

A Physical Act

Since the Mormon god is a physical man, preoccupied at Kolob with the work of procreation, it must also be that he had physical relations with Mary, to purposely "beget" Jesus. The prophet Brigham Young said that the Holy Ghost could not be involved; otherwise it would not be safe to lay hands on the young women of the Church for the receiving of the Holy Ghost because the Holy Ghost would make them pregnant and bring great shame to the elders of the Church.[12]

The Word of God clearly destroys this blasphemy. Mary was with child of the Holy Ghost (Matthew 1:18; Luke 1:34,35). It was prophesied that He would be born of the seed of woman (Genesis 3:15) and He would be born of a virgin (Isaiah 7:14).

The Gravest Heresy of All

The gravest heresy among so many is the Mormon doctrine of Jesus Christ: a son of one god of many gods, our elder brother, and a polygamist, whose death on Calvary gives all mankind physical resurrection so that we can be judged for our sins and pay the penalties for all sin not covered by our works! To believe this would require the removal of the major portion of the New Testament and a good amount of the Old Testament. It would need a latter-day prophet whose words would supersede even the mighty Word of God. It would need a Joseph Smith and a people who would believe the lie the Mormons call the Law of Eternal Progression.

The Way of Escape

The Mormon must come to understand that we all sin and come short of God's best for us (Romans 3:23). But God loved us, even though we separated ourselves from Him so very long ago. He sent His Son to reconcile us with Him. He became sin for us (2 Corinthians 5:21). He became our Passover Lamb (1 Corinthians 5:7). For while we were enemies of God, we were restored through Calvary (Romans 5:8-10). We, in Christ, are redeemed from the curse of the law (Galatians 3:13). Through the shedding of His blood, we have the forgiveness of sin (Ephesians 1:6,7) and are accepted by God, raised up, and seated together with Christ in heavenly places (Ephesians 2:6).

This reconciliation is not of our works of righteousness, but through His death at Calvary. It is our acceptance of this fact that makes us holy and unblameable and unreprovable in His sight (Colossians 1:21,22).

The laws and ordinances that were against us (and still against the Mormon people) were moved out of the way 2000 years ago by Christ, who nailed them to the cross (Colossians 2:14).

The Mormon leaders have removed the one true sin offering— the only one possible. *What a grievous error!* They have taken God's perfect gift—His perfect love—and replaced Calvary with their own judgment, their own version of the first covenant. They have taken the shed blood of Calvary away from Jesus.

The doctrines of Mormonism cannot stand the test of the Word of God. We are told in Scripture that false teachers will come, fleeing from sound doctrine, and will turn away their followers from the truth to fables (2 Timothy 4:4). How true that is of the Mormon leaders! "For the leaders of them shall cause them to err, and they that are led of them are destroyed" (Isaiah 9:16).

The tragedy of all this is that such beautiful, hardworking, and committed people are spiritually blinded people, with the light of the glorious gospel of Christ hid from them by Satan (2 Corinthians 4:3,4). The Mormon people are not the enemies of God, but victims of a horrible and wicked hoax fed to them by evil teachers, who are of their father, the devil.

Only those sent by God, with the knowledge of God, using the Word of God, can set them free. Are you one who can reach out to them and bring them the living light? We pray that you can and that you will!

A Warning to Christians

With the constant barrage of Mormon advertising and proselytizing, the Christian church must again be warned in the strongest way to stay true to sound biblical teaching. Don't buy the lie.

Christians must realize that the Mormon hope of outwardly appearing Christian is not reflected in their foundational teaching. Mormons still believe that all Christian pastors are part of the great whore of all the earth. They still have the hope of becoming gods and goddesses. The Mormon Jesus is still the brother of Lucifer. They still teach that our holy God was once a man, and has a body. That Jesus was begotten through a sexual relationship between the Father and Mary. That the Garden of Eden was in Missouri. That the Bible is missing many plain and precious parts. That the Book of Mormon is the most correct of any book on earth. That plural marriage is a holy principle.

They still follow the teachings of a false prophet. They still usurp the holy priesthood of Christ. They still baptize for the dead. They still wear occult underwear with Masonic markings. They still believe they must offer up secret handshakes and secret names to enter into God's presence. They still teach that all the Christian creeds are an abomination in God's sight.

God's Word is still reliable, without vacillation, and Mormonism is still in direct violation of the Word of God. One cannot "revise" Mormonism enough; one has to repent of it.

A Spiritual Battle

There is no basic difference between being led to hell through the doctrines and gods of Mormonism and being led there through the gods and doctrines of the pagan New Age movement, or Hinduism, or Buddhism.

I (Ed) had this point strongly brought home to me while speaking at a church recently. I was sitting quietly in the back row of the church as I waited for the congregation to file in for the service. I have always marveled at the speed with which a church can be filled in those last few moments before the start of a service. It's as though every family has worked out the very minutes and seconds it takes to rise, shower, dress, eat, drive to church, and walk from the parking lot to their favorite pews. It is an amazing example of human engineering.

Looking about me, I noticed a magazine sitting on the pew next to me. Its front cover and lead story caught my eye. The headline read: *Buddhism: Golden Temples, Empty Hearts*. I picked up the magazine and turned to the article inside.

The author, Robert Houlihan, shared his dismay as he visited the Buddhist Shwedagon Pagoda in Yangon, Myanmar:

> Why would anyone worship such idols? Why would people pay money to pour water over stone gods that are eroded from years of usage? Why would they teach their children to bow before gods that look like devils, show no compassion and have the vile nature of humanity?[13]

In his article, Houlihan shares his zeal for bringing the glorious message of Jesus Christ to the 300 million souls in over 1000 people groups who are bound by the power of Buddhism.

In a follow-up article titled "Warfare in the Temple," an unidentified missionary speaks of the spiritual battle for souls lost to the demonic powers of Buddhism:

> I stood in the temple doorway and stared at the Buddha. All around me pilgrims prostrated themselves before the idol. The temple was lit only by oil lamps. Hot air, laden with the stench of sweaty bodies and rancid oil, hung over me. In my spirit I felt the heavy bondage of the worshippers. This temple was a stronghold of the devil, and these people were his captives. "I come here in the name of Jesus," I declared aloud. "He is going to tear down this stronghold. He is going to set the captives free."[14]

My own heart raced as I read those words. Just getting a church to agree to hear a message on the tragedy of the millions of people lost to the spiritual darkness of Mormonism is itself a victory these days.

People in churches like the one I was sitting in easily understood the mighty battle when it came to Buddhism, but experience had taught me that I was going to have a difficult time stirring their hearts to engage in spiritual battle for the souls of their friends and neighbors lost in Mormonism.

Something Special in the Air

The church had miraculously filled as I finished the article, and I went forward to sit with the pastor, saying my hellos as I worked my way to the platform and climbed the few stairs to sit at his side in front of the choir. The service quickly got underway, but my own thoughts drifted back several years to a time when my friend Ron Carlson and I spoke at a series of meetings throughout the Philippine Islands.

One morning our host took us to a Buddhist temple outside the city we were visiting. I remembered the ornate structure, the giant statue of Buddha, and the prostrate pilgrims. The smells of the place were burned indelibly in my mind, and they returned to me in the middle of this church service as fresh as though I had just experienced them. I remembered how Ron and I both felt the intense heaviness of spiritual darkness in the air of that place and how it remained with us until we stepped outside the gardens surrounding the property and returned to the street.

Our hearts had been broken for those souls lost in that terrible darkness. There was no doubt in either of our minds that this temple was truly a stronghold of the devil.

Not long after my return to the United States, I went to Utah for a conference. One weekday morning I took advantage of a break in the schedule to take a solitary walk around downtown Salt Lake City to reflect on the ministry in which I was involved and to pray for the Mormon people. Like most walks through downtown Salt Lake, mine ended at Temple Square. I walked through the gates and felt the intense heaviness of spiritual darkness that I remembered from our visit to the Buddhist temple.

I determined to go quietly through both the North and South Visitor Centers and pray for the Mormon people held in bondage to that demonic power I felt in such control of the place. Much like the missionary in the magazine article, I kept praying that God would break the spiritual stranglehold the devil held over these people in the mighty name of Jesus!

I walked through every display area, entered presentation rooms that were largely empty at that hour of the workday, and continued through each level of each building and along every pathway between.

Finally I made my way down to the lower level of the Visitor Center nearest the Assembly Hall, which housed the famous baptismal font, a great basin that stands on the backs of 12 bronze oxen representing the 12 tribes and is a replica of the ones used in Mormon Temples for baptisms for the dead. The place was deserted. I went into a little theater area, and by some automatic mechanism or the hidden hand of an attendant, I watched an animated Book of Mormon presentation.

When it was over I sat there, alone in that dark and quiet place, asking God what to do, how to reach these lost people with His message of freedom. I saw clearly that the Mormon people were not the enemies of God, but victims who had fallen prey to the wiles of the devil. I saw clearly that Lucifer was the god of that place, blinding even those who loved God and sought only to serve Him. They were bondslaves to the prince of darkness. I wept that morning for the Mormon people, with groanings from deep within my soul. I knew that the battle was "not against flesh and blood, but against principalities, against powers, against the rulers of the darkness of this world, against spiritual wickedness in high places" (Ephesians 6:12).

I stepped back into the hallway and, rounding a corner, headed for an escalator that would return me to the main floor. As I neared the escalator, I startled a small, elderly lady who was apparently asleep on a comfortable bench against the wall. She jumped up and brushed her clothes, straightening her white hair and her hostess badge, a bit embarrassed to be caught sleeping at her post. She smiled sweetly at me, and as I stepped onto the escalator she said:

> My, My! Isn't this the most peaceful place on earth? Don't you feel that special something in the air, smell that holy aroma? Have you ever experienced anything like that before?

I already knew about the special heaviness she was describing, but I didn't have the heart to tell this sweet dear lady. I smiled back at her and kept my lips closed, letting her comment slip into the air. But God had other plans. The escalator stopped in its tracks. There I stood and there she stood, waiting for my response to her inquiry. Our eyes locked. Seconds seemed like minutes. Finally I spoke:

> Yes, I recognize it. It is the very same heavy air of spiritual darkness that I found in a Buddhist temple in

the Philippines. It has the same weight, the same
aroma. My heart broke for those lost in *that* terrible
darkness because there was not a shred of doubt in my
mind that temple was truly a stronghold of the devil. I
am sorry, but I am convinced that it holds true of this
place as well.

Looking down at the dead escalator, I added, " I think the Lord
wanted you to know that."

The lady looked at me for a moment, and then I saw the silent
tears falling from her eyes. The escalator started again at just that
moment, and I silently rose away from her view.

Appendix
Testing the Book of Mormon

SETTING ASIDE ALL THE MORMON CLAIMS of divine illumination for the moment, let's seriously consider the Book of Mormon on its own merit. In an undated LDS tract titled "The Challenge the Book of Mormon Makes to the World," the last paragraph states: "The first thing to do in examining any ancient text is to consider it in the light of the origin and background that is claimed for it. If it fits into that background, there is no need to look any farther since historical forgery is virtually impossible." While this is not necessarily true, we can use it as a fair statement of the *Mormon position* with regard to the Book of Mormon. Does the Book of Mormon measure up to even this simple test?

Let's Start at the Very Beginning

There is no better starting point than the very first page of the Book of Mormon. In the first book of Nephi we read the account of Lehi, the key prophet of what Mormons call the second migration. It is through this man that the actual Book of Mormon story comes. In 1 Nephi 1:4 we are told:

> It came to pass in the commencement of the first year of the reign of Zedekiah, King of Judah (my father, Lehi, having dwelt at Jerusalem in all his days); and in that same year there came many prophets, prophesying unto the people that they must repent, or the great city Jerusalem must be destroyed.

Throughout the rest of chapters 1 and 2 we see that Lehi is portrayed as a mighty prophet of the Lord, and after much danger leaves the city of Jerusalem at the Lord's bidding. Let's assume that this is true for the time being and "consider it in the light of the origin and background that is claimed for it. If it fits into that background, there is no need to look any farther since historical forgery is virtually impossible."

Using the clue that we are dealing with the reign of Zedekiah, it is possible to go to the Bible and examine 2 Kings 24:17,18. We see that Zedekiah reigned for 11 years, starting about 600 B.C. and ending his reign with the fourth and last siege of Jerusalem. This siege was conducted by Nebuchadnezzar and ended with the destruction of Jerusalem and the Babylonian captivity.

At that time Daniel and Ezekiel had already been taken captive to Babylon—Daniel in the first siege and Ezekiel in the third siege. The only prophet left in Jerusalem during Zedekiah's reign was Jeremiah, and he makes it perfectly clear that he was the only prophet speaking for God in that city in that time:

Jeremiah 2:8: "The prophets prophesied by Baal."

Jeremiah 5:31: "The prophets prophesy falsely."

Jeremiah 6:13: "From the prophet even unto the priest every one dealeth falsely."

Jeremiah 8:10: "Every one dealeth falsely."

Jeremiah 14:14: "The prophets prophesy lies in my name: I sent them not. . . . They prophesy unto you a false vision and divination."

Jeremiah 23:16: "Hearken not unto the words of the prophets that prophesy unto you."

Jeremiah 23:21: "I have not sent these prophets, yet they ran; I have not spoken unto them yet they prophesied."

Jeremiah 27:14-17: "Therefore hearken not unto the words of the prophets that speak unto you, saying, ye shall serve not the King of Babylon; for they prophesy a lie unto you. . . . Hearken not to the words of your prophets that prophesy unto you. . . . Hearken not unto them; serve the King of Babylon, and live."

Jeremiah 29:8,9: "Let not your prophets and your diviners, that be in the midst of you, deceive you . . . for they prophesy falsely unto you in my name: I have not sent them, saith the Lord."

All these Scriptures clearly warn the people not to listen to any of the other prophets because they were all false and spoke lies. It is quite clear that the words Jeremiah spoke (especially Jeremiah 27:14-17) would certainly include the prophet Lehi, whom the Book of Mormon claims was shouting a prophetic word that was in *direct* opposition to that of Jeremiah, in the *same* city at the *same* time.

Since God didn't deliver Ezekiel, Daniel, and Jeremiah from bondage, but wanted all the people to serve the King of Babylon, why would he favor a prophet who is not mentioned in the Bible with a message in total contradiction to the one given to Jeremiah for the whole nation of Israel? God gave absolutely no indication in the Bible that some people had to serve in Babylon, but some would be spared. In fact, He gave some pretty severe warnings to those who would attempt to escape captivity. In Jeremiah 28 we read about the false prophet Hananiah, who taught rebellion against the Lord, telling the people to flee the city. That act brought swift judgment and death to many.

If the judgment of the Lord against Hananiah was death, why would God call and send forth another prophet, Lehi, with the same rebellious message to the very same people and call him a true prophet? *Impossible!* If the Book of Mormon were true Scripture, Lehi would have to be in direct disobedience to God in leaving Jerusalem to escape capture and bondage in Babylon.

So, coming back to page 1 of the Book of Mormon, it immediately fails the basic test. It does not fit into its time frame correctly as true Scripture. One need not go a page further to know that we are dealing with a false prophet. Yes, Lehi does fit into the biblical picture, but only as a false prophet! The wise reader would put down the Book of Mormon after reading just one page.

Out of the Dust

Let's look at it from another angle. The late LeGrand Richards was often called the Gentle Apostle. In his famous missionary book *A Marvelous Work and a Wonder*, which is given away to people investigating Mormonism by the hundreds of thousands, Richards describes the biblical prophecies fulfilled by the Book of Mormon. He uses Isaiah 29:4 as a proof text for the creation of the Book of Mormon:

> And thou shalt be brought down, and shalt speak out of
> the ground, and thy speech shall be low out of the dust, and

thy voice shall be, as of one that hath a familiar spirit, out of
the ground, and thy speech shall whisper out of the dust.

Richards comments:

Now, obviously, the only way a dead people could speak
"out of the ground" or "out of the dust" would be by the
written word and this was done through the Book of Mormon. Truly, it has a familiar spirit, for it contains the words
of the prophets of the God of Israel.[1]

Unfortunately for Book of Mormon scholarship, the Hebrew word
for "familiar spirit" in this passage of Isaiah is the word *Ob*, which is
translated in the King James Bible as "familiar spirit." In the Hebrew,
the word means *necromancer* or *a spirit of witchcraft*. There are 15 Old
Testament references to familiar spirits, and all of them deal with
witchcraft.

The apostle LeGrand Richards and the hundreds of thousands of
Mormons who have used his words as evidence that the Book of Mormon has this same "familiar spirit" tie their scripture solidly to witchcraft. They are heartily welcome to the label. Again, the Book of
Mormon fails its own challenge.

Sticks and Scrolls

Of the several other biblical prophecies used to substantiate the
Book of Mormon, one other stands out as the most common of all LDS
"proof" scriptures. It is used almost every time the missionaries teach
on the Book of Mormon.

Ezekiel 37:15-17 reads:

The Word of the Lord came again unto me, saying,
Moreover, thou son of man, take thee one stick, and write
upon it, for Judah, and for the children of Israel his companions; then take another stick, and write upon it, for
Joseph, the stick of Ephraim, and for all the house of Israel
his companions; and join them one to another into one
stick; and they shall become one in thine hand.

The Mormon Church teaches that the sticks mentioned in this prophecy are two books that would become one witness as they are joined

together by the Mormon Church. Mormon leaders say this Scripture speaks of the Bible and the Book of Mormon! This is made clearly evident in the LDS scripture: "... and with Moroni, whom I have sent unto you to reveal the Book of Mormon, containing the fullness of my everlasting gospel, to whom I have committed the keys of the record of the stick of Ephraim" (*Doctrine and Covenants* 27:5).

In actuality, the Hebrew word used here for stick is *es* or *ets*, meaning wood, tree, or stick. The Hebrew words for "scroll," "roll," "book," or "writing" include *sepher*, *dabar*, *sephar*, and *siphrah*. The Old Testament talks about sticks, rolls, books, writings, scrolls, and so on. Yet in no case has God ever used the word for stick to mean anything but a piece of wood. He never interchanged these words. The LDS Church has applied the wrong meaning to the words.

What was really happening in this Scripture? If you read the very next few verses, the people ask Ezekiel what he meant by what he said, and he explains that the sticks represent the two kingdoms of Israel, which will be joined together just as the sticks were in his hands (vv. 18-22). Unfortunately for the cause of reasonable scholarship, it is evident that Mormon theologians have missed those later verses for 150 years.

Further, it was Ezekiel who wrote on both sticks. He obviously did not write both the Bible and the Book of Mormon. Again, the point is that the evidence of the Mormon interpretation for this prophecy just does not exist. Ezekiel clearly defined the exact conditions and scope of the prophecy, and we have concrete historical evidence of its fulfillment.

There is no evidence from the Bible of any future set of scriptures such as the Mormons claim. The LDS effort to fit the Book of Mormon into biblical context has no point of reference, except the one which they have contrived.

The People Who Weren't There

Let's look at the history found in the Book of Mormon. God is not obtuse. If this great Nephite society described in the Book of Mormon really existed in the Americas, the evidence would have to be there. Sandra Tanner, one researcher on the Mormon question, commented:

> The Book of Mormon claims to be an actual historical record translated from real plates that Joseph Smith unearthed in a hill in New York. Now, if this is a genuine

history, one would assume you could study this, just as you would study any historical book.

When I study the Bible, I can approach it as a total atheist or as a believer in Christ, but either way I can study the book historically. It does not require a "testimony." You can determine where Jerusalem is; you can determine that there was a Hebrew language. When we turn to the Book of Mormon we have nothing. There is no Nephite language; there are no Nephite cities; there is not a map in any Book of Mormon; you cannot locate any sites. There is no evidence for the book, and yet it's supposed to be an historical record.[2]

When asked about this during the filming of a segment of *The God Makers* in London, LDS Mission President Harold Goodman commented:

Many people do not understand the Book of Mormon. This is a history of the people that inhabited the American Continent—North, South and Central America, from about 600 B.C. to about 420 A.D., and we have much evidence, of course, of people having lived there.[3]

We all know that a large, complex society did exist there during those years of Book of Mormon history. But were they the descendants of Jewish immigrants? The question is still, "Does the Book of Mormon fit the time frame?" We do not think it does. Yet with fervent zeal and that same burning testimony, the Mormons claim it does. President Goodman is aware that Mormon missionaries throughout the world are converting people to the Mormon Church by explaining to them that archaeology has proved the Book of Mormon to be true. Slide presentations, special fireside meetings, and filmstrips are used along with volumes of specialty books on the subject, available from Mormon publishers.

Where are the so-called "evidences" claimed to be so readily available as proof? Either they exist as presented by the Mormons or they don't. We can't play games with historical facts.

In the LDS Visitor Centers throughout the country, a painting by artist John Scott is displayed. Copies are available in great abundance wherever LDS materials are sold. The painting is called "The Resurrected Christ in America." What is so important about this painting? It represents Christ standing before the multitudes in front of several of the temples in Meso-America, graphically tying in, for the millions of people who have viewed this painting of Jesus, the Book of Mormon and the temples of these early civilizations. *What is wrong?* Neither temple depicted in the painting existed until about A.D. 1000, almost ten centuries after the supposed appearance of the Mormon Christ in the Americas!

The two temples are actually very well-known: They are El Castillo and El Caracol. They are also used in one of the well-known LDS proof works, *The Trial of the Stick of Joseph,* by Bishop Jack West. In both representations, their use can only be out of blind ignorance or blatant deception.

The fact that the painting is an artist's rendition is not important. It *is* important that it is published widely by the Mormon Church as an expression of implied fact. The same painting is used, in part, as the cover of an LDS pamphlet, "Christ in America," written by apostle Mark E. Petersen and published in 1983. Jack West's representation may be waved away as the work of an individual, yet it is used widely to convert people out of the Christian body through the use of open deception.

Could the Mormon Church and people like Jack West simply be blind to the facts? We think not. A friend, Jack Sande, wrote to John L. Sorenson, Chairman of the Department of Anthropology at Brigham Young University, and asked him about this problem after he received a copy of the West book from a Mormon bishop.

In a letter to Jack, dated October 5, 1981, John Sorenson replied:

> I understand that people who have not had educational experiences concerning archaeology could be enthusiastic about books like these of West or Farnsworth when they see these as supporting the Book of Mormon in which they strongly believe. I presume the Bishop who gave you the West volume would fall into that class—overcome by zeal. Nevertheless, the fact remains that those books are worse than useless, because they are not reasonably close to the truth. I wish the zealous had other options open to them in the way of truthful books, but at the moment, that is a problem.

Significant Insights

John Sorenson sounded like a pretty straightforward scholar. We went to a book of his, dated 1980, and found that he had made several very significant observations. First, regarding the Bible, Sorenson said:

> Learning about context seems unimportant to some readers of the book [Book of Mormon]; others consider it impossible. To me the Bible is a model in this regard. Biblical scholarship has illuminated certain inobvious meanings of that scriptural text showing the complex interplay between human and divine influences and establishing the Bible as a record all the more profound, because it is anchored in a complex reality of time, space and behavior. I have wanted that same illumination for Lehi's people and their book.

And what of that book, the Book of Mormon? He made no evasive apologies, but hit directly home with his point:

> After nearly 150 years since the Nephite record was first published by Joseph Smith, we Mormons have been unable confidently to pin down the location of a single city, identify even one route they traversed, or sketch an accurate picture of any segment of the life they lived in their American promised land. In many respects, the Book of Mormon remains a sealed book to us because we have been incapable of placing it in its specific setting.[4]

John Sorenson is not the only Mormon scholar who is a realist in this matter. Dr. Ross T. Christensen, BYU professor and head of the Society for Early Historic Archeology, stands by his side. More than 20 years earlier, in an article for the University Archaeological Society, Christensen wrote:

> In the first place, the statement that the Book of Mormon has already been proved by archaeology is misleading. The truth of the matter is that we are only beginning to see even the outlines of the archaeological time-periods which could compare with those of the Book of Mormon. How, then, can the matter have been settled once and for all?

Christensen continued:

> That such an idea could exist indicates the ignorance of
> many of our people with regard to what is going on in the
> historical and anthropological sciences. With the excep-
> tion of Latter-day Saint archaeologists, members of the
> archaeological profession do not, and never have espoused
> the Book of Mormon in any sense of which I am aware.

He added:

> As for the notion that the Book of Mormon has already
> been proved by archaeology, I must say with Shakespeare,
> "Lay not that flattering unction to your soul" (Hamlet III:4).[5]

Another honest Mormon scholar, Dee F. Green, asserts, "The first
myth we need to eliminate is that Book of Mormon archaeology exists."[6]

In the January/February 1981 issue of *Sunstone* magazine, Martin
Raish, a doctoral candidate and teacher of art history at BYU, wrote
one of the best scholarly reports we have read on this subject of amateur
attempts to prove the Book of Mormon through historic evidence.

He goes through the works of such well-known Mormon men as Jack
West, Dewey Farnsworth, Paul Cheesman, and Wayne Hamby, showing the exact manner in which the reader of their works is manipulated
with sweeping assumptions, questionable artifacts, misdated archaeology, and mismatched scriptures and pictures, all designed to assure the
reader that the Book of Mormon is fact. Raish cautions the LDS community that these pseudoscholarly tactics thwart the best efforts of the
LDS professionals. He concludes:

> I do not think that we will ever prove the Book of Mor-
> mon to be true through archaeological evidences any more
> than we can yet prove the date of the Creation through
> scientific means alone.[7]

A Leap of Faith

So we fall back again on the pamphlet "Challenge the Book of
Mormon Makes to the World," which we spoke of earlier. Its premise

was that an authentic historical text has to fit the time frame of which it speaks. This is not only reasonable but imperative. Yet, while it is the proven standard for the Bible, it appears to be impossible for the Book of Mormon.

Charles Crane has spent most of his life studying the Bible and also the LDS scriptures. He is an active student of both Bible and Mormon archaeology. He emphasized the difference to us. "The simple facts," he said, "are that the truth does not match the LDS stories. While the accuracy of the Bible has been vindicated time and again, we have yet to find the first Book of Mormon city. Not one city as named in the Book of Mormon has ever been found . . . not one."[8]

The Mormon nonscholars keep trying to "associate" Book of Mormon archaeology with the historic evidences of the Aztec and Mayan temple builders. Yet at every corner warning flags leap up. On March 26, 1982, the Utah Museum of Natural History held a presentation by Nicholas M. Hellmuth. His subject: "The Human Sacrificial Practices of the Maya." If the Mormons want to be associated with butchers who killed innocent people in their religious ceremonies, they are of course free to do that, but to say then that "restored" Christianity sprang from that well is ludicrous!

More than a decade ago *New York Times* writer Boyce Rensberger listed archaeological findings that push back the Mayan origins to 9000 B.C.[9] However, Lehi and his people supposedly arrived in Meso-America around 600 B.C., over 8000 years off schedule. That certainly stretches the Book of Mormon time frame.

Jesus the Feathered Serpent

In his book *Christ in Ancient America*, Milton R. Hunter, then a member of the First Council of the Seventy, described Quetzalcoatl, god of the Aztecs and the Olmecs, as Jesus. He states:

> Quetzalcoatl could have been none other than Jesus the Christ, the Lord and God of this earth, and the Savior of the human family. Thus Jesus Christ and Quetzalcoatl are identical.

He further quotes LDS President and Prophet John Taylor, who in 1882 stated:

The story of the life of the Mexican divinity, Quetzal-coatl, closely resembles that of the Savior; so closely, indeed, that we can come to no other conclusion than that Quetzal-coatl and Christ are the same being.[10]

Hunter explains that Quetzalcoatl was represented as the "Feathered Serpent," which is identified with the "Plumed Serpent" of Egyptian origin and the serpent in the Garden of Eden [or Satan]. He says, "The serpent, in early times, was also identified with the Crucifixion, and hence was also a symbol of the Son of Man." He goes on to explain, "In this Chapter and throughout the book, the serpent will be presented as a symbol of Quetzalcoatl or Jesus and no further reference will be made to its identification with the Prince of Darkness, or Lucifer."[11]

This is absolute, utter nonsense. Quetzalcoatl dates back into the far distance long before the Book of Mormon era began. He was the god of learning and civilization, and he appeared in the Olmec religion around 2000 B.C. The Feathered Serpent was a pagan idol requiring blood sacrifice. From this point and all through the temple-building eras of the Book of Mormon dating, the Feathered Serpent God cult began to take over and the once-beneficent Quetzalcoatl was incarnated into the bloodthirsty Feathered Serpent. Untold hundreds of thousands of inno-cent victims died to offer up their still-beating hearts to this bloody idol during the so-called Book of Mormon years. That serpent is a blood-thirsty demon, not the Jesus Christ of the Bible.

It wasn't until many hundreds of years after the Book of Mormon era that a Toltec king named Ce Acatal Topiltzin ascended the throne and took the name of Quetzalcoatl and sought to reestablish the gentle theology of the original god as the principal deity of the Toltec nation. This took place in A.D. 968. The bloodthirsty priests disgraced and banished him from the nation. This gentle king promised to return in a "one-reed year" (according to the Mayan calendar), and hence the legend of the return of Quetzalcoatl. By the way, Spanish explorer Hernando Cortés landed in 1519, a "one-reed year," which is one of the reasons the native people accepted him with such open arms.[12]

Returning again to the difficult task of trying to fit the Book of Mor-mon into its own background and time frame, let's look at another of literally hundreds of conditions that make it impossible. Remember our earlier test: to examine the Book of Mormon in the light of the origin and background that is claimed for it. If it fits into that background, "there is no need to look any farther since historical forgery is virtually impossible," and if it doesn't fit in, it is simply a forgery.

Assuming that Lehi was right and Jeremiah wrong, and assuming that Jewish travelers truly did land on the western shores of the Americas somewhere, then let's evaluate one of the major activities of this group in light of this test of history and fact.

In the Book of Mormon, 2 Nephi, chapter 5, Nephi separates himself and his family from his very difficult brother, Laman. He takes several other of his relatives and all those who would go with him. These people become the foundation of the Nephite nation. Bear in mind that this whole story takes place before 30 years have passed since they left Jerusalem. Just getting to the boat took enough time that Jacob and Joseph, sons of Lehi, were born, so we can't be talking about much more than 20 to 25 years at best.

In all, we can't be talking about more than a half-dozen grown men, some young boys, and a very small number of women and children. You can't build a nation of much size in one single generation, starting from the travelers on the tiny vessel that supposedly brought them from Jerusalem, especially when that nation is split away from the whole. Yet, in 2 Nephi 5:15-17, Nephi describes how they built a mighty temple constructed after the manner of the Temple of Solomon.

Just try to envision at best a few dozen able-bodied people building a temple "like unto Solomon's." The Bible says that Solomon's Temple was built of stone, precious metals, and enough cedar to keep 80,000 hewers of wood busy (1 Kings 5:13-15). It took Solomon over seven years (1 Kings 6:38), and well over 150,000 full-time workers (2 Chronicles 2:18).

In verse 15, Nephi claims to have taught his people to build with all manner of wood, iron, steel (not found in the Americas for another 1500 years), gold, silver, and precious ores, which "were in great abundance." Then, in the very next verse, he states that they could not use these things in the temple since they were not to be found upon the land.

At the completion of this great temple, and still within 30 years of leaving Jerusalem, Nephi reports that the people desired that he should be made king. Remember, this is a small clan of only about two dozen people—men, women, and children. Where is this mighty temple today? Has God taken it away as he supposedly took the gold plates? He must have, to hide such a temple from the plundering hands (and records) of the Spanish explorers.

Again, the Book of Mormon cannot fit into its background and time frame. It cannot be what it pretends to be.

Jewish Distinctions

There is another item of significance that is totally outside anything we have read about the Book of Mormon in any of its promoters' claims or its critics' challenges.

If we were to gather together four or five families and leave for an unknown land to be able to worship in our own manner, we would probably take our scriptures and our form of worship and develop our religious practices in a very fundamentalist manner—a form of worship that would have a lasting effect upon our new society. This is easily seen in the arrival in North America of the Pilgrims and the Puritans. Likewise, if the Book of Mormon were true, we would certainly see this same determination in the Jewish people of the Book of Mormon.

One thing for which the Jewish people are noted is their tenacity over centuries of time to maintain their own identity. Yet there is not a shred of evidence anywhere in the Americas of a Jewish influx as described in the Book of Mormon. Another unmovable Jewish trait is the utter inability of anyone to destroy the Hebrew language throughout centuries of time. Again, not even one example of genuine Hebrew writing appears. Instead, we are asked to believe that devout Jewish scholars would transcribe their most sacred Scriptures in "reformed Egyptian." Bear in mind that the Hebrew people were forbidden to deal with anything Egyptian. To do so would have defiled the priesthood of God (Nehemiah 13:23-31)!

Check the Calendar

Lastly, if we were to embark on such a journey, we would take our calendar! This is the final flaw in their mimicry. Jewish people who fled across a perilous ocean rather than submit to a Babylonian king who would not let them worship as Jews are not going to give up their calendar and holy days. They would die first.

What about the Book of Mormon people? Did the people who lived in the Americas between 600 B.C. and A.D. 420 have anything even remotely resembling the Jewish 360-day calendar? Did their months and holidays bear any name resemblance? *If not, they could not have been Jewish!*

In actuality, approximately 3000 years ago, on the coastal plain of southern Mexico, a priest received a revelation from the Sun God that not only determined the course of history for Meso-America, but destroyed the remotest possibility of the Book of Mormon being a true history of these people.

"At precisely noon on the date we call August 13, probably in the year 1358 B.C., the priest noticed that no tree, pillar or post cast a shadow." Counting the days to the next such experience, he was finally rewarded 260 days later. After another 105 days, on the next August 13, the same phenomenon repeated itself.

These events took place at Izapa, a ceremonial center on the Mexico-Guatemala border. And here began a sacred calendar of a 13-unit cycle with 20 day names, known as the "Tzolkin" or "Tonalamatl." Once in place, this almanac became the basis of all religions, art, and science in the civilizations that followed on this part of the continent.

The Izapans used the sacred calendar names to name their chiefs and nobles. These names were designated by "one of 20 animals important to the local mythology, such as Alligator, Buzzard, Eagle, Jaguar, Snake, Deer, etc."

The 365-day solar calendar tied together the nations and religions of this entire part of the world. Under no circumstance could such a complex calendar exist and extend its influence out across the many centuries if the advanced civilization of the thousand-year Book of Mormon era ever existed.[13]

What More Can We Say?

What more can we say? The Book of Mormon has had over 4000 changes made to it, and yet it is supposed to be the "most perfect book in the world," according to its translator. Eleven men bore witness to its reality, yet eight of these left the Mormon Church as apostates. There has never been found a gold plate of such type as described by Joseph Smith, nor brass plates such as the ones described as containing the Jewish Scriptures taken from Jerusalem. Not one exists anywhere in the Jewish world.

Further, why would God speak to Joseph Smith, a nineteenth-century American, in archaic, seventeenth-century English? Would He speak that way to a Peruvian? Is God limited to King James English as His official language? Where do we stop and call the Mormon Church to account for what has been said? The Bible talks about people who mock the truth: "For this cause God shall send them strong delusion, that they should believe a lie" (2 Thessalonians 2:11).

Notes

Introduction—A Truly Modern Religion

1. *Saints Alive* (newsletter), published by Saints Alive in Jesus, P.O. Box 1076, Issaquah, WA 98027, Sep. 1989, p. 3, quoting *The Latter Day Sun.*

Chapter 1—Mass-Marketing Mormonism

1. Book of Mormon, 1 Nephi 14:10.
2. Bruce R. McConkie, *Mormon Doctrine* (Salt Lake City: BookCraft, 1966), p. 670.
3. Jeffrey Sheler and Betsy Wagner, "Latter-day Struggles: The Prosperous Mormon Church Is at Theological Crossroads," *U.S. News & World Report*, Sep. 28, 1992, pp. 73-78.
4. Ibid., p. 73.
5. Andy Hall, Jerry Kammer, Mark Trahant, and Richard Robertson, "Mormon Inc., Finances and Faith," a four-part series beginning Jun. 30, 1991, *Arizona Republic*, Jul. 1, 1991, p. 9.
6. Maurine J. Proctor, "Communicating the Church," *This People*, Spring 1989, pp. 18-23.
7. Ibid.
8. John Heinerman, video interview, Feb. 27, 1988, on file, Jeremiah Films (P.O. Box 1710, Hemet, CA 92546); see John Heinerman and Anson Shupe, *Mormon Corporate Empire* (Boston: Beacon Press, 1985), pp. 62, 72, for further information.
9. *Saints Alive* (newsletter), May 1990, quoting *Salt Lake Tribune*, Jan. 23, 1990.
10. *Salt Lake Tribune*, Jan. 27, 1988, p. A8.
11. Ibid.
12. *Encyclopedia of Mormonism*, vol. 2 (New York: Macmillan, 1992), pp. 537-38.
13. "Digging Up Your Roots," *Rocky Mountain News*, Mar. 9, 1990, Lifestyles section, p. 75.
14. "A Church Center Offers Chance to Research Roots," *Philadelphia Inquirer*, Jan. 9, 1991, Living section.
15. Ibid.
16. *Church News*, week ending Feb. 6, 1988, p. 4.
17. *Encyclopedia of Mormonism*, vol. 2, pp. 950-52.
18. *Church News*, week ending Feb. 20, 1988, p. 10.
19. Mike Cannon, "Valuable Tool in Bringing Young Men to Christ," *Church News*, week ending Feb. 2, 1991, p. 7.
20. *Church News*, week ending Feb. 13, 1988, p. 11.
21. *Saints Alive* (newsletter), Aug. 1990, p. 3, quoting various *Church News* articles.
22. Sheler and Wagner, "Latter-day Struggles," pp. 73-78.
23. Roy Rivenburg, "Mormons' Stronghold of Faith," *Contra Costa Times*, Oct. 2, 1992, p. C5.
24. Ibid.
25. Ibid.
26. *Church News*, week ending Jan. 9, 1988, pp. 3, 7.
27. *Encyclodpedia of Mormonism*, vol. 4, p. 1526.

Chapter 2—The Other Side of Family Home Evening

1. *The Evangel*, May-Jun. 1992, p. 10, quoting the *Salt Lake Tribune*, Jan. 13, 1992.
2. Bill Schnoebelen, video interview, Feb. 27, 1988, on file, Jeremiah Films.
3. Heinerman, video interview.
4. Ibid.
5. Dean Huffaker, "Homosexuality at BYU," a two-part series, *Seventh East Press*, Provo, Utah, Mar. 27, 1982 and Apr. 12, 1982, p. 1, both issues.
6. Ibid.
7. Dawn House, "Evergreen Holds Private Meet for LDS Bishops, Gays," *Salt Lake Tribune*, May 7, 1990, p. 2B.
8. "Utah Divorce Rate Still High," *Saints Alive* (update report), Feb. 1990, p. 4, cites *Salt Lake Tribune*, Jan. 11, 1990.
9. "Concern about Domestic Violence Increases," *Saints Alive* (update report), Mar. 1992, p. 3, cites *Salt Lake Tribune*, Jan. 4, 1992.
10. "Child Abuse and Neglect Jump 20%," *Inner Circle* (Marlow, OK), Jul. 1992, p. 1, cites the Utah Division of Family Service's Report 1991.
11. "Zion Going Downhill," *Saints Alive* (update report), Jun.-Jul. 1992, p. 3, cites *Salt Lake Tribune*, Apr. 8, 1992 and Apr. 12, 1992.
12. "Utah High in Child Labor-Law Violations," *Saints Alive* (update report), cites *Salt Lake Tribune*, Apr. 24, 1990.
13. "Unwed Teen Pregnancies Reaching Crisis," *Saints Alive* (update report), Jan. 1991, p. 4, cites *Utah Holiday*, Nov. 1990.
14. "Utah Ranks Fourth for Its Prison Population in 1989," *Provo Daily Herald*, May 24, 1990.
15. Utah Criminal Code #76-5-406.5.
16. "Utah Child Abuse Rises 44% in Two Years," *Saints Alive* (newsletter), Feb. 1990, p. 2, cites *Salt Lake Tribune*, Jan. 24, 1990.

231

17. "Coddling Sex Offenders?" *Saints Alive* (newsletter). Feb.-Mar. 1989, p. 3, cites *Salt Lake Tribune*, Feb. 16, 1989.
18. "Circumstances Required for Probation or Suspension of Sentence for Sex Offense Against a Child," Utah Criminal Code 76-5-406.5, Section 1.h.
19. Paul Rolly, "Did God Influence Jury?" *Salt Lake Tribune*, Mar. 17, 1988, p. B4.
20. Fax on file, transcript on file, Saints Alive in Jesus, Issaquah, WA.
21. Peggy Fletcher Stack, "Attacking LDS Church Is Way of Life for Some," *Salt Lake Tribune*, Dec. 7, 1992, p. D1.

Chapter 3—The Changing Face of Mormonism
1. *Encyclopedia of Mormonism*, vol. 3, pp. 1363-64.
2. Ibid.
3. Chuck Sackett, *What's Going On in There?* (Thousand Oaks, CA: Sword of the Shepherd Ministries, 1982), p. 62. Letter rescinding oath, Apostle George F. Richards, Feb. 15, 1927.
4. Ibid.
5. McConkie, *Mormon Doctrine*, p. 538.
6. *Encyclopedia of Mormonism*, vol. 1, p. 423.
7. Joseph Smith, *History of the Church*, vol. 5 (Salt Lake City: Deseret Books, 1978), pp. 217-18.
8. Brigham Young, *Journal of Discourses*, vol. 7 (1955 edition), pp. 290-91.
9. Ibid., vol. 10, p. 110.
10. John Taylor, *Journal of Discourses*, vol. 22, p. 304.
11. Joseph Fielding Smith, *The Way to Perfection* (Salt Lake City: Deseret Books, 1975), pp. 101-02.
12. Joseph Fielding Smith, *Look*, Oct. 22, 1963.
13. John Heinerman and Anson Shupe, *The Mormon Corporate Empire* (Boston: Beacon Press, 1985), pp. 69-72.
14. Ibid., pp. 71, 72.
15. "Latter-day Struggles," *U.S. News & World Report*, Sep. 28, 1992, p. 77.
16. Ibid.
17. "The Mormon Gender Gap," *U.S. News & World Report*, May 14, 1990, p. 14.
18. Vern Anderson, "Historian Explores LDS Women and Priesthood," *Provo Daily Herald*, Dec. 25, 1992, p. A11.
19. Elder Boyd K. Packer of the Council of the Twelve Apostles during a Priesthood Restoration fireside, May 1989. Cited in *Provo Daily Herald*, Dec. 25, 1992, p. A11.
20. "LDS Leader: Don't Limit Family Size," *Salt Lake Tribune*, Feb. 23, 1987.
21. "Pres. Benson Affirms Home Is Heart of Gospel, *Deseret News*, Church News Section, Feb. 28, 1987, p. 3.
22. "Female Elder of Church Dies at 78," *Rocky Mountain News*, May 26, 1990, p. 32.

Chapter 4—Reach Out and Touch Someone
1. Billy Graham, *Seattle Post Intelligencer* Newspaper, circa 1985, column.
2. Gordon R. Lewis, *Confronting the Cults* (Philipsburg, NJ: Presbyterian and Reformed Publishing Co., 1966), p. 3.
3. *Concerned Christians & Former Mormons* (newsletter), Whittier, CA, Jul. 1992, p. 3.
4. "A Baptist Ward Each Week," *Latter-Day Sentinel*, Apr. 2, 1988, Church Digest section.
5. Walford Erickson, "Mormon Tries to Reach Out to Other Faiths," *Journal American* (Bellevue, WA), May 21, 1988, Religion page.
6. Ed Decker, "Peril to Churches," *Journal American* (Bellevue, WA), Jun. 4, 1988, letter to editor.
7. Darl Anderson, *Soft Answers to Hard Questions* (self-published, 1987), available in LDS bookstores.
8. *Latter-Day Sentinel* (Phoenix, AZ), Aug. 10, 1986.
9. "Missionaries to Zion," *Inner Circle* (Marlow, OK), Sep. 1992, p. 7.
10. *Latter-Day Sentinel*, Aug. 6, 1988, p. 3.
11. Richard Hamilton, VISN letter of invitation to area ministers, Jan. 6, 1992.
12. Don and Brennan Kingsland, "Dear Pastor," Platen Publications form letter, Aug. 11, 1987.
13. David Briggs, "Mormons Smooth Relations with Other Denominations," *Journal American*, Jun. 16, 1990, Religion page.
14. Ed Decker, letter to Rev. Harry Applewhite, pastor, First Congregational Church, Bellevue, WA, Jan. 19, 1989.
15. *Inner Circle*, Jul. 1992, p. 1.
16. Book of Mormon, 1 Nephi 14:10.
17. Robert McKay, *The Evangel*. Jul.-Aug. 1992, p. 6.
18. "Mormons Forge Links with Other Faiths," *Orange County Register* (CA), Oct. 20, 1990, p. E11.
19. Ibid.
20. Chuck Sackett, video interview, Nov. 7, 1991, on file, Jeremiah Films.
21. Ibid.

Chapter 5—Astonishing Changes in the Unchangeable Temple
1. Sackett, *What's Going On in There?*
2. Spencer and Schnoebelen, *Mormonism's Temple of Doom* (Triple J Publishers, P.O. Box 8656, Boise, ID 83707, 1987).
3. Sackett, *Shocking News of the Secret Renovation of the LDS Temple Ritual* (Thousand Oaks, CA: Sword of the Shepherd Ministries, Inc., Apr. 15, 1990).
4. Sandra Tanner, *Evolution of the Mormon Temple Ceremony: 1842-1990* (Salt Lake City: Utah Lighthouse, 1990).
5. Sackett, *Shocking News*.
6. Sackett, *What's Going On in There?* p. 33.
7. Kim Sue Lia Perkes (Religion editor), "Mormon Temple Rite Gets Major Revision," *Arizona Republic*, Apr. 28, 1990.

8. John Dart, "Mormons Summon Those Who Spoke to Media of Temple Rites," *Los Angeles Times*, Jun. 2, 1990.
9. "Historian: LDS Church Wants 'Cookie-Cutter' Members," *Salt Lake Tribune*, Dec. 6, 1992, p. C3.
10. Bill Claudin, video interview, Jul. 30, 1990, on file, Jeremiah Films.

Chapter 6—Purging the Radicals

1. Chris Jorgensen and Peggy Fletcher Stack, "It's Judgment Day for Far Right: LDS Church Purges Survivalists," *Salt Lake Tribune*, Nov. 29, 1992, pp. A1, A2.
2. Christopher Smith, "Hero Turned Heretic? Gritz May Be Leading LDS Flock into Wilderness," *Salt Lake Tribune*, Nov. 29, 1992, p. A5.
3. Christopher Smith, "Ultraconservative Gritz Remains As Bold As Ever," *Salt Lake Tribune*, Dec. 7, 1992, p. B1.
4. "Pro-Lifers Being Excommunicated," transcription of KTVX (Channel 4) Salt Lake City 10:00 P.M. News, Dec. 11, 1992 (complete text is shown in book).
5. Peggy Stack, "LDS Apostasy Investigation Launched Against Historian," *Salt Lake Tribune*, Feb. 13, 1993, pp. A6, A7.
6. Ibid.
7. Vern Anderson, "BYU Bans Students Who Quit LDS Church," *Salt Lake Tribune*, Mar. 20, 1993, p. C1.

Chapter 7—The Birth of Heresy

1. *Pearl of Great Price*, 1:14-19.
2. Ibid., 1:30-35.
3. *Doctrine and Covenants*, Section 135.
4. Dr. David Breese, video interview, 1992, on file, Jeremiah Films.
5. Fawn M. Brodie, *No Man Knows My History, The Life of Joseph Smith* (Alfred Knopf Publishers, 1971), p. 457.
6. *Nauvoo Expositor* (IL), Jun. 7, 1844.
7. *History of the Church*, vol. 6, pp. 616-19.
8. Ibid, p. 408.

Chapter 8—False Prophecies of Joseph Smith

1. *Vine's Expository Dictionary of New Testament Words* (McLean, VA: MacDonald, n.d.), under the entry "prophet," p. 904.
2. Smith, *History of the Church*, vol. 2, pp. 380-81.
3. Ibid., p. 187. See for a list of the twelve apostles chosen.
4. Ibid., p. 528.
5. Ibid., vol. 3, p. 20.
6. Ibid., pp. 31-32.
7. Ibid., pp. 166-67.
8. Ibid., vol. 7, p. 483.
9. *Doctrine and Covenants*, Official Declaration 1, pp. 291-92, 1981 edition.
10. Larry S. Jonas, *Mormon Claims Examined* (Grand Rapids, MI: Baker Books, 1961), p. 52.
11. *The Evening and Morning Star*, vol. 1, issue 8.
12. Letter from Dick and Patty Baer, dated Oct. 10, 1981, p. 9.
13. *History of the Church*, vol. 1, pp. 315-16.
14. Ibid., vol. 5, p. 336.
15. Ibid., p. 394.
16. Ibid., vol. 6, pp. 408-09.
17. Ibid., p. 618.
18. Joseph Fielding Smith, *Teachings of the Prophet Joseph Smith* (Salt Lake City: Deseret Books, 1972), p. 368.
19. Smith, *History of the Church*, vol. 6, p. 308 (delivered Apr. 1844).
20. "Ward Teachers' Message for Jun. 1945," *Deseret News*, May 26, 1945.
21. S. Dilworth Young, BYU Stake Fireside, May 5, 1974.
22. "Pres. Benson pleads, 'Follow the Prophet!'" Brigham Young University TODAY speech delivered Feb. 26, 1980, in Marriot Center.
23. Neal A. Maxwell, *Scriptures for the Modern World*, ed. Paul R. Cheesman and C. Wilfred Griggs (Provo, Utah: Religious Studies Center, 1984), p. 1.
24. *A New Witness for the Articles of Faith* (Salt Lake City: Deseret Books, 1985), pp. 348-50.
25. Brigitte Greenberg, "As Membership Grows, Mormon President Wanes," *Journal American* (Bellevue, WA), Feb. 20, 1993, p. B1.
26. Wendy Ogata, "Benson Too Frail to Attend [General Conference]." See picture accompanying article, *Ogden Standard Examiner*, Oct. 4, 1992, Religion page.
27. "Debates by Mormon Leaders Preceded 'Revelations,' Book Says," *Los Angeles Times*, Dec. 3, 1988, Sec. II, pp. 6-7.

Chapter 9—A Tangled Tale of Scripture

1. *Pearl Of Great Price* (1981 edition), p. 60.
2. Orson Pratt, "The Bible Alone an Insufficient Guide," early LDS pamplet, pp. 44-47.
3. Joseph F. Smith, *The Teachings of the Prophet Joseph Smith* (1938), p. 327.
4. *Doctrine and Covenants*, Section 9:8,9.
5. *Ensign*, Oct. 1979, p. 18.

6. Edvalson and Smith, *Plain and Precious Parts* (Provo, UT: Seventy's Mission Bookstore, 1977), pp. 62-63.
7. Richard A. Parker, "The Joseph Smith Papyri, A Preliminary Report," *Dialogue*, Summer 1968, p. 86.
8. Klaus Baer, "The Breathing Permit of Hor," *Dialogue*, Summer 1968, pp. 109-10, 119.
9. Dr. Edward H. Ashment, "The Facsimiles of the Book of Abraham," *Sunstone*, vol. 4, nos. 5 and 6, pp. 33-48.

Chapter 10—Present-Day Polygamy and Blood Atonement
1. *Doctrine and Covenants*, Section 132:1-4.
2. Ibid, verses 20, 21.
3. Fawn M. Brodie, *No Man Knows My History* (1945), pp. 335-36.
4. Ibid, pp. 458-59.
5. Brigham Young, *Journal of Discourses*, vol. 11, p. 269.
6. *Doctrine and Covenants*, Official Declaration 1. See also Heinerman and Shupe, *Mormon Corporate Empire*, p. 10.
7. Margaretta Spencer, video interview, Jul. 22, 1988, on file, Jeremiah Films.
8. James Spencer, video interview, Jul. 22, 1988. on file, Jeremiah Films.
9. Harold Schindler, "Leaders, Descendants to Dedicate Monument at Mountain Meadows," *Salt Lake Tribune*, Sep. 9, 1990, p. B3.
10. Thelma Geer, video interview, Sep. 7, 1988, on file, Jeremiah Films.
11. Art Buella, video interview, Oct. 14, 1988, on file, Jeremiah Films.
12. Lillian Chynoweth, video interview, Sep. 25, 1988, on file, Jeremiah Films.
13. Evan Moore, "Dead Cult Leader's Doctrine Still Leaving Trail of Blood, *Houston Chronicle*, Jun. 28, 1988, p. A11. See also Hanson and Liebrum, "Four Killings Tied to LeBaron Cultists," same paper and day, p. A1.
14. J.M. Grant, *Journal of Discourses*, vol. 4, p. 51.
15. Brigham Young, *Journal of Discourses*, vol. 4, p. 220.
16. AP Report, "Blood Atonement Concerns Church," *Daily Herald* (Provo, Utah), Apr. 30, 1989, p. A5.
17. *Doctrine and Covenants*, Section 132.
18. *Come Unto Christ*, Melchizedek Priesthood personal study guide, 1986 edition, Lesson 20, "Joseph Smith: The Prophet of the Restoration," pp. 139-45.
19. Eyewitness News report, Jun. 27, 1988, video copy on file, Jeremiah Films.
20. AP Report, "Three Polygamists Convicted in Slayings of Wayward Members," Houston, TX, Jan. 21, 1993.
21. McConkie, *Mormon Doctrine*, p. 92.
22. Art Buella, video interview, Oct. 14, 1988, on file, Jeremiah Films.
23. Thelma Geer, video interview #2, Sep. 17, 1991, on file, Jeremiah Films. Also see Thelma Geer, *Mormonism, Mama and Me* (Tucson, AZ: Calvary Missionary Press, 1983), pp. 117-23.
24. Art Buella, video interview, Oct. 14, 1988, on file, Jeremiah Films.

Chapter 11—The Satanic Connection
1. Bishop Glenn L. Pace, Memorandum: Jul. 19, 1990, to the Strengthening Church Members Committee re: Ritualistic Child Abuse, pp. 1, 5.
2. Ed Decker, "The Sure Sign of the Nail," *Saints Alive* (newsletter), Spring 1987, pp. 9-10.
3. William J. Schnoebelen and James R. Spencer, *Mormonism's Temple of Doom* (1987) and *Whited Sepulchers: The Hidden Language of the Mormon Temple* (1990), from Triple J Publications, Box 8656, Boise, ID 83707.
4. Sackett, *What's Going On in There?* p. 57.
5. Lucy Mack Smith, "History." Manuscript trans. by Martha Jane Coray in 1845, photocopy, Special Collections in the J. Willard Marriott Library, University of Utah, Salt Lake City, p. 46.
6. Court records found by Rev. Wesley P. Walters, Oct. 28, 1971, certified by E.M. Crumb, Clerk of the Board, Mar. 31, 1980.
7. D. Michael Quinn, *Early Mormonism and the Magic World View* (Salt Lake City: Signature Books, 1987), pp. 118-32.
8. Guinn Williams, "A Necromantic Incident in Palmyra, NY" (Issaquah, WA: Saints Alive in Jesus, 1988, pp. 2-12.
9. C.R. Stafford, "The Naked Truth About Mormonism," Jan. 1888, p. 3.
10. William Stafford, sworn affidavit; and Francis W. Kirkham, *A New Witness for Christ in America*, vol. 2 (1959), p. 367.
11. Reed C. Durham, *No Help for the Widow's Son* (Nauvoo, IL: Martin Publishing, 1980), pp. 22ff.
12. Schnoebelen and Spencer, *Mormonism's Temple of Doom* and *Whited Sepulchers*.
13. Pace Memorandum, p. 5.
14. Ibid., p. 4.
15. Ibid.
16. J. Tanner, "The Lucifer-God Doctrine," Nov. 1987, quoted in *Lucifer-God Doctrine—Shadow or Reality?* (Issaquah, WA: Saints Alive, 1987).
17. Bill Schnoebelen, "Joseph Smith and the Temple of Doom," Saints Alive tapes, Capstone, 1986. Tanner, "Covering Up Syn" (Salt Lake City: Utah Lighthouse), Apr. 1988. See also Jim Spencer, attack on *Mormonism's Temple of Doom*, Through the Maze Ministries, P.O. Box 8656, Boise, ID 83707, 38-page response.
18. Ed Decker and Bill Schnoebelen, *Lucifer-God Doctrine—Shadow or Reality?* (Issaquah, WA: Saints Alive in Jesus), Dec. 12, 1987, 60-page response.
19. Dr. David Breese, video interview, 1992, on file, Jeremiah Films.

Chapter 12—Secrets of a Wealthy Kingdom
1. "Mormon, Inc., Finances and Faith."
2. John Heinerman, video interview, Feb. 27, 1988, on file, Jeremiah Films.

3. Ibid.
4. Heinerman and Shupe, *Mormon Corporate Empire*, pp. 32-75.
5. Ibid., pp. 72-74.
6. Ibid., pp. 66-69.
7. Ibid., pp. 58-61.
8. Peter H. Brown, "Tales Told out of Church: The Rumblings Over 'Mormon Murders,'" *Washington Post*, Jan. 22, 1989, p. G1.
9. John L. Smith, video interview, undated, on file, Jeremiah Films.

Chapter 13—The Hinckley Affair
1. "President Hinckley Charged," *Saints Alive* (newsletter), Oct. 1988, p. 3.
2. Charles Van Damm, video interview, Sep. 8, 1988, on file, Jeremiah Films. All quotations attributed to Charles Van Damm in this book are from this interview.
3. Sisco, Huff, Wright, "Hidden Population: What Does It Mean to Be Homosexual in Utah?" *Salt Lake Tribune*, Jan. 12, 1992, p. A1.
4. Ben, video interview, Oct. 14, 1988, on file, Jeremiah Films. All quotations attributed to Ben in this book are from this interview.
5. Louie, video interview, Oct. 14, 1988, on file, Jeremiah Films. All quotations attributed to Louie in this book are from this interview.
6. Deed to house, showing Van Damm's ownership, on file, Jeremiah Films.
7. Viola, video interview, Oct. 25, 1988, on file, Jeremiah Films. All quotations attributed to Viola in this book are from this interview.
8. Charles Van Damm, video interview, Sep. 8, 1988, on file, Jeremiah Films.
9. Bill Claudin, video interview #2, Jul. 30, 1990, on file, Jeremiah Films.
10. Bill Claudin, video interview, Hinckley protest, Oct. 14, 1988, on file, Jeremiah Films.
11. Protestors, video interview, Hinckley protest, Oct. 14, 1988, on file, Jeremiah Films.
12. "Hinckley Prescribes Chastity and Fidelity to Battle AIDS Epidemic," *Deseret News*, Apr. 5, 1987, p. A7.
13. "Hoover: Documentary Says Mob, Homosexuality, Gambling Dominated His Private Life," *USA Today*, Feb. 8, 1993, p. A3.

Chapter 14—Back to Basics
1. *Ensign*, May 1977, p. 49.
2. *Journal of Discourses*, vol. 6, pp. 3-5.
3. Orson Pratt, *The Seer*, pp. 37-38.
4. McConkie, *Mormon Doctrine*, pp. 163-64.
5. Joseph Smith, *Doctrines of Salvation*, vol. 1, pp. 64-66.
6. *Journal of Discourses*, vol. 8, p. 115; McConkie, *Mormon Doctrine*, pp. 742-43.
7. *Journal of Discourses*, vol. 1, pp. 345-46.
8. James Talmage, *Articles of Faith* (Salt Lake City: Church of Jesus Christ of Latter-day Saints, 1973), pp. 85-87.
9. LDS pamphlet, "What the Mormons Think of Christ," p. 22.
10. Smith, *Doctrines of Salvation*, vol. 2, pp. 44-46.
11. *Journal of Discourses*, vol. 4, p. 271.
12. Ibid, vol. 1, p. 51.
13. Robert Houlihan, "Mountain Movers," Nov. 1992, *Assemblies of God Missions* (Springfield, MO), pp. 7-9.
14. Ibid., pp. 16-17.

Appendix—Testing the Book of Mormon
1. LeGrand Richards, *A Marvelous Work and a Wonder* (Salt Lake City: Deseret Book Co., 1976), pp. 67-68.
2. Sandra Tanner, *The God Makers* video, 1982, Jeremiah Films.
3. Harold Goodman, *The God Makers* video, 1982, Jeremiah Films.
4. John L. Sorenson, *An Ancient American Setting for the Book of Mormon* (1980), pp. 0/2-0/3.
5. Dr. Ross T. Christensen, *University Archaeological Society Report*, Dec. 1960, pp. 8-9.
6. Michael Coe, "Mormons and Archaeology, An Outside View," *Dialogue: A Journal of Mormon Thought*, Summer 1969, pp. 70-78.
7. Martin Raish, "All That Glitters: Uncovering Fool's Gold in Book of Mormon Archaeology," *Sunstone*, vol. 6, no. 1, pp. 10-15.
8. Dr. Charles Crane, *The Bible and Mormon Scriptures Compared* (Joplin, MO: College Press, 1992).
9. Boyce Rensberger, *Salt Lake Tribune*, May 25, 1980, p. G1.
10. Milton R. Hunter, *Christ in Ancient America*, vol. 2 (Salt Lake City: Deseret Books), pp. 51-53.
11. Ibid., p. 121.
12. James Witham, "Archaeology and the Book of Mormon," a slide presentation with notes (Issaquah, WA: Saints Alive in Jesus), pp. 5-8.
13. Vincent H. Malmstrom, "Where Time Began," *Science Digest*, Dec. 1981, pp. 56-59, 112-13.

Other Good
Harvest House Reading

THE GOD MAKERS
by *Ed Decker* and *Dave Hunt*

This unique exposé on Mormonism is factual, carefully researched, and fully documented. *The God Makers* provides staggering new insights that go beyond the explosive film of the same title. An excellent tool in reaching Mormons.

THE EVOLUTION CONSPIRACY
by *Caryl Matrisciana* and *Roger Oakland*

What was once a classroom debate has made a quantum leap into our everyday lives in surprising and alarming ways. This highly readable, comprehensive, well-documented exposé shows that the raging war between evolution and creation is not a battle between science and religion, but rather a battle between religion and religion—with eternal consequences for us and our children.

WHAT YOU NEED TO KNOW
ABOUT MORMONS
by *Ed Decker*

In this informative book, the differences between Mormonism and Christianity are clearly presented. Through a series of conversations between neighbors, Decker presents the basic tenets of Mormonism and the countering truths of the Bible.

EVERYTHING YOU EVER WANTED TO KNOW ABOUT
MORMONISM
by *John Ankerberg* and *John Weldon*

Like no book before it, this definitive work covers every aspect of the history, beliefs, and practices of the largest, wealthiest, and most influential sect in America, comprehensively tracing its early schemes and modern deceptions in nearly 300 detailed and information-packed pages.

COPING WITH THE CULTS
by *Lorri MacGregor*

Hands on, down-to-earth explanations and an evangelistic focus make *Coping with the Cults* the winning choice in a popular guide to the cults. The author's extensive personal ministry to cult groups for the past 15 years lets her target the main points quickly and thoroughly in simple, nontechnical language. Easy-to-remember questions help readers determine whether an unfamiliar group is a cult.

Dear Reader:

We would appreciate hearing from you regarding this Harvest House nonfiction book. It will enable us to continue to give you the best in Christian publishing.

1. What most influenced you to purchase *The God Makers II*?
   - ☐ Author
   - ☐ Subject matter
   - ☐ Backcover copy
   - ☐ Recommendations
   - ☐ Cover/Title
   - ☐ _____

2. Where did you purchase this book?
   - ☐ Christian bookstore
   - ☐ General bookstore
   - ☐ Department store
   - ☐ Grocery store
   - ☐ Other

3. Your overall rating of this book:
   - ☐ Excellent   ☐ Very good   ☐ Good   ☐ Fair   ☐ Poor

4. How likely would you be to purchase other books by this author?
   - ☐ Very likely
   - ☐ Somewhat likely
   - ☐ Not very likely
   - ☐ Not at all

5. What types of books most interest you?
   (check all that apply)
   - ☐ Women's Books
   - ☐ Marriage Books
   - ☐ Current Issues
   - ☐ Self Help/Psychology
   - ☐ Bible Studies
   - ☐ Fiction
   - ☐ Biographies
   - ☐ Children's Books
   - ☐ Youth Books
   - ☐ Other _____

6. Please check the box next to your age group.
   - ☐ Under 18
   - ☐ 18-24
   - ☐ 25-34
   - ☐ 35-44
   - ☐ 45-54
   - ☐ 55 and over

Mail to: Editorial Director
Harvest House Publishers
1075 Arrowsmith
Eugene, OR 97402

Name _____

Address _____

City _____ State _____ Zip _____

**Thank you for helping us to help you
in future publications!**